Adolescent Counselling Psychology

I0130450

Adolescent Counselling Psychology: Theory, Research and Practice provides a thorough introduction to therapeutic practice with young people. As an edited text, it brings together some of the leading authorities on such work into one digestible volume.

The text is divided into three major sections. The first provides a context to therapeutic work with young people. This outlines the historical background to such work, the types of settings in which individuals work and the allied professions that they will encounter. Following on from this, the second section introduces the psychology of adolescence and provides an overview of the research into youth counselling. Finally, the third section considers more applied issues. Initially the infrastructure of counselling services is discussed before moving on to reflect upon pluralistic therapeutic practice. To end, the ways in which outcomes may be assessed in such work are described.

In covering such a wide territory this text acts as an essential resôurce to practising counselling psychologists and other mental health professionals. It provides a foundation to the work that individuals are undertaking in this arena and advocates that individuals enter into therapeutic work in a critically informed way. At the heart of such considerations is the need to utilise psychological theory alongside research findings to inform therapeutic decision making.

Terry Hanley is a Lecturer in Counselling Psychology at the University of Manchester, Editor of Counselling Psychology Review and an Associate Fellow of the British Psychological Society.

Neil Humphrey is Professor of Psychology of Education at the University of Manchester.

Clare Lennie is joint Programme Director of the Doctorate in Counselling Psychology at the University of Manchester.

Adolescent Counselling Psychology

Theory, research and practice

Edited by Terry Hanley,
Neil Humphrey, and
Clare Lennie

Routledge
Taylor & Francis Group

LONDON AND NEW YORK

First published 2013 by Routledge
27 Church Road, Hove, East Sussex, BN3 2FA

Simultaneously published in the USA and Canada
by Routledge
711 Third Avenue, New York NY 10017

Routledge is an imprint of the Taylor & Francis Group, an Informa business

British Library Cataloguing in Publication Data
A catalogue record for this book is available from the British Library

Library of Congress Cataloging in Publication Data
Adolescent counselling psychology : theory, research, and practice / edited by
Terry Hanley, Neil Humphrey, Clare Lennie.
    p. cm.
  1. Adolescent psychotherapy. 2. Adolescence–Counselling of. I. Hanley,
Terry. II. Humphrey, Neil, Ph. D. III. Lennie, Clare.
  RJ503.A3138 2012
  618.92'8914–dc23   2012004149

ISBN: 978-0-415-58025-0 (hbk)
ISBN: 978-0-415-58026-7 (pbk)
ISBN: 978-0-203-10317-3 (ebk)

Typeset in Times New Roman by
Swales & Willis Ltd, Exeter, Devon

Contents

Illustrations

Tables

Boxes

Figures

Contributors

Laura Cutts is presently a trainee on the Doctorate in Counselling Psychology at the University of Manchester. She has worked as a volunteer for a number of not-for-profit organisations, most recently including Anxiety UK and Stockport Progress and Recovery Centre. Her doctoral thesis is looking at the social justice interest and commitment of counselling psychologists, and her practice is currently based both within NHS primary care and for a local charitable organisation, Beacon Counselling.

Terry Hanley is joint Programme Director of the Doctorate in Counselling Psychology at the University of Manchester and an experienced youth counsellor. He is an Associate Fellow of the British Psychological Society (BPS) and the Research Lead for the Division of Counselling Psychology (DCoP) within the same organisation. He has published widely in the field of youth counselling and is also the Editor of the DCoP's research publication *Counselling Psychology Review*. For his therapeutic practice he is registered in the UK by Health Professions Council as a counselling psychologist and is a British Psychological Society chartered psychologist.

Neil Humphrey is Professor of Psychology of Education at the University of Manchester. His research interests include social and emotional learning and mental health in educational contexts. Neil has led several major projects in this field, including the national evaluations of the primary social and emotional learning (SEAL) small-group work element and secondary SEAL programme, in addition to a recent systematic review of measures of social and emotional competence for children and young people. He has published his work in journals such as *Educational Psychology*, *School Psychology International*, *Educational and Psychological Measurement* and the *International Journal of Emotional Education*.

Peter Jenkins is a Senior Lecturer in Counselling at the University of Manchester and a member of the Ethics Committee of the UK Council for Psychotherapy. He has extensive experience of training counselling practitioners and organisations on legal aspects of therapy, and has researched and published widely on this topic. His publications include *Counselling, Psychotherapy and the Law*

(Sage, 2007) and, as co-author with Debbie Daniels, *Therapy with Children: Children's Rights, Confidentiality and the Law* (Sage, 2010).

Ann Lendrum is Programme Director of the Masters in Psychology of Education at the University of Manchester, lecturing on qualitative research methods, human development and the social psychology of education. Her principal research interests reflect her experience as a practitioner and lie in two key areas: the inclusion and support of pupils with special educational needs in mainstream settings; and the issues involved in the effective implementation of both targeted and universal interventions. Ann's most recent research includes the evaluation of the small-group work element of the SEAL intervention in primary schools, the national evaluation of SEAL in secondary schools and an evaluation of the Achievement for All initiative.

Clare Lennie is a chartered counselling psychologist and teacher. She currently works at the University of Manchester where she is joint programme director of the Doctorate in Counselling Psychology. Her research interests are around the positioning of counselling psychology in different organisational settings and related staff welfare issues. She has a particular interest in the prison setting and the role that counselling psychology might offer there. In her past life she was a teacher of vocational and non-vocational courses in the sixth-form setting, before training in counselling to develop her pastoral skills and moving into student counselling and teacher training.

Emma Lindley is Senior Researcher on the Social Brain Project at the Royal Society for the encouragement of Arts, Manufactures and Commerce (RSA). Emma holds a first-class degree in English Language and Literature from Liverpool University, an MSc in Educational Research and an Economic and Social Research Council-funded PhD, both from the University of Manchester. Emma has also worked in publishing, student guidance at Leeds College of Music, events management for Opera North, and theatre-in-education in the third sector. Her doctoral thesis focused on antistigma mental health education and involved an exploration of young people's understandings of mental illness. Emma's work led to the development of the inclusive dialogue approach to education about mental illness and has received media attention from the BBC and the *Times Educational Supplement*.

Gill Parkinson is an Honorary Research Fellow of the University of Manchester, former senior lecturer and researcher in neuropsychology and subjects relating to people with complex health, education and communication/social support needs. She has worked in a range of health, education and voluntary sector settings as a consultant speech and language therapist. This work has continued to inform her interest in training, writing and teaching counsellors and allied professions to work with disabled people who may have communication impairments who wish to use counselling and allied psychological support services. She is a member of the Health Professions Council and British Psychological Society.

Sue Pattison is Director of the Integrated PhD in Education and Communication at Newcastle University, UK. She lectures, consults and researches in the field of counselling children and young people and manages a small private practice providing clinical supervision, counselling and therapeutic play.

Maggie Robson is currently Director of Counselling Psychology at Keele University where they offer both a full-time and part-time MSc in Counselling Psychology, both of which are a route of training accredited by the British Association for Counselling and Psychotherapy (first 2 years of the part-time route). As well as being an experienced and Health Professions Council-registered counselling psychologist, Maggie is a qualified play therapist and has worked therapeutically with children and young people in a variety of settings. Her research interests are mainly focused in this area.

Kate Sapin, author of *Essential Skills for Youth Work Practice* (Sage, 2009), has been a director and tutor of community and youth work learning programmes at the University of Manchester for over 25 years and has a keen interest in the development of innovative and appropriate informal youth work and research with young people. She has developed short-course provision on counselling skills for community and youth work and convened workshops and conferences on a relevant topics, including, for example, 'How Do You Do It: Sharing ideas about youth participation' (2011) and 'Risk and Resilience on Issues and Practice Related to Mental Health and LGBT Young People' (2008).

Aaron Sefi is an online youth counsellor for Kooth. He was initially trained in Gestalt therapy, which has been broadened into an integrative practice, using research-informed humanistic interventions and a pluralistic framework. He has honed this practice for online (textual) work and is excited about the possibilities within computer-mediated therapy. He has an MA in Counselling, which sparked an interest in outcome measures used to capture effectiveness in counselling. He has been developing applicable measures for online practice and a research design to compare face-to-face and online counselling.

Matt Shorrock is a UK Council for Psychotherapy-registered psychotherapist, a certified transactional analyst and guest lecturer at the University of Manchester. He is also in private practice and is Director of the Oak Tree Therapy, Training and Research Institute, based in Manchester and Vienna. He is currently completing a Doctorate in counselling psychology at University of Manchester, whilst researching for his upcoming book concerning the treatment of internet addiction. With over ten years' experience working with groups throughout Europe and Asia, he remains passionate about working with the therapeutic group process.

Garry Squires is Director for the professional doctorate in educational psychology at the University of Manchester and formerly worked as an educational psychologist, providing training to teachers and psychologists in the area of special educational needs (SEN) and inclusion. He is an Associate Fellow of the British Psychological Society and is registered with the Health Professions Council as a practitioner psychologist. His research is in the areas of SEN, inclusion and mental health and has been published in popular SEN magazines and peer-reviewed journals; he has presented papers at UK and international conferences. He is on the editorial board of *School Mental Health.*

Panos Vostanis is Professor of Child and Adolescent Psychiatry at the University of Leicester in the UK, and Consultant at the Leicestershire child mental health service. In his clinical capacity, he works with a mental health service designated for vulnerable children, young people and families, that is, those looked after by local authorities, homeless, adopted, refugees and young offenders. In his academic capacity, Panos is actively involved in a number of research projects on the assessment of mental health needs, evaluation of treatment and services for traumatised children and young people. He also participates in the evaluation of mental health interventions in schools; the development and evaluation of training intervention for child mental health practitioners to improve joint working with schools; and he is interested in the impact of trauma on children living in war zones.

Dr Michael Wigelsworth is a lecturer in the Psychology of Education and Educational Research at the University of Manchester, specialising in quantitative methods and statistics. His work focuses on the mental health and well-being of children, specifically in the area of social and emotional learning. Recently completed projections include evaluations of UK-based intervention programmes for improving social and emotional well-being (primary and secondary SEAL) and assessing outcomes for children with special educational needs and disabilities (Achievement for All).

Gareth Williams is currently a senior counsellor for North Staffs Mind. Gareth has also worked for Rethink and Visyon and at Lothlorien therapeutic community. During his 15 years' experience in the field of mental health, he has worked in a variety of settings (including online, in schools and in the community) and developed special interests in creativity, mindfulness, therapeutic common factors and working with young people and their families. Gareth has a BSc in psychology, as well as Master's degrees in both counselling and music. He is in the process of establishing a private practice as therapist, supervisor and teacher.

Miranda Wolpert is Director of the Child and Adolescent Mental Health Services' (CAMHS) Evidence-Based Practice Unit (EBPU), an academic and service development unit located across University College London and Anna Freud Centre. The unit undertakes research and dissemination and runs courses for senior CAMHS managers and practitioners to aid development of evidence-based and outcomes-focused practice. Miranda chairs the CAMHS Outcome Research Consortium, a collaboration of the majority of CAMHS in England committed to routine outcome evaluation and to using this approach to develop and enhance services. Miranda is a clinical psychologist by background.

Chapter 1

Introduction

Terry Hanley, Neil Humphrey and Clare Lennie

Overview

This chapter aims to provide the reader with a brief reflection upon the conception of this text and to provide an overview of what is to follow. Thus, the rationale for entering into this project is presented in the first instance before moving on to define some of key terms utilised within this text. Finally, the order of the text is presented. This attempts to give the reader a sense of our reasoning behind the structure that we have adopted in the book and the presentation styles used.

Rationale for the text

Before entering into the main content of the text we provide a brief rationale for this project. We have included this part because we hope to provide a transparent overview of its positioning in order to give you a sense of its general ethos and an idea of whether or not you are going to get on with it. We also hope that providing this overview will give you an idea of the parts of the book that you might dip into, although of course we hope that in dipping into the book we can entice you to engage with the whole text!

As the awareness of the needs of young people becomes heightened, support services have gained a higher profile. One major area of growth has been the emergence of therapeutic services for children, young people and young adults. This increase in prevalence of youth counselling services is not an indicator that being an adolescent has become more difficult within contemporary society. However, there is a clearer awareness that individuals can gain benefit from further support in navigating through this difficult life stage. Such services, although still not readily available to all, have become relatively commonplace within the environments that this group inhabit and, with this in mind, it is on this burgeoning area of development that this text focuses.

In a time when the notion of evidence-based practice has become a juggernaut that is difficult to turn, this text attempts to present an alternative way of utilising research when offering youth-friendly therapeutic services. This is not to challenge the potential that evidence-based models have, but to acknowledge that there are other avenues which may prove fruitful and first, reflect real-world scenarios more accurately, and second, provide a more rounded response to young people who are seeking support. With this in mind, this text aims to present a framework in which research can, alongside a multitude of other influences such as psychological theory and personal experience, be used to inform practice. Such a research-informed approach would contrast with research-directed approaches that are more commonly presented as a consequence of evidence-based models.

Unlike the more prescriptive nature of research-directed approaches of therapy, a research-informed approach could prove rather disparate in its make-up. Thus, in advocating therapeutic practice that can potentially be so varied, the pluralistic framework of counselling and psychotherapy, which was originally conceived by Professors Mick Cooper and John McLeod (2007, 2011), has been utilised to connect the thinking within this text. Such a framework provides a pragmatic harnessing feature in a world where so many individuals have been trained in a multitude of potentially helpful approaches of psychological therapy. Furthermore, it is felt that such a framework can: (1) acknowledge that different therapeutic approaches are likely to be suitable for different people at different points in their lives; (2) provide a means of working with an age group where pure models of therapy may prove less appropriate and are commonly utilised flexibly; and (3) enable practitioners to work to their strengths (e.g. utilising core therapeutic training, personal experience or professional background, continuing professional development and supervision as dynamic resources) rather than be constrained by rigid frameworks of practice.

Although we hope that this text is a relatively pleasant and informative read, the framework presented here does not provide a step-by-step guide to working as a counselling psychologist with young people. We do however feel that it can be part of the process that therapists working with this age group might use to bridge their core training, which is generally focused on working with older populations, when entering the field of youth counselling. In doing so, the content of the text outlines some of the core facets necessary for making this move. For instance, the three major parts of the text reflect upon the context in which such work is offered (Part 1: counselling young people in context), the notion of psychological change within this age group (Part 2: psychological change for young people) and core issues related to offering therapy to adolescents (Part 3: counselling young people in action).

As is probably evident from the notes above, the major audience for this text is those people who have completed a generic professional therapeutic training and now find themselves working (or considering working) with younger populations. It is primarily focused upon situating such work within the discipline of counselling psychology; however, it is acknowledged that other professions (e.g. other applied psychology disciplines such as clinical or educational, counselling and psycho-therapy) are also likely to find the contents of interest. Furthermore, it is hoped that the text is written in an accessible yet professional way that will enable those interested in the subject matter, but not directly familiar with such work (e.g. health professionals, teachers, parents), to benefit from its contents.

Note about terminology

Prior to continuing it is important to outline the stance that this text has upon two key terms.

First, the term 'adolescence' (or 'adolescent') is utilised to describe those individuals aged between 11 and 25 years. It is utilised interchangeably within this text with alternative terms such as 'young person' or 'young adult'. Although some might use the term 'children' to describe those in the younger age of this spread, it is not used within this text.

Second, there are numerous words to describe the therapeutic activities of a counselling psychologist. Within this text the terms 'counselling' (counsellor), 'psychotherapy' (psychotherapist) and 'therapy' (therapist) are viewed as synonymous. It should be noted that, within the UK, the term 'counselling psychologist' is a protected title, and anyone utilising it should be registered with the Health Professions Council.

An overview of the text

The editors

To economise on words, we direct you to the list of contributors at the beginning of the book for a brief biography of each editor. In summary, however, each of the editors has a passion for supporting developments within this field and has been working for many years in this area as either a counselling psychologist or a researcher. It is this closeness to the subject matter that has led to the conception of the text.

The contributors

A great number of people have been involved in the writing of this text. Each of these individuals has been selected for their particular strengths in the area they are writing. They are mentioned in the overview of the chapters below and briefly introduced in the list of contributors at the beginning of this text.

The content

The three major parts to this book are outlined below. Within each part the chapters are briefly introduced and their content is described.

Part I: Counselling young people in context

CHAPTER 2: HISTORICAL CONTEXT (TERRY HANLEY, AARON SEFI,
LAURA CUTTS AND CLARE LENNIE)

This chapter offers a conceptual framework for adolescent counselling psychology and examines the historical context of counselling young people. It includes the following:

- What counselling psychology is (and isn't)
  This part introduces how the term 'counselling psychology' is utilised in this text. It emphasises how it can be conceptualised in work with young people and outlines how such work differs from similar professions (e.g. counselling and clinical psychology). It then briefly introduces the dominant theoretical perspectives in this area and considers their influence on therapeutic practice. Additionally it provides an overview of the variety of approaches that practitioners may adopt with this client group (individual, group and family therapy) and emphasises the focus upon individual therapy within this text.
- A brief history of counselling for young people
  This provides a chronology of the role of counselling in supporting young people over the last few decades. It begins by outlining the need for therapeutic work with young people and then introduces the different types of support that are now on offer.

CHAPTER 3: DIFFERENT SETTINGS (NEIL HUMPHREY, MIRANDA WOLPERT,
MATT SHORROCK, AARON SEFI AND TERRY HANLEY)

This chapter focuses on the major settings in which youth counselling occurs. For each setting, experienced practitioners provide an insight into the different contextual factors of which individuals should be aware. The settings and authors are as follows:

- Counselling young people in clinical settings (Miranda Wolpert)
  This section provides an overview of the key issues involved in counselling young people in traditional clinical settings (e.g. Child and Adolescent Mental Health Services). In particular it examines the impact of recent developments in policy and legislation on practice in this setting.
- School-based counselling for young people (Aaron Sefi and Terry Hanley)
  This section describes the development of counselling for young people within schools. It introduces the way in which such services have developed and considers the political landscape in which they are situated.
- Counselling young people in the community (Matt Shorrock)
  This section examines the variety of community settings in which young people can access counselling support. It explores some of the key issues pertinent to this type of work and provides some examples from practice.

- Online and telephone counselling for young people (Terry Hanley and Aaron Sefi)
  This section introduces an often-ignored area of youth counselling. It reflects upon the development of mediated therapy and particularly focuses on the recent emergence of online counselling. As with other sections, the prevalence of such work is considered and key issues pertinent to this setting are introduced.

CHAPTER 4: ALLIED INTERVENTIONS

This chapter briefly outlines the relevance of being aware of allied resources and professions. It emphasises the need to be mindful of the types of interventions offered and to work in a collegiate manner with relevant professions. The chapter outlines a variety of allied interventions available to young people alongside counselling. The different interventions to be discussed are as follows:

- School-based strategies: social emotional aspects of learning (Neil Humphrey)
- Raising awareness and reducing stigma (Emma Lindley)
- Youth work (Kate Sapin)
- Educational psychology (Garry Squires)
- Support for disabled young people (Gill Parkinson)
- Psychiatry/medication (Panos Vostanis)

Part 2: Psychological change for young people

CHAPTER 5: ADOLESCENCE IN CONTEXT (CLARE LENNIE AND TERRY HANLEY)

This chapter begins by providing a historical context to the construct of adolescence. Following on from this, the major theories of adolescence are introduced and are then considered in relation to major perspectives of counselling young people.

- What is adolescence?
  This section explains the relatively recent emergence of adolescence as a concept and associated cross-cultural variations within this. Taking these issues into account, it then attempts to define this stage of development.
- The psychology of adolescence
  The main theories of adolescence are discussed. The major proponents are introduced and the four major categories of biological, behavioural and social learning theories, psychoanalytic and cognitive stage theories are considered. Following this, we present key issues that young people might face at this stage in development, for example social roles and drugs.
- Counselling adolescents

Following the discussion of the major theories of adolescence and some of the key issues faced, the focus shifts to consider the extent to which developmental theories can complement and inform models of counselling. Particular focus is placed upon the person-centred, psychodynamic and cognitive-behavioural approaches of therapy. This chapter ends with a reflection upon integrative counselling approaches that have developed to work with young people. These include Geldard and Geldard's proactive approach and the pluralist framework of Mick Cooper and John McLeod.

CHAPTER 6: RESEARCH INTO YOUTH COUNSELLING: A RATIONALE FOR RESEARCH-INFORMED PLURALISTIC PRACTICE (TERRY HANLEY, AARON SEFI, LAURA CUTTS AND SUE PATTISON)

This chapter initially outlines the main research findings that relate to counselling young people. It then moves on to discuss the notion of research-informed practice and presents a pluralistic framework for making use of resources to hand (e.g. research, psychological theory and personal experience). The framework presented is based upon Cooper and McLeod's (2011) pluralistic approach to counselling and psychotherapy.

- Evaluating youth counselling
  The main research findings regarding counselling young people are outlined in this section. In particular, the work reflects upon research studies examining the effectiveness of youth counselling, the therapeutic alliance in youth counselling and what research suggests young people want from youth counselling.
- Developing a research-informed approach
  Reflecting on the findings above, and pre-empting the following section, the notion of research-informed therapy, rather than research-directed therapy, is introduced. The key tenets to the pluralistic approach to counselling psychology introduced here are then presented.

Part 3: Counselling young people in action

CHAPTER 7: THE COUNSELLING INFRASTRUCTURE (TERRY HANLEY, PETER JENKINS, SUE PATTISON, MAGGIE ROBSON AND GARETH WILLIAMS)

This chapter focuses upon the practical issues that surround offering counselling psychology services to adolescents. In particular the work focuses upon the following areas:

- Ethics and the law (Peter Jenkins)
  This section briefly introduces some of the major ethical and legal considerations when working with the client group. In particular, the issue of client

competence is introduced and the potential need to gain parental consent is discussed. Additionally, this section raises issues of confidentiality and considers when it may be necessary to breach confidentiality.
- Policies and procedures (Peter Jenkins)
  This section reflects upon the issues that youth counselling organisations commonly face. These include developing referral pathways, conducting assessments and completing appropriate paperwork.
- The contract (Sue Pattison and Maggie Robson)
  In relation to the previous sections of this chapter, this section will focus upon the need to create an appropriate working contract with adolescent clients. Key issues and examples of good practice are discussed.
- Supervision (Gareth Williams)
  Issues relevant to supervising counselling psychologists working with adolescents are introduced here. These include reflecting upon the adolescent–counsellor relationship and the power imbalances that may occur.

CHAPTER 8: PLURALISTIC COUNSELLING PSYCHOLOGY FOR YOUNG PEOPLE (TERRY HANLEY, AARON SEFI AND GARETH WILLIAMS)

This chapter focuses upon the applied issues that surround offering counselling psychology services to adolescents. It includes the following:

- Pluralistic counselling psychology for young people
  This section builds upon the content of Chapter 6 by briefly recapping the importance of the therapeutic alliance in therapeutic work with young people. It then outlines how these common therapeutic factors might manifest with young clients. In particular, challenges faced in developing a therapeutic bond are discussed alongside the goals that young people have, the therapeutic tasks they engage with in therapy and the methods that are collaboratively employed.
- Examples of how the pluralistic framework may look in practice
  The second half of this chapter outlines three examples of how the pluralistic framework might look in real-world practice. The three examples reflect work that has been delivered in school, community and online settings and describe how goals, tasks and methods manifest within individual cases.

CHAPTER 9: ASSESSING THERAPEUTIC OUTCOMES (NEIL HUMPHREY, TERRY HANLEY, CLARE LENNIE, ANN LENDRUM AND MICHAEL WIGELSWORTH)

This chapter focuses upon assessing the outcomes of therapeutic interventions. It includes coverage of the following:

- Research with children and young people
- The importance of research and routine outcome measurement
- Commonly applied research designs, including:

- – Before-and-after designs
- – Non-randomised trials
- • Therapeutic outcome measures, including:
  - – YP-CORE
  - – SDQ
  - – HoNOSCA
- • Issues in interpreting and analysing outcome data, including:
  - – Statistical significance
  - – Effect size
  - – Reliable and clinically significant change
  - – Differential results
- • Assessment of process (and perspectives)
- • A suggested model for assessing therapeutic outcomes in practice.

At the end of the book a brief summary is presented. Chapter 10 brings together the key threads within the work. In particular, it highlights the need for counselling psychologists to have a good understanding of the influence of their own backgrounds, the context and setting in which they find themselves working, to be informed of the psychological theory that influences their practice, and to allow research to inform, rather than direct, their practice.

We hope that you find the chapters that follow helpful and enjoyable.

References

Cooper, M. and McLeod, J. (2007). A pluralistic framework for counselling and psychotherapy: implications for research. *Counselling and Psychotherapy Research,* 7 (3), 135–43.

Cooper, M. and McLeod, J. (2011). *Pluralistic Counselling and Psychotherapy.* Sage: London.

Part I

Counselling young people in context

Chapter 2

Historical context

Terry Hanley, Aaron Sefi,
Laura Cutts and Clare Lennie

Overview

This chapter aims to provide a transparent basis for what follows within this text. It begins by placing the profession of counselling psychology within context, specifically aiming to address how it is viewed by the editors of this text, and to define some of its parameters within this work. In doing so, the discipline of counselling psychology is reflected upon within both UK and international perspectives, its core values are introduced and it is contrasted with allied/related professions. Following on from this, we move to introduce therapeutic work with young people. This section begins by introducing the arena of adolescent mental health care, placing it within a current political context in the UK, and introduces the complex concept of adolescence. It then goes on to introduce briefly the youth counselling movement and outlines some of the important nuances which are developed throughout this text.

What counselling psychology is (and isn't)

Counselling psychology is a relatively new discipline within the UK and with this newness come some confusion and misunderstanding. For instance, in a survey of counselling psychology trainees, Cross and Watts (2002) found that the popular and diverse descriptors of counselling psychology could be reasonably described as 'nebulous and vague' (p.293). More recently, voices from the applied psychology world have suggested that counselling psychology may best serve itself by allowing itself to be 'assimilated' into the realms of clinical psychology (Kinderman, 2009, p.16). These misunderstandings appear to be partly perpetuated by the problems counselling psychologists have with articulating the key tenets of the profession. Such suggestions potentially question the foundations on which an increasingly popular profession lies. With this in mind, this section hopes to provide a brief overview of the core elements to this profession, as perceived by the editors. Here we should clarify that it does not profess to provide definitive answers but it is hoped that it will prove useful in making sense of the content which follows.

As a point of departure we ask you to undertake a brief reflective activity to consider the impact of professional titles on our work. We explain our motivations following the activity instructions. In the box below there are a number of the titles that professionals use when working with young people around issues of mental health and well-being. With these in mind, and when considering issues of mental health, we ask that you consider them in relation to the following broad questions:

- Which does society view as the most clinically effective?
- Which does society view as the most cost-effective?
- Which does society view as the most powerful?

(You may wish to make a note of your answers, noting one as the most important profession and ten as the least important.)

- Life coach
- Counselling psychologist
- Psychiatrist
- Psychotherapist
- Teacher
- Educational psychologist
- Youth worker
- Clinical psychologist
- Counsellor
- Mentor

Often, when trainees are asked to undertake this activity, it raises important issues regarding therapeutic impact and level of therapeutic training – for instance, clinical psychologists are often rated as potentially more effective than counsellors, and likewise counsellors as more effective than teachers, but is this really the case? (Does a higher level of training really reflect a higher level of skill?) In contrast, counsellors are often viewed as more cost-effective than psychiatrists, but once again, is this really the case? (Does lower pay equate to a more cost-effective service? A factor that links directly to the first question). Furthermore, it inevitably raises questions about the impact of the perceived power of professionals upon therapeutic impact – for instance, psychiatrists are often rated as most powerful but not the most clinically effective. (Does a professional with more status really understand the needs of the young person?) Finally, professions that are not explicitly targeting mental health, such as youth workers, mentors, teachers and (potentially) life coaches, are often viewed as having an inferior impact to those with explicit motivations to support individuals in making such changes. Once again, it can be asked, is this really the case? All these questions come before we even get to consider the question: how do we measure impact anyway?

Now if we change the instruction slightly, what do you think?

- Which do you view as the most clinically effective?
- Which do you view as the most cost-effective?
- Which do you view as the most powerful?

(Once again, you may wish to note your answers from one to ten to reflect on how your views may differ from your perception of society's views.)

Our aim here is not to claim there are right and wrong answers but to raise awareness of your own positioning of the title 'counselling psychology'. This exercise is without doubt a blunt tool, but we hope that it has got you thinking about the fuzzy parameters that mental health professionals inhabit. In relation to the latter part of the activity, we anticipate that for you, just as for trainees who are asked this question, counselling psychologists fall somewhere in the middle of many of your thoughts. They are not likely to be the cheapest or most expensive, they are not likely to be the most or least powerful and, given the likely audience of this text, we anticipate that you would rate them as fairly clinically effective.

The potential cross-over between professions is a major reason for the conception of this text. There is need for some clarity over the role of counselling psychologists within the field of adolescent mental health and this text hopes to situate itself in this gap. So, as a starting point, we will reflect upon what counselling psychology is.

What is counselling psychology?

As was evident within the first reflective exercise, there are numerous professionals working in the field of adolescent mental health. The work of counselling psychologists is therefore likely to overlap with the work of others. For instance, the therapeutic work engaged in is clearly similar to the work of counsellors and psychotherapists. Likewise, its link to psychology places it in a similar playing field to educational and clinical psychologists. Furthermore, its leaning towards models of well-being may also situate itself alongside more systemic interventions such as considering the social and emotional aspects of learning. Thus, in presenting an overview of what counselling psychology is we consider: (1) the central tenets of the profession; (2) a brief history of the profession both in the UK and internationally; and (3) the Health Professions Council's Standards of Proficiency for counselling psychologists (Health Professions Council, 2009b), and the way in which these values and expectations impact upon training programmes.

In considering the central tenets of the profession of counselling psychology in the UK, the British Psychological Society's Division of Counselling Psychology provides a useful starting point. The website briefly describes the setting of counselling psychology (http://dcop.bps.org.uk): developing from the humanistic movement, counselling and psychotherapy, and from the science of psychology. An interesting point to note here is that in the most recent third edition of the

Handbook of Counselling Psychology, Strawbridge and Woolfe (2010) remark upon this combination of counselling and psychology as a creative synthesis, due to the possible clash between existential-phenomenological counselling approaches and the scientific nature of psychology.

The Division of Counselling Psychology website then goes on to set out the core intentions underpinning models of practice within the profession, which in plain language are as follows:

1. We concentrate on the self-reliance of the person with the problem.
2. We work together with the person with the problem to understand the internal world and all its social pressures.
3. We apply the best of scientific evidence and leading-edge professional practice in the field to that healing relationship towards the goal of the client's well-being.
4. We seek to relate to the whole person with the problem, regardless of the way in which he or she may be perceived by wider society.

These points nicely demonstrate the way in which counselling psychology brings together the emphasis on the holistic nature of the person and humanistic values from counselling, and the ideas around the use of scientific research as applied to practice from psychology.

Counselling psychologists work in a variety of settings, including private practice, other areas of the private sector such as for individual companies in employee assistance programmes, forensic settings such as prisons, charities and the voluntary sector, and a wide range of NHS services such as hospitals, general practitioner surgeries and Improving Access to Psychological Therapies services. Within these services, counselling psychologists work with a variety of people, ranging from those who have severe and enduring mental health problems, to those who are struggling with challenges in their life, such as stress or bereavement. Counselling psychologists look to the medical context regarding mental health problems but work with particular individuals' subjective psychological experience to empower their recovery.

Such an introduction hopefully reflects the breadth of a profession which acknowledges the influence of pluralistic and phenomenological models of therapeutic practice, and values practice-based evidence. Additionally, the following statements, written by Ray Woolfe (1990), are often viewed as core elements of the profession. These are presented in turn below followed by a brief statement reflecting the substance which could be attributed to them.

•   An increasing awareness among many psychologists of the importance of the helping relationship as a significant variable in facilitating the therapeutic endeavour.

As the notion that all therapeutic approaches have the potential to support individuals becomes accepted within the therapeutic field (Luborsky *et al.*, 1975), the focus of how we might improve the success of counselling has begun to change. Therefore, increasingly, there is an interest in the common factors that are associated with successful therapy, an approach that brings the quality of the therapeutic relationship to the fore. With this in mind, the relationship has often been reported to be one of the major influences on positive change (Asay and Lambert, 1999) and provides a central factor at the heart of the profession of counselling psychology.

• A growing questioning of what is often described as the medical model of professional–client relationships and a move towards a more humanistic value base.

Often psychological approaches attempt to understand people's distress by breaking it up into treatable chunks, or diagnoses, by a qualified professional. Such a perspective has clearly provided numerous benefits to many people, and proves a fruitful model in health care in a broader sense; however it can also be viewed as a reductionist stance that does not sufficiently account for what it means to be a person in distress. Counselling psychologists therefore often advocate a more holistic view of the person in distress and are often cautious when considering the implications of diagnoses (Douglas, 2010). This can often be aligned with the principles of humanistic psychology (Bugental, 1964) and promotes a more egalitarian professional–client relationship in which those in need are viewed as individuals with agency (Bohart and Tallman, 1999).

• A developing focus in the work of helpers on facilitating well-being as opposed to responding to sickness or pathology

Linked to the previous point, the notion that psychological health can be treated by using the same mind set as treating a broken leg may be misplaced. Whereas many medical procedures have an observable ailment, this is not often the case with psychological issues. Maybe developments in neuropsychology will change this in the future, but for now we rely upon relatively crude psychometric tests that estimate levels of distress and limitations on functioning. Such a reactive model again proves understandable given the financial constraints of any service provider, but could also be perceived as short-sighted. The emphasis upon well-being that counselling psychologists have acknowledges that psychological support relies upon proactive ongoing care, rather than solely responding to high levels of distress.

With the above in mind, counselling psychologists work with a core value system that flows throughout their work. This ethos provides a foundation for a professional decision-making process that is respectful and, importantly, places great emphasis on the collaborative nature of therapy. This may not be specific to counselling psychology, and other professionals (e.g. clinical psychologists, counsellors and psychotherapists) may share these sentiments; it does, however, provide a unifying factor for the profession. When considering similar professions, the following co-created statement from a recent proposal to create a *British Journal of Counselling Psychology* may be useful:

> in contrast to clinical psychology, counselling psychology has an orientation towards well-being (vs pathology), growth (vs remediation), and is not solely focused on clinical diagnostic criteria. Furthermore, in contrast to the related professions of counselling and psychotherapy (as it is in the UK), it is rooted in psychological knowledge, and explicitly draws on practices and theories from a plurality of orientations (Proposed British Journal of Counselling Psychology Editorial Board, 2011, p.1).

A brief overview of the historical context of counselling psychology

As noted at the outset of this chapter, counselling psychology is a relatively new profession within the UK. It began its life within the British Psychological Society as a special-interest group in 1979, before moving on to become a section in 1982, with the formal Division of Counselling Psychology only coming to life in 1994. Such developments went hand in hand with the desire of those involved to situate counselling as a discipline back within the field of psychology:

> [C]ounselling (and psychotherapy), in Britain, largely developed separately, outside the profession of psychology, and counselling psychology represents a return to psychology initiated by psychologists trained in counselling and psychotherapy (Strawbridge and Woolfe, 2003, p.4).

Up until this date, counselling in the UK had evolved with a relatively different focus. Many early voluntary services began to develop with no direct link to the profession of psychology. For instance, the Marriage Guidance Council (now Relate) was set up in 1938 and the first university counselling service was set up at Keele in 1963. Such movements led to organisational development and the Association of Student Counsellors was created in 1970; this steadily grew into the broader British Association for Counselling (BAC), created in 1977 (now the British Association for Counselling and Psychotherapy (BACP)). Thus, the creation of a Division of Counselling Psychology represented a major push by those psychologists with additional training in counselling and psychotherapy to join up the dots between these two disciplines. At the point of writing, in 2011, counselling psychology occupies a major place within the British Psychological Society, as the third largest division (behind clinical psychology and occupational psychology), and is the second fastest-growing.

Outside the UK, counselling psychology is showing great strides in establishing itself. The USA proves the most dominant force in the field, having the longest-established counselling psychology profession. The terms 'counseling psychologist' and 'counseling psychology' were introduced at the 1951 Northwestern Conference (Munley *et al.*, 2004). Once again, the profession had historical roots in humanistic psychology, vocational guidance and counselling and psychotherapy. In the USA now the focus in counselling psychology appears to primarily be on the multicultural and social justice movements, and emphasising a philosophy of prevention and well-being across diversity.

Beyond the USA, there exists a counselling psychology profession to some degree in Australia, New Zealand, Hong Kong, China, South Korea, South Africa, Israel, Portugal and Germany (Orlans and van Scoyoc, 2009). There is however a considerable degree of variance around the extent to which the profession is demarcated or considered a specialty in itself.

As with other applied disciplines of psychology in the UK, counselling psychology made the move to standardise all training programmes at Doctorate level in 2005. Such a move also emerged at a similar time as the Health Professions Council became the official regulatory body for practitioner psychologists. This body developed Standards of Education and Training, with which all training programmes must comply (Health Professions Council, 2009a), and ensures that all trainees have evidenced coverage of the Standards of Proficiency, as stipulated by the same professional body (Health Professions Council, 2009b). The British Psychological Society provides a further value-added accreditation for counselling psychology programmes. The main components of such training programmes support the development of the core values of the profession, discussed above. All practitioners must:

- Be competent, reflective, ethically sound, resourceful and informed practitioners of counselling psychology able to work in therapeutic and non-therapeutic contexts
- Value the imaginative, interpretive, personal and intimate aspects of the practice of counselling psychology
- Commit themselves to on-going personal and professional development and inquiry
- Understand, develop and apply models of psychological inquiry for the creation of new knowledge which is appropriate to the multi-dimensional nature of relationships between people
- Appreciate the significance of wider social, cultural and political domains within which counselling psychology operates
- Adopt a questioning and evaluative approach to philosophy, practice, research and theory which constitutes counselling psychology

(British Psychological Society, 2010)

In the above sections we have outlined the developing profession of counselling psychology. We have briefly introduced some historical developments in the field and discussed the core values on which it is founded. In doing so, we hope to have provided a background to the conception of such a text and reflected upon the ethos which we hope resonates throughout the work.

A brief history of counselling for young people

This section reflects upon the development of therapeutic services for young people. It briefly discusses recent developments within adolescent mental health care in the UK and highlights some of the key issues that revolve around such service delivery. This section therefore sews numerous seeds for many of the issues which are further developed at later stages within this text.

Adolescent mental health

Adolescence is renowned for being a particularly challenging life phase. Broadly, it is viewed as a relatively new phenomenon that became commonplace within the UK during the middle part of the twentieth century; it has been defined as a life stage which emerged as full-time education took over from full-time employment as the primary activity of young people (Furstenberg, 2000). It is also a period of life full of contradictions, with adult care-givers fluctuating from supporting individuals in developing their own autonomous thinking on the one hand and condemning them for their self-centredness on the other (Farkas and Johnson, 1997). Alongside the inconsistent treatment from adult figures comes the need to negotiate pathways through great physical changes and to ally themselves successfully with individuals in their peer group who will support them on their journey. There is an abundance of literature around the challenges that adolescents face and Chapter 5 develops the ideas introduced here.

The transitional nature of adolescence, combined with the limited resources that young people have to control their lives, is likely to lead to an increase in psychological problems (Coleman, 2010). Within studies which examine how the mental health of the nation's young people is changing, it is commonly reported that conduct disorders, depression and suicide have all increased since the Second World War (Rutter and Smith, 1995; Fombonne, 1998; Collishaw et al., 2004). These changes have led to a great prevalence of mental health difficulties within this age group, and at the turn of the century the Mental Health Foundation claimed that up to one in five children and young people experience some form of psychological problem (Mental Health Foundation, 1999).

The difficulties which adolescents face manifest in numerous ways. In attempting to provide an overview of how this may occur, Downey (2003) notes that young people either internalise problems, for example by anxiously ruminating, or externalise problems, for example by becoming aggressive with others. Without a doubt these activities vary greatly in severity; however, there are an increasing number of reports outlining how commonplace some of the more extreme manifestations of psychological difficulties may be. For instance, conclusions have been drawn stating that 'Roughly 1 in 10 children have at least one DSM-IV disorder, involving a level of distress or social impairment likely to warrant treatment' (Ford *et al.*, 2003, p.1203), one in three young people have contemplated suicide (Steinberg, 1996) and 24,000 potentially self-harmed in 1999 (Oxford Centre for Suicide Research, 1998). This list could continue to include a multitude of other reports that display the alarming ways that some adolescents cope with the challenges of everyday life.

In response to the pressures that young people are facing, and accounting for the increased awareness of the need for support, attempts are being made to develop appropriate mental health provision for this age group. Within the UK the Green Paper *Every Child Matters* (Boateng, 2003) and the new *Children Act* (Department for Education and Skills, 2004) prove significant in highlighting government backing for the development of joined-up mental health care for children and young people. This is also evident within government strategies which outline the need for educational establishments to support their students in a more holistic way (see, for example, The Healthy Schools Initiative (Department for Education and Skills, 1999)). Developing on from such policy documents comes guidance to consider offering counselling as a response when supporting young people with emotional and behavioural difficulties (Department for Education and Skills, 2001). The next section moves on to consider developments within the field of youth counselling.

The development of counselling services for young people

Counselling services for young people have steadily begun to increase within the UK. This trend stems from research such as that presented above, which outlines the challenges faced by adolescents and their need for additional support. It is an area of debate that has provoked high-profile youth organisations such as the National Society for the Prevention of Cruelty to Children (NSPCC) and government ministers to call for all young people in the UK to have easy access to professional counselling services (see NSPCC, 2004, and Hodge, 2004, respectively). Below we introduce some of the central debates that revolve around offering therapy to young people.

Since the turn of the twentieth century, hundreds of therapeutic approaches have been devised to support children and young people. Individuals often pinpoint Freud's work with Little Hans as the first chronicled case of adolescent psychotherapy (Weisz *et al.*, 2005) and these humble beginnings have now led to the creation of over 550 distinct treatments (Kazdin, 2000). Such interventions can be categorised into four major categories: (1) community approaches; (2) family approaches; (3) group approaches; and (4) individual approaches (Downey, 2003). For the purposes of this book the focus becomes the last of these perspectives; however there is a great deal of potential overlap between much of the content.

Counselling services for young people have traditionally developed in clinical settings in much the same way that adult services have. More recently, there has been a move to tailor services to the needs of the client group. Such 'youth-friendly counselling services' (Pope, 2002) acknowledge that young people may not fit seamlessly into the frameworks of existing adult services. In particular, a recurring important issue is that of accessibility – Griffiths (2003) sums it up concisely when he notes that services should be 'accessible, appropriate, friendly and relevant to adolescents' (p.26). In creating a service that complies with these recommendations, individuals need to be mindful of both practical issues (e.g. Where is the service hosted? and Who offers it?) and theoretical issues (e.g. What therapeutic approach is adopted?). Importantly, it is suggested that such considerations can ultimately impact upon the quality of the therapeutic alliance between counsellor and client (French *et al.*, 2003).

In considering the practical issues of service development, great strides have been made in the provision of youth counselling. Issues essential to safe and ethical practice with this age group have increasingly received necessary attention (Daniels and Jenkins, 2010; Welsh Assembly Government and British Association for Counselling and Psychotherapy, 2011) and services have begun to develop outside traditional clinical settings. On this latter point, counselling services have emerged within independent community settings, educational establishments and in mediated formats (both online and using the telephone). The purpose of doing so has been to increase access pathways for those individuals who would not ordinarily access traditional therapeutic services.

Counselling within educational settings has been one of the major areas of development in the past decade. Up until recently, little was known about how prevalent work in this area is (Baginsky, 2004); however two major surveys have begun to provide insight into this matter (Jenkins and Polat, 2005; Pattison *et al.*, 2008). The most recent of these studies examined the provision of counselling within Welsh schools. It found that three-quarters of the secondary schools who responded to the survey ($n = 76$) reported providing a formal counselling service (Pattison et al., 2008). The earlier study noted that, of 607 respondents, almost three-quarters claimed to offer 'therapeutic individual support' (Jenkins and Polat, 2005). Such findings show that schools and colleges are now beginning to view counselling as an important part of their pastoral infrastructure (see also Hanley *et al.*, 2012, for further discussion). Research examining the quality of the therapeutic work in these settings not only displays the effectiveness of the work being carried out, it also consistently indicates that service users are themselves highly satisfied with these services (see Chapter 6 for an overview of this literature). With such positive developments in the work conducted within educational settings, it is necessary to note that other non-traditional settings have received much less attention to date (see Chapter 3 for further discussion regarding different settings).

The development of therapeutic services within environments which are distanced from traditional medical settings, and therefore potentially more youth-friendly, goes hand in hand with the move to create youth-friendly therapeutic approaches. Historically practitioners have been mindful of developmental differences between young people and adult therapists and attempted to create appropriate therapeutic models. For instance, Bettelheim (1976) during the mid-1970s introduced the notion that working imaginatively with fairy tales can be incredibly insightful with regard to young people's conscious and unconscious processes. Such creative practices have now become commonplace and counsellors regularly report using art, music and creative writing in youth settings. Although psychologists do adopt purist models of therapy with young people, quite often youth-friendly models acknowledge a need to bridge both the relational aspects of therapy and the technical aspects of such work. For instance, the quality of the relationship is viewed as fundamental to the work of youth counsellors (DiGiuseppe et al., 1996) and, without paying attention to its subtleties, therapeutic engagement may not be possible (French et al., 2003). In addition, therapists are aware that at times there may be a need to make developmentally appropriate technical interventions (see texts outlining evidence-based practice, for example, Kazdin and Weisz (2003) and Fonagy et al., 2003). The integration of such components is reflected in numerous theoretical frameworks which focus upon working therapeutically with children and young people (see, for instance, Geldard and Geldard's (2010) proactive approach to counselling adolescents).

The view that young service users can positively impact upon the direction of service delivery proves another area that has come to the fore in recent years. Historically the creation of services for young people was directed solely using an adult-centred top-down approach; however this view has begun to change. It is now accepted that the opinions of this age group can provide a unique insight into adolescents' experiences of health services (Docherty and Sandelowski, 1999). These views are also recognised to give service developers incredibly rich information about the wants and needs of the client group being catered for (Buston, 2002; Kirby, 2004; Hanley, 2012). In addition to the benefits to the service in question, the young people involved in such consultation exercises can also benefit (see Kirby, 2004, for a list of seven reasons why young people can benefit from being involved in service development). Undertaking such work needs a great deal of forward planning and strategies of appropriately engaging individuals need to be considered thoroughly. This is particularly important as many consultation exercises with young people can be criticised for being tokenistic or even exploitative of those involved (Kirby, 2004). Presently there is limited evidence of user involvement within the development of therapeutic services for adolescents; however significant political pushes in the UK acknowledge the importance of such involvement (Wade and Badham, 2003; Department for Education and Skills, 2005). One notable contribution comes in the arena of school-based counselling. The Welsh Assembly, in partnership with the BACP and a number of universities, actively liaised with the youth group The Funky Dragon regarding the development of such provision (see Pattison et al., 2008, for a detailed summary of this work). Such collaborations once again highlight the value of enabling young service users to have a voice in services that potentially impact upon their lives.

Conclusion

Counselling psychology is a relatively new discipline within the UK: the Division of Counselling Psychology in the British Psychological Society was formed in 1994. Since then it has been growing and carving a unique identity within the landscape of British psychology, distinct from the areas of counselling, clinical psychology and psychotherapy. It is a profession which emphasises the importance of the collaborative therapeutic relationship where the psychologist works alongside clients, empowering them to achieve their individual goals for therapy.

Evidence around the therapeutic relationship and its link to improved outcomes is also at the heart of work within adolescent counselling services. Due to the psychological difficulties faced by many adolescents and young people in the UK, services are being developed specifically for this population group which aim to foster a therapeutic relationship and find appropriate ways of working therapeutically with young people. Since the turn of the century, various services, models, and approaches have been developed. More recently there has been a shift towards creating services specifically tailored for young people as a distinct population group, and recognising the need to involve young people in the planning of their services.

Summary

- Counselling psychology brings together the traditions of counselling and psychology and therefore combines the values of the humanistic movement with more traditional models of scientific psychology. The profession has been evolving in the UK since 1979 and is present to some degree in numerous other countries across the globe.
- Counselling psychology looks to promote well-being and prevention whilst questioning the validity of the traditional medical model when applied to psychological distress, and emphasises the importance of the therapeutic relationship and client agency in contributing to outcome for the client.
- Counselling psychology training is now at Doctorate level, and is accredited by both the Health Professions Council and the British Psychological Society. The Health Professions Council is the official regulatory body for practitioner psychologists in the UK.
- There is a high rate of mental health difficulties among young people, attributable in part to the transitional nature of the developmental period, and the lack of control young people may have at this stage. Due to increased levels of psychological distress, youth counselling and mental health services are steadily on the increase, particularly in educational settings.
- Specific youth counselling services have developed in non-traditional therapeutic formats, such as being delivered through mediated formats, using art, music and creative writing therapeutically. The core focus of working with young people has been the need to develop a therapeutic relationship in order for therapeutic work to be done.

- There is now a move towards including young people in the development of adolescent counselling services, as it has begun to be acknowledged that the opinions of young people themselves can provide service developers with rich and insightful information.

Further reading

A good place to start in relation to counselling psychology in the UK is the *Handbook of Counselling Psychology*, edited by Ray Woolfe, Sheelagh Strawbridge, Barbara Douglas and Windy Dryden, currently in its third edition (London: Sage, 2010). Another introductory text which looks at some of the historical and contextual issues is *A Short Introduction to Counselling Psychology*, by Vanja Orlans and Susan van Scoyoc (London: Sage, 2009).

In relation to training of counselling psychologists and the Health Professions Council, see the following websites: www.bps.org.uk and www.hpc-uk.org.

References

Asay, T. P. and Lambert, M. J. (1999). The empirical case for the common factors in therapy: quantitative findings. In B. L. Duncan, M. A. Hubble and S. D. Miller (eds) *The Heart and Soul of Change* (pp.23–55). Washington, DC: American Psychological Association.

Baginsky, M. (2004). *Evaluation of the NSPCC's Schools Teams Service*. London: NSPCC.

Bettelheim, B. (1976). *The Uses of Enchantment: The meaning and importance of fairy tales*. London: Penguin Books.

Boateng, P. (2003). *Every Child Matters*. London: Stationery Office.

Bohart, A. C. and Tallman, K. (1999). *How Clients Make Therapy Work: The process of active self-healing*. Washington, DC: American Psychological Association.

British Psychological Society (2010). *Accreditation Through Partnership Handbook: Guidance for counselling psychology programmes*. Leicester: BPS.

Bugental, J. F. T. (1964). The third force in psychology. *Journal of Humanistic Psychology*, 4 (1), 19–26.

Buston, K. (2002). Adolescents with mental health problems: what do they say about health services? *Journal of Adolescence*, 25, 231–42.

Coleman, J. (2010). *The Nature of Adolescence* (4th edition). London: Routledge.

Collishaw, S., Maughan, B., Goodman, R. and Pickles, A. (2004). Time trends in adolescent mental health. *Journal of Child Psychology and Psychiatry*, 45 (8), 1350–62.

Cross, M. and Watts, M. (2002). Trainee perspectives on counselling psychology: articulating a representation of the discipline. *Counselling Psychology Quarterly*, 15 (4), 293–305.

Daniels, D. and Jenkins, P. (2010). *Therapy with Children: Children's' Rights, Confidentiality and the Law* (2nd edition). London: Sage.

Department for Education and Skills. (1999). *National Healthy School Standard (NHSS)*. London: HMI.

Department for Education and Skills. (2001). *Promoting Children's Mental Health in the Early Years and in School Settings*. London: DfEE Publications.

Department for Education and Skills. (2004). *Children Act.* London: HMSO.

Department for Education and Skills. (2005). *Youth Matters.* London: HMSO.

DiGiuseppe, R., Linscott, J. and Jilton, R. (1996). Developing the therapeutic alliance in child-adolescent psychotherapy. *Applied and Preventive Psychology*, 5, 85–100.

Docherty, S. and Sandelowski, M. (1999). Focus on qualitative methods: interviewing children. *Research in Nursing and Health*, 22,177–85.

Douglas, B. (2010). Disorder and its discontents. In R. Woolfe, S. Strawbridge, B. Douglas and W. Dryden (eds) *Handbook of Counselling Psychology* (3rd edition) (pp.23–33). London: Sage.

Downey, J. (2003). Psychological counselliong of children and young people. In R. Woolfe, W. Dryden and S. Strawbridge (eds). *Handbook of Counselling Psychology* (2nd edition) (pp.322–42). London: Sage.

Farkas, S. and Johnson, J. (1997). *Kids These Days: What Americans really think about the next generation.* New York: Public Agenda.

Fombonne, E. (1998). Increased rates of psychosocial disorders in youth. *European Archives of Psychiatry and Clinical Neuroscience*, 248, 14–21.

Fonagy, P., Target, M., Cottrell, D., Philips, J. and Kurtz, Z. (2003). *What Works for Whom? A critical review of treatments for children and adolescents.* New York: Guildford Press.

Ford, T., Goodman, R. and Meltzer, H. (2003). The British Child and Adolescent Mental Health Survey 1999: the prevalence of DSM-IV disorders. *Journal of the American Academy of Child and Adolescent Psychiatry*, 42 (10), 1203–11.

French, R., Reardon, M. and Smith, P. (2003). Engaging with a mental health service: perspectives of at-risk youth. *Child and Adolescent Social Work Journal*, 20 (6), 529–48.

Furstenberg, F. (2000). The sociology of adolescence and youth in the 1990s: a critical commentary. *Journal of Marriage and the Family*, 62, 896–910.

Geldard, K. and Geldard, D. (2010). *Counselling Adolescents: The proactive approach for young people* (3rd edition). London: Sage.

Griffiths, M. (2003). Terms of engagement. *Young Minds Magazine*, 62, 23–6.

Hanley, T. (2012). Understanding the online therapeutic alliance through the eyes of adolescent service users, *Counselling and Psychotherapy Research*, 12, 35–43..

Hanley, T., Humphrey, N. and Lennie, C. (2012). The therapeutic classroom. In D. Armstrong and G. Squires (eds) *Contemporary Issues in Special Educational Needs: Considering the whole child.* London: Open University Press/McGraw-Hill Education.

Health Professions Council. (2009a). *Standards of Education and Training Guidance.* London: HPC.

Health Professions Council. (2009b). *Standards of Proficiency – Practitioner Psychologists.* London: HPC.

Hodge, M. (2004). Virtual conversations. *Counselling in Education*, Spring, 14–15.

Jenkins, P. and Polat, F. (2005). *The Current Provision of Counselling Services in Secondary Schools in England and Wales.* Manchester: University of Manchester.

Kazdin, A. (2000). *Psychotherapy for Children and Adolescents: Directions for research and practice.* Oxford: Oxford University Press.

Kazdin, A. and Weisz, J. (eds) (2003). *Evidence-based Psychotherapies for Children and Adolescents.* New York: Guilford Press.

Kinderman, P. (2009). The future of counselling psychology: a view from outside. *Counselling Psychology Review*, 24 (1), 16–21.

Kirby, P. (2004). *A Guide to Actively Involving Young People in Research: For researchers, research commissioners and managers.* Hampshire: Involve.

Luborsky, L., Singer, B. and Luborsky, L. (1975). Is it true that 'Everyone has won and all must have prizes'? *Archives of General Psychiatry, 32* (8), 995–1008.

Mental Health Foundation. (1999). *Bright Futures: Promoting children and young people's mental health.* London: Mental Health Foundation.

Munley, P. H., Duncan, L. E., McDonnell, K. A. and Sauer, E. M. (2004). Counseling psychology in the United States of America. *Counselling Psychology Quarterly* 17 (3), 247–71.

National Society for the Prevention of Cruelty to Children. (2004). *Someone to Turn to.* London: NSPCC.

Orlans, V. and van Scoyoc, S. (2009). *A Short Introduction to Counselling Psychology.* London: Sage.

Oxford Centre for Suicide Research. (1998). *Annual Report on Suicide Statistics.* Oxford: University of Oxford.

Pattison, S., Rowland, N., Cromarty, K., Richards, K., Jenkins, P., Cooper, M., Polat, F. and Couchman, A. (2008). *Counselling in Schools: A research study into the services for children and young people' commissioned by the Welsh Assembly Government.* Lutterworth: British Association for Counselling and Psychotherapy.

Pope, P. (2002). Youth-friendly counselling. *Counselling and Psychotherapy Journal,* February, 18–19.

Proposed British Journal of Counselling Psychology Editorial Board. (2011). *Proposal to Create the British Journal of Counselling Psychology.* Unpublished document.

Rutter, M. and Smith, D. (1995). Psychosocial disorders in young people: time trends and their causes. Chichester: John Wiley.

Steinberg, L. (1996*). Beyond the Classroom: Why school reform has failed and what parents need to do.* New York: Simon Schuster.

Strawbridge, S. and Woolfe, R. (2003). Counselling psychology in context. In R. Woolfe, W. Dryden and S. Strawbridge (eds) *Handbook of Counselling Psychology* (2nd edition). London: Sage.

Strawbridge, S. and Woolfe, R. (2010). Counselling psychology: origins, developments and challenges. In R. Woolfe, S. Strawbridge, B. Douglas and W. Dryden (eds) *Handbook of Counselling Psychology* (3rd edition) (pp.3–22). London: Sage.

Wade, H. and Badham, B. (2003). *Hear By Right: Standards for active involvement of young people in democracy.* UK: The National Youth Agency/Local Government Association.

Weisz, J., Sandler, I., Durlak, J. and Anton, B. (2005). Promoting and protecting youth mental health through evidence-based prevention and treatment. *American Psychologist,* 60 (6), 628–48.

Welsh Assembly Government and British Association for Counselling and Psychotherapy (2011). *School Based Counselling Operating Kit* (including Welsh version). Cardiff: WAG.

Woolfe, R. (1990). Counselling psychology in Britain: an idea whose time has come. *The Psychologist,* 3 (12), 531–5.

Chapter 3

Different settings

Neil Humphrey, Miranda Wolpert,
Terry Hanley, Aaron Sefi and Matt Shorrock

Overview

Adolescent counselling psychology services come in many shapes and sizes. This chapter provides an overview of some of the major settings in which such services can be found and the major considerations related to them. In turn, the different settings include Child and Adolescent Mental Health Services (CAMHS), school-based counselling services, counselling in the community and online and telephone counselling. Each of these sections has been written by an individual, or individuals, working at the leading edge of such development and aims to highlight some of the key factors related to such ways of working. As is noted at the end of the chapter, these sections will hopefully provide a useful resource for considering therapeutic practice in these different settings.

Child and Adolescent Mental Health Services

Counselling for young people in clinical settings generally takes place as part of CAMHS. Whilst in some areas specialist adolescent provision is available, in the majority of areas CAMHS cover the age group up to 18 years. In 2009 the national mapping service identified 128 CAMHS across England, employing the equivalent of 11,000 full-time staff and seeing just under a quarter of a million children and young people each year (www.camhsmapping.org.uk).

CAMHS generally comprise multidisciplinary teams made up of a range of professionals, such as psychiatrists, psychologists, nurses, social workers, primary mental health workers, family therapists, psychotherapists, educational professionals and other allied therapists. They see children and young people who experience a wide range of problems, including anxiety disorders, depression, trauma following abuse, attention deficit disorder, self-harm and early-onset psychosis. A range of interventions are offered which may include counselling but may also include structured psychological interventions such as cognitive-behavioural therapy (CBT), pharmacological interventions, group treatment, family therapy, art therapy and play therapy.

CAMHS provision grew out of two traditions – the tradition of child psychiatry on the one hand and the tradition of child guidance on the other. It can be argued that the tension between these two traditions can still be felt today. Child psychiatry traditionally focuses on more severe difficulties and disorders (such as early-onset psychosis), may draw on medical models, and looks particularly to links with adult mental health services. Child guidance traditionally focuses on milder difficulties (such as anxiety) and has had stronger links with educational and social care models of provision. Both elements can be seen as present in CAMHS and services still struggle at both a local and national level between the need to link with adult mental health and the need to link with child services (including health, social care and education) whilst not being entirely subsumed within either.

Most CAMHS today are still located in clinical settings in the NHS but there is increasing push for delivery in other settings, such as in community venues and schools. Also, there is an increasing push for collaboration between statutory and voluntary sector provision and for possible greater development of the independent sector.

Policy direction for CAMHS was set under the Labour administration by the National Service Framework in 2003 (Department of Health, 2004), which set a ten-year direction of travel and has been subject to periodic review, including the CAMHS Review (2008). The emphasis was on the development of equality of access across the country, the need to ensure that particularly vulnerable groups (such as children looked after by the state) received appropriate support, the need to increase overall capacity, the need to improve outcomes by encouraging focus on key targets and the need to develop more evidence-based practice.

Interventions provided by CAMHS have become increasingly guided by National Institute for Health and Clinical Excellence guidelines. These set out to summarise the research evidence and have this reviewed by professional experts and service user groups, who come together to agree best-care packages for different problems, to which services should adhere. There has also been an emphasis on developing more user involvement in CAMHS provision at all levels, including service development. The work of the advocacy group YoungMinds has been particularly powerful in developing models of user involvement and championing a manifesto of children's and young people's priorities in relation to CAMHS developments.

During the Labour government, dedicated funds were put into service development and used to finance a number of initiatives, including the development of a National CAMHS Support Service (Rees, 2007), which consisted of a network of regional workers who helped develop models of best practice in services. The development of learning collaborations across services such as the CAMHS Outcomes Research Consortium, whereby CAMHS joined together to develop meaningful outcome protocols (this collaboration is chaired by Miranda Wolpert, one of the co-authors of this chapter) and the Quality Network for Community CAMHS, whereby teams joined together to establish peer review mechanisms to set standards for best practice, have contributed to shared views of what might constitute aspects of best practice in CAMHS.

However, it remains the case that most services have grown up *ad hoc*, with service prioritisation based on clinician interest and passion rather than coherent analysis of need. Moreover, there are often difficult relationships with potential colleagues in allied organisations such as schools and adult mental health services. CAMHS remain very small compared to size of need and it is estimated that only 10–25% of those severe enough to require specialist mental health provision currently access this. Waiting lists remain long in some areas and referral routes may be complicated and hard for the majority to access. A number of initiatives have been launched in recent years to try to manage capacity and bring increasingly rational ways of working, including the Choice and Partnership Approach, which promoted a model of managing workloads within multidisciplinary teams and developing models for helping service users access most appropriate services and care for their particular difficulties (York and Kingsbury, 2011).

With the new Coalition administration (2010 onwards), the emphasis has remained on evidence-based practice but this has been combined with an increasing emphasis on ensuring a focus on outcomes and not outputs, a reduced emphasis on targets and an increased emphasis on the need for choice and shared decision making and on the importance of the role of the voluntary and independent sectors as potential providers of CAMHS.

Whilst some CAMHS across the country in 2011 were experiencing cuts, others were expanding (Gillen and Hayes, 2011). Throughout both the Labour and Coalition periods there has been an emphasis on the need for more competitive commissioning to encourage service improvement and a range of commissioning guidelines were developed. Increasing numbers of areas set up systems whereby services were put into competition with each other to allow commissioners to choose a provider from a range of possibilities.

One particular new policy initiative launched for CAMHS provision in 2011 is Children and Young People – Improving Access to Psychological Therapies (CYP IAPT). This initiative draws on adult mental health IAPT but is different from it in that it does not look to develop a new service but rather to 'transform existing services'. Central to this vision is the idea of developing more skills in key evidence-based treatments such as CBT and parent training. Collaboratives of universities and service providers were invited to bid for funds to develop training and service transformation programmes across a range of services. Central to this programme is the focus on the use of regular outcome monitoring based on client report during contact with CAMHS.

There is an increasing interest in ensuring such services are providing positive outcomes and value for money (Department of Health, 2010a, 2010b). There is also an increasing interest in value for money in the provision of services, reflected in developments such as payment by results (PBR), which aims to develop a process whereby care is costed according to provision (and in time outcomes) rather than as old block contracts. Whilst PBR in CAMHS is still in its infancy, it is likely to develop further in future years. However, it remains to be seen what impact this actually has and how much becomes truly 'payment by results' rather than 'payment by processes'.

Meanwhile, at the heart of the young person's experience within CAMHS remains the relationship between the young person and those trying to help that individual. There is an increasing emphasis on trying to make this as positive an experience as possible for all groups. Recent policy has reinforced the emphasis on the importance of practice that is informed and guided by input from clients, and allows them fully informed choice at all points. The guiding principal is 'no decision about me without me' (Department of Health, 2010a, 2010b). Research suggests that allowing service users to inform their own treatment can lead to more appropriate service use, promote adherence to treatment and improve coping skills (Coulter, 2011).

In summary, CAMHS remains a key focus of policy interest. Riots in England in 2011 reignited debates about how best to prevent and respond to behavioural disturbance in young people and several reports in the early 2000s focused on meeting the emotional and psychological needs of children and young people as a key focus for any government (Layard, 2011). Yet services remain small relative to need and judgements about how best to help particular groups of young people with particular difficulties and where it is most cost-effective to target provision remain much debated. What does seem to be clear is that the level of need remains high and unlikely to be reducing any time soon.

School-based counselling

It is often noted that school-based counselling had a surge of interest in the early 1960s after the Newsom Report (1963) recommended counselling for under-achieving children (see National Society for the Prevention of Cruelty to Children (NSPCC) report by Baginsky, 2004). This led to the first university courses, training experienced teachers to become school counsellors. By this time, counselling in schools had already been established in the USA, mainly through the work of child psychologists, some of whom came to the UK and helped develop the movement in this country.

The surge of interest in school-based counselling in the 1960s has its roots even further back in the emergence of child psychology and child guidance in the first half of the twentieth century. As Freud (1962) articulated his five psychosexual phases, and Piaget (1977) set out his developmental models, developmental psychology, and the understanding of how to intervene in adolescent processes, was born. Arguably, we can see some 'counselling' roots even further back eighteenth century (King, 1999). These schools were almost all church-based Sunday schools, with the Bible as their only text. Yet with this benevolent drive towards helping slum boys discover their innate goodness (Rousseau, 1997), this pastoral ideology is arguably as much a root of modern school-based counselling as is the development of child psychology.

It is noteworthy, and arguably inevitable, that right from the outset school-based counselling was perceived as a tool for behaviour modification. Indeed, the recent wave of interest in such practice has coincided with media-driven perceptions of 'problem youth'. Whilst increased awareness has developed a more altruistic motivation to help young people at risk in recent times, this conformative motivation may be reflected in how young people and their families and teachers have perceived counselling across the ages, and to the present day. As mentioned later in more detail, recent surveys (Jenkins and Polat, 2005) indicate that counselling is still emphasised as benefiting the school through its social, educational and pupil behavioural merits, over and above the drive for self-actualisation (Rogers, 1961) of young people, which may in turn be the bias for the majority of counsellors. A recent randomised controlled trial conducted on school-based counselling also identified self-reported improvements in educational attainment as a result of receiving counselling (McArthur *et al.*, 2011). It is contentiously important that counsellors are able to show this level of change, beyond therapeutic improvement.

It is important to point out that this initial surge was relatively localised within the UK, uncoordinated (Lang, 1999) and unintegrated (Robinson, 1996) into the school system. Also, a large part of the counselling was informally undertaken by teachers. Bor and colleagues (2002) point out that recently this trend has switched. The implementation of the National Curriculum in the UK has meant that the role of teachers in helping achieve academic attainment has taken precedence in recent times. Yet at the same time *The Children Act 1989* recognised the need to protect at-risk young people (HMSO, 2011). Thus, the recent wave of formal school-based counselling correlates with a decline in this pastoral role of teachers, and a growing momentum to protect young people. The importance of an independent counsellor to do this work has become increasingly recognised in schools (Burnison, 2003). The value in this independence takes a greater emphasis when considering the need to separate the perception of counselling from the mechanics of school discipline. However, in saying this, the recent initiative of social and emotional aspects of learning (SEAL) in schools (Department for Children, Schools and Families, 2007) has attempted to bring these two aspects of school life together. How independent counselling fits into the SEAL criteria is an area that requires closer attention if counselling services are to complement this initiative more than is presently the case.

Another initiative which has addressed the mental health of school pupils is the Targeted Mental Health in Schools programme which ran from 2008 to 2011. Initial reports from the initiative indicate that around ten per cent of pupils are experiencing adverse emotional and behavioural problems. This figure is consistent with other large studies (Department for Children, Schools and Families, 2008). This project has also been reflected in the roll-out of IAPT for children and young people (Department of Health, 2011). This government strategy is committed to improving access to evidence-based talking therapies for young people, with a particular focus on looked-after children and body confidence.

Until recently there was very little knowledge of the overall provision of therapy in schools in the UK. Since this fact was highlighted in the NSPCC review (2004), Jenkins and Polat (2005) undertook a survey of schools and local education authorities in the UK. Their key findings were that almost 75% of schools claim to provide 'therapeutic individual counselling' (2005, p.8). However, the format of this varies greatly from school to school, with the majority of counselling (42%) provided by external counsellors employed on a sessional basis, and the next highest being members of teaching staff (26%). The provision tends to be *ad hoc* and demand-led. It is also characterised by being decentralised, non-statutory and school-funded.

The nature of this provision is being challenged to take a more multiagency focus in recent years. The Green Paper, *Every Child Matters* (Boateng, 2003) preceded the *Children Act 2004*, which radically reshaped service delivery for children, took in the role of extended schools in 'providing pastoral care to all children' (Boateng, 2003, p.63). These recommendations were echoed by former Minister for Children Margaret Hodge (2004). She called for counselling provision in all schools, which joined up with multidisciplinary teams of professionals. This call has been echoed recently by the 'think tank' the Institute for Public Policy Research, whose commissioned report (Sodha and Margo, 2008) called for counsellors to be introduced into every school in the UK, starting with those in deprived areas. It argues that these counsellors should be well versed in the local pathways of outside agencies, and be able to provide a bridge to these services.

While there is this considerable political will, echoed by the local education authorities, for counselling to become embedded within schools and sit within a Tier 2 framework and link much more closely with CAMHS and other external agencies, anecdotal evidence would suggest that this is happening on an ad hoc basis only within England. However, within Wales there has been more focus on strategy, where the Welsh Assembly Government has backed up a commitment to providing counselling in all schools, by commissioning research offering evidence-based guidelines to inform provision strategy (Pattison *et al.*, 2009). Considering the key role that school-based counselling could take in early detection, intervention and prevention, this aspect needs further research. This is just beginning to take place in England, with the British Association for Counselling and Psychotherapy (BACP) undertaking initial exploration in this area, with the creation of a practice research network to examine existing provision in England, and how lessons can be learned to extend the provision effectively in this country, with priority being placed on getting counsellors into schools in the poorer communities, where provision from other services may be more sparse (Pattison *et al.,* 2009).

Outside England, as mentioned, the lead has been taken by the commitment to provide counselling in all schools in Wales. The nature of this provision is varied, particularly in some areas of Wales, with anecdotal evidence of a preference in some schools to outsource counselling to online and other service providers. However, this commitment shows the priority now being placed on school-based counselling in these areas of the UK, one which is hoped to be reflected in England. With this commitment is a greater need to show the efficacy of such practice (see Chapter 6 for developments in this area). Inevitably, this commitment also requires the funding to achieve its goal. Field research in Wales (Welsh Assembly Government, 2008; Pattison *et al.*, 2009) indicated that the majority of schools were dissatisfied with the current provision for funding, most of these being schools that have to fund the service from within their own budgets (just under half the schools surveyed, while another third of the schools used local authority funding). As well as a recommendation for more sustainable funding for schools, this Welsh Assembly Government-commissioned research also recognised that there was a need for more 'hard' evaluation (using quantitative measures), and to achieve this, a need for counsellors and managers of services to be better informed about how to apply this level of monitoring. Clearly, as school-based counselling takes a more prevalent role in young people's lives, and as budgets become tighter, the need for this informed evidence-based approach grows stronger.

The practice of school-based counselling now has clear guidelines and standards in place offered by the BACP toolkit for practitioners (BACP, 2011). This offers guidance on how services should operate within the school setting; how to work within the ethical standards of the BACP in schools; the role of the counsellor and link person in the school; and recommendations of how the relationship with the school and parents can be maintained considering practical issues of confidentiality and accountability.

Counselling in the community: working with disaffected young people

Throughout my training to become a psychotherapist and psychologist, I was employed as a social worker and social services manager, and was commissioned by the local authority to develop service provision for disaffected children and young people leaving the care system. In partnership with the Connexions Service (the national agency developed as part of a government strategy to reduce social exclusion among young people), I embarked on an extensive piece of research exploring gaps in service provision for young people; the causes of the disaffection of those leaving local authority care; and community-based models of best and innovative practice (Shorrock, 2006). I will refer to the impact of this research, and the implications for future research and service delivery shortly.

In terms of government policy, *Every Child Matters* (HM Treasury, 2003) and subsequently the *Children Act 2004* have resulted in significant organisational changes, forging the development of children's trusts and local safeguarding children boards in each local authority in England, intended to ensure the delivery of integrated services focused primarily on early intervention and prevention of disaffection in children and young people. Other developments, such as the frameworks introduced for assessing children with additional needs (Department of Health/Department for Education and Employment/Home Office, 2000;

Department for Children, Schools and Families, 2006), highlight the impact that community-level factors can have in shaping the well-being of children and young people (Bronfenbrenner, 1979; Jack, 2000).

Talking to young people, in a variety of community settings, not only allows volunteers, local residents and practitioners to learn directly of their experiences, it also communicates a clear message that their views are significant and that adults value them as agents of change who are capable of shaping their own lives (Gill, 2008). Sadly, there an abundance of evidence supporting the contrasting view, and children and young people rarely consider that their views are listened to or taken seriously by adults (Kloep *et al.*, 2010). In the absence of active listening networks many young people are left feeling alienated and vulnerable (Jack and Gill, 2010).

In a fascinating study, exploring the views of young people in two deprived communities, Kloep *et al.* (2010) found that a generalised picture of how disaffected youth cope in such adversity cannot be established as conditions leading to resilience or vulnerability are unique for each individual, given the complex interactions among personal qualities, environmental/community influences and social relationships. Another significant finding was how vitally importance it is for young people to feel they are 'good at something':

> In our sample the aptitudes and abilities mentioned varied widely, from music, dance and sports to academic skills. These adolescents do not necessarily aspire to Olympian heights, but just wish to develop competence in 'something', at least to a level that enhances confidence and self-belief. Most importantly, this seems to trigger the creation of other resources and skills: It gives them a valued position vis-à-vis peers and adults, gains them the attention of possible mentors, goals to aspire to, and convincing reasons to stay out of trouble. Similarly, the opportunity to care for, and take responsibility for somebody who needs help, can have this effect.
>
> One-factor solutions to community problems are too simplistic, let alone a 'blaming the victim' approach which justifies much social policy today. Our findings show that reality is far too complex for single factors to have effects on young people's transitions independently of the other interacting and for ever changing elements and events occurring in each individual's life (Kloep *et al.*, 2010, p.523).

We have already started to take significant steps in developing community-based therapeutic interventions for young people, born of a culture of listening to the young people themselves (Shorrock, 2006). There is now an extensive assortment of therapeutic services within community settings for young people, ranging from intensive individual and group psychotherapies to psychoeducational input trainings, where 'therapeutic' discussion is facilitated. Forward-thinking services will often integrate several approaches within a therapeutic intervention; for example, impromptu 'talks' with a counsellor whilst undertaking an outdoor pursuit session. The rationale of fostering an environment where the young person is 'good at something' is an intelligent therapeutic gateway into the world of the disaffected young person.

Over the years we have learnt that great benefits can be reaped by engaging with young people in their own environment and flexibly accommodating their needs. Mounting evidence indicates how hard to reach these individuals can be, which comes as no surprise to those of us who have worked with or parented even the healthiest young people. Building rapport with a young person who has become deeply disenchanted with adults and the adult world, after years of abuse and neglect, can be a common challenge for the most experienced of therapists.

For instance, I currently manage a team of therapists providing consultancy, training and supervision to support staff who provide residential care to young people. Typically, residential care providers, offering homes to young people from dysfunctional families, struggle with staff retention, as support workers and their front-line managers experience extremely high stress and burn-out. A psychodynamic model would lend itself well to explaining the intense 'acting out' of young people with insecure attachments. As consultants, we provide psychoeducational training to staff, considered risk assessments and therapeutic intervention strategies, by way of nurturing a therapeutic environment within the young person's own home. However, it takes an experienced counselling psychologist, with many years of advanced clinical training, to identify the more sophisticated forms of transferences within therapeutic relationships, and so the confusion and despair of a foundation-level-trained support worker are understandable when experiencing such a phenomenon as projective identification countertransference from a young person who has been repeatedly abused.

Of the few therapeutic community projects that are the subject of research, perhaps one of the most inspiring is the Fife Intensive Therapy Team (FITT) project, a nurse therapist-led team, which is part of a wider network of specialist CAMHS teams and clinical services comprising psychological practitioners from a range of disciplines (Simpson *et al.,* 2010). Working with young people in their own homes or in a suitably safe community facility, the FITT team sustains therapeutic engagement with young people and their carers through an assortment of interventions. These include risk assessment, individual therapy, group therapy, family therapy, psychoeducation for the patient and family, assistance in accessing alternative sources of support and social integration. Each young person is engaged in an ongoing process of assessment, intensive therapeutic intervention and review. This approach enables a multidimensional understanding of an individual patient's needs within humanistic, bio-psycho-social and systemic frameworks. Responsive and adaptive interventions ensure that flexible packages of care mirror the level and nature of the assessed individual need.

My own research (Shorrock, 2006) identifying the needs of, and gaps in provision for, young people leaving care ('care-leavers') supports the findings of the studies above. Using a mixed methods approach, collation and analysis of the views of care-leavers and professionals (social workers, social service management and clinicians) and models of best and innovative practice, were presented at a conference in Westminster. This provided a format and protocol for delivering therapeutic services to young people, which was embraced by local authorities and the Connexions Service at a national level. In summary, the key recommendations were rolled out using the following NEET-2-EET model (NEET being the government's acronym for those young people 'not engaged in education, employment or training'):

Stage 1: Intensive psychoeducational programme

This six-week training focused on supporting care-leavers to identify their personal strengths and 'growing edges', as well as providing opportunities to develop emotional awareness. It is essential that activities and engagement with attendees remain flexible and accommodate the often unspoken needs of the care-leaver.

Stage 2: Flexible work placements within local authorities

As the 'corporate parent', training and support were provided to council service departments in offering care-leavers an experience of work. A 'buddy system' involved the identification and specialist support of an employee to mentor the young person. Upon completion of a four-week placement, young people were offered an extended stay or the option of another work placement.

Stage 3: Progression on to becoming a 'peer mentor'

Upon successful completion of the stages above, care-leavers were afforded the opportunity to receive additional training and support in becoming a mentor for a care-leaver entering the programme at stage 1. The credibility and authority that peer mentors effortlessly attracted serve to foster a belief of hope and 'if they can do it, then so can I!' mind set within the incoming young person – not to be underestimated as a vital ingredient within the model.

I believe the success of the programme lies within the skill sets of its facilitator. I was a counselling psychologist in-the-making, and a keen reflexive scientist practitioner. A willingness to think laterally, the ability to identify and flexibly accommodate the young person's needs, and receptivity to be research-informed are just three of the key humanistic qualities necessary. This potent, yet simple three-step model continues to sustain many young people leaving local authority care with a growing sense of worth and self-confidence.

In looking towards the future, therapeutic community practitioners working with young people must continue to foster a multidimensional awareness of a young person's needs within humanistic, bio-psycho-social and systemic frameworks. It is fitting that counselling psychologists are specifically trained to develop such competencies (Health Professions Council, 2011), and are attracted to this way of working in the first instance because of their postmodernist philosophical position;

it is hard to imagine a professional candidate better suited to working with disaffected young people within their own communities.

Online and telephone counselling

It is important to begin this section by highlighting that there are those who would challenge the view that therapy mediated through the internet or telephone is not 'real' therapy. The authors of this section do not adhere to this view and acknowledge the important role that such service providers offer in providing a lifeline to some young people. It is also true that many services that offer support using these means do so without directly describing the service as counselling, or utilise the term 'counselling' in a rather *ad hoc* way. Thus, for the purposes of this section, we intend to reflect briefly upon the work of those who explicitly describe what they do as 'counselling' and employ individuals with a substantial therapeutic training. Furthermore, although both telephone and online counselling services have developed a foothold in the delivery of support for young people, due to limitations of space this chapter focuses on the development of online services (many of the discussions being parallel to telephone work). For more information regarding telephone counselling we would signpost you towards Coman *et al.* (2001) for general information and King *et al.* (2006a) for a comparison of telephone and online counselling with young people.

To begin, it feels important to reflect upon whether adolescents are actually using mediated counselling services. This seems particularly relevant as there is research suggesting that young people are not overly keen on using the internet as a means of accessing support and advice services (Livingstone and Bober, 2005). However, there is a significant body of evidence developing which suggests that young people will access and are using online counselling services. For instance, a service based in the UK reports over 2,400 young people took part in over 8,000 'live' counselling sessions and 5,100 young people used the service to send messages to a counsellor during a 12-month period (Xenzone, 2011). Reports from Australia's national service Kids Helpline note that in 2009 '8,197 real time web counseling sessions were provided and all of the 11,737 email contacts received a reply' (Kids Helpline, 2010, p.6). Users of both these services also report that they would never have sought help if online counselling were not available (Kids Helpline, 2003; Hanley, 2012) and there is a growing body of evidence to suggest that young people present with complex issues online (Kids Helpline, 2010; Sefi and Hanley, 2012). Both the UK service (Kooth) and Kids Helpline therefore display that online therapy is accessed by young people seeking support and there are indications that there may be unique features to the client group using the services.

In examining adolescents' motives for using online counselling services, the work of King *et al.* (2006b) sheds light on such trends of usage. King and his colleagues (2006b) ran focus groups which involved 39 young people who accessed the Kids Helpline online counselling service. They found three key themes emerged within the discussions: (1) the privacy and emotionally safe environment; (2) the impact of communication through text; and (3) the waiting time. The first two related to issues that proved to be positive motivators, notably that online communication appeared safer than other forms of counselling and that some users felt more comfortable communicating through text. In contrast, a number of users felt that communicating only through text meant that it was difficult to convey feelings and that their dialogue was open to misinterpretation. The third theme related to the long waiting times and the limited duration of the sessions available. Such work reflects that adolescents do not necessarily view the internet as the ideal forum to access counselling; however the privacy and convenience that come with such services can prove more attractive than alternatives.

The major motivation for developing online services proves to be that it would increase access for individuals who would not ordinarily approach therapeutic services. One service notes that individuals may access them because they:

- live in a rural area or are unable to get transport to one of [the organisation's face-to-face] counselling services bases;
- have a physical disability that makes it difficult/impossible for them [to access the face-to-face service];
- have other commitments/time limits that mean they wouldn't ordinarily seek counselling;
- have concerns or fears about approaching a counselling service;
- prefer to communicate online (Hanley, 2004, p.48).

Such a rationale appears consistent throughout the world. In addition, papers cite that such practice may be cost-effective (Mehta and Chalhoub, 2006), session notes can easily be made from the work conducted (King et al., 2003; Mehta and Chalhoub, 2006), online work may lead to face-to-face engagement (Campbell, 2004; Mehta and Chalhoub, 2006;), individuals can be more honest to the counsellor online (Roy and Gillett, 2008; Hanley, 2012), and the adult–adolescent power imbalance may be readdressed (Mehta and Chalhoub, 2006; Roy and Gillett, 2008; Hanley, 2009, 2012). Other reasons can be transposed from the motivations for developing adult services; however the issues of accessibility and adult–adolescent power imbalance are factors that prove distinct to youth counselling.

There is a growing amount of online counselling services for young people. Primarily these are free at the point of delivery, although access routes vary greatly. There are also a number of therapeutic responses that appear to be used. Predominantly these involve the use of asynchronous email exchanges but synchronous chat is also a popular mode of delivery. Other services utilise online forum spaces and offer counsellor-led online group therapy (Vossler and Hanley, 2010); however such interventions presently appear very much in the minority. Additionally, the use of increasingly available videoconference technologies does not appear to have taken off as yet.

Inevitably the development of online counselling services for young people raises numerous challenges. As with adult online counselling, these include philosophical, ethical and practical concerns (see Rochlen *et al.*, 2004, for more discussion on general issues about online counselling). Some of these challenges, such as the need for practitioners to become competent in 'netiquette' and online language skills, may also be magnified with this age group. Additionally, there are specific difficulties that are more common to online work with adolescents. For instance, many services for this age group prove to be free at the point of delivery, a factor that opens up the potential for individuals to access them from all around the world. Some services therefore fear becoming swamped by users and having to respond to a multitude of 'test' messages (Hanley, 2004). Additionally, as some sites allow individuals to access the service without providing identifiable information, unique difficulties can occur where the safety of a young person is in question (Hanley, 2004). Some additional issues that have been raised include the potential to alienate those individuals who are not capable of accessing services online (Mehta and Chalhoub, 2006) and that practitioners working on the sites need to receive appropriate training (Campbell, 2004) and supervision (Hanley and Morris, 2007).

In response to these difficulties, services have had to become technologically savvy and pioneering in developing appropriate protocols and procedures. Services such as Kooth and Kids Helpline have developed web-based platforms to host counselling sessions and have been proactive in creating working policies that respond to the nuances of working online. Additionally, some individuals have provided tips for practitioners entering this arena (Mehta and Chalhoub, 2006). These include reference to practical issues, such as ensuring that you have appropriate insurance and keep records appropriately safe. They also cover practice issues such as how to respond solely using text. Likewise a small study consulting online counsellors about working with young people outlines a number of minimum requirements for which UK-based organisations should take some responsibility. These were summarised as:

- ensuring that practitioners have appropriate levels of training or experience. This falls into three distinct areas:
  - Counsellor training (minimum of a Diploma in Counselling).
  - Relevant experience or training in working with young people.
  - Relevant experience or training in developing therapeutic relationships online.
- ensuring that individuals offering online counselling services for young people are aware of the appropriate legalities of running such a service . . .

And a final responsibility may also be to:

- ensure that practitioners are working within an appropriate and recognised set of ethical guidelines and are member of a professional counselling body (Hanley, 2006, p.184).

Although not all of the advice relates to every online service, such tips and recommendations outline some of the major challenges for those who work online with this age group. Additionally, as services become more commonplace, it becomes ever-more essential that frameworks of good practice are developed for those working in this medium.

Conclusion

Counselling psychologists work with young people in a wide array of settings. There is a common acknowledgement that professionals now need to be open to meeting this client group in familiar territory, or at least being mindful of the power dynamics that could be present within less familiar ones. In the sections above it is clear that numerous innovative and creative practices are being developed to support young people actively in obtaining the support that they need. It is also evident that such practices will continue to develop as technology advances. Although this chapter just scratches the surface of the burgeoning territory, we hope that these contributions provide some thought-provoking insights into the settings in which counselling psychologists might find themselves working with adolescents.

Summary

- Adolescent counselling psychology services come in numerous shapes and sizes. This chapter provides a rich overview of four distinct settings. These are considered in turn and major issues related to them presented.
- CAMHS often comprise multidisciplinary teams who offer a wide range of therapeutic interventions. This work is primarily situated in clinical settings, but moves into settings such as schools are increasing. One of the guiding principles behind CAMHS work is that no decision should be made without the informed input from the young clients themselves (Department of Health, 2010a, 2010b).
- School-based counselling is an area of major growth within the UK. A majority of schools now report having a counsellor in school and there is an increased body of research developing around the effectiveness of such provision.
- Just as school-based counselling services attempt to meet young people on their own territory, other therapeutic interventions are being developed within community settings. These can vary widely in how they manifest in practice (e.g. one-to-one counselling or group interventions) and may prove more flexible in their nature due to the messy nature of the environment.
- Mediated counselling services have developed a major presence within youth counselling. Although these can be challenged due to perceived limitations in technology, they provide distinct advantages for some young people. These

include the potential to increase access to individuals and the attractiveness of the anonymous nature of communication.

Further reading

Further reading is not directly suggested here as the sources referred to by the contributing authors provide numerous directions for consideration.

References

Child and Adolescent Mental Health Services

Child and Adolescent Mental Health Services review. (2008). *Children and Young People in Mind; The final report of the National CAMHS review.* Retrieved 05/10/2011 from www.dcsf.gov.uk/CAMHSreview/downloads/CAMHSReview-Bookmark.pdf.

Coulter, A. (2011). *Engaging Patients in Healthcare.* Maidenhead: Open University Press.

Department of Health. (2004). *CAMHS Standard, National Service Framework for Children, Young People and Maternity Services: The mental health and psychological well-being of children and young people.* London: Department of Health Publications.

Department of Health. (2010a). *Transparency in Outcomes: A framework for the NHS.* London: The Stationery Office.

Department of Health. (2010b). *Getting it Right for Children and Young People: Overcoming cultural barriers in the NHS so as to meet their needs. A review by Professor Sir Ian Kennedy.* Leicester: Department of Health.

Gillen, S. and Hayes, D. (2011). Cuts begin to bite for some. *YoungMinds Magazine,* 113, 25–7.

Layard, R. (2011). *Happiness: Lessons from a new science.* London: Penguin.

Rees, D. (2007). *The National CAMHS Support Service: Learning perspectives from a national service improvement programme.* Leicester: Department of Health.

York, A. and Kingsbury, S. (2011). What is CAPA? Retrieved 05/10/2011 from www.camhsnetwork.co.uk/Basics/basics_whatiscapataster.htm.

School-based counselling

Baginsky, W. (2004) *School Counselling in England, Wales and Northern Ireland: A review.* London: NSPCC.

Boateng, P. (2003). *Every Child Matters.* Cm 5860. London: Stationery Office.

Bor, R., Ebner-Landy, J., Gill, S. and Brace, C. (2002). *Counselling in Schools.* London: Sage.

British Association of Counselling and Psychotherapy. (2011). *School Based Counselling Operating Toolkit.* Retrieved 11/04/2011 from www.bacp.co.uk/information/school Toolkit.php.

Burnison, B. (2003). *It's OK to See the Counsellor.* Belfast: NSPCC.

Department for Children, Schools and Families (2007). *Social and Emotional Aspects of Learning for Secondary Schools.* Nottingham: DCSF Publications.

Department for Children, Schools and Families (2008). *Pastoral Support Programme Guidance.* London: DCSF.

Department of Health. (2011). *No Health Without Mental Health: A cross government mental health outcomes strategy for people of all ages.* Retrieved 11/04/11 from www.dh.gov.uk/en/Healthcare/Mentalhealth/MentalHealthStrategy/index.htm.

Freud, S. (1962). *Three Essays on the Theory of Sexuality*, translated by Strachey, J. New York: Basic Books.

HMSO (2011). *The Children Act 1989.* Retrieved 06/6/2011 from www.legislation.gov.uk/ukpga/1989/41/contents.

Hodge, M. (2004). Virtual conversations. *Counselling in Education*, Spring, 14–15.

Jenkins, P. and Polat, F. (2005). *The Current Provision of Counselling Services in Secondary Schools in England and Wales.* Manchester: University of Manchester.

King, G. (1999). *Counselling Skills for Teachers: Talking matters.* Buckingham: Open University Press.

Lang, P. (1999). Counselling, counselling skills and encouraging pupils to talk: clarifying and addressing confusion. *British Journal of Guidance and Counselling,* 27 (1), 23–33.

McArthur, K., Cooper, M. and Berdondini, L. (2011). A pilot randomised controlled trial to assess the impact of school-based counselling on young people's wellbeing, using pastoral care referral. Paper presented at the British Association for Counselling and Psychotherapy Research Conference, Liverpool.

National Society for Prevention of Cruelty to Children. (2004). *School Counselling in England, Wales and Northern Ireland: A review.* London: NSPCC.

Newsom Report. (1963). *Half our Future: A report of the Central Advisory Council for Education.* London: HMSO.

Pattison, S., Rowland, N., Cromarty, K., Richards, K., Jenkins, P. and Polat, F. (2009). School counselling in Wales. Recommendations for good practice. *Counselling and Psychotherapy Research*, 9 (3), 169–73.

Piaget, J. (1977). *The Grasp of Consciousness: Action and concept in the young child.* London: Routledge and Kegan Paul.

Robinson, B. D. (1996). School counsellors in England and Wales, 1965–1995; a flawed innovation? *Pastoral Care in Education,* 14 (3), 12–19.

Rogers, C.R. (1961). *On Becoming a Person.* London: Constable.

Rousseau, J (1997). *'The Discourses' and Other Early Political Writings*, translated by Gourevitch, V. Cambridge: Cambridge University Press.

Sodha, S. and Margo, J. (2008). *Thursday's Child.* Newcastle Upon Tyne: Institute for Public Policy Research.

Welsh Assembly Government (2008). *School-based Counselling Services in Wales: A national strategy.* Cardiff: Welsh Assembly Government, DELLS.

Counselling in the community

Bronfenbrenner, U. (1979). *The Ecology of Human Development.* Harvard University Press: Cambridge.

Department for Children, Schools and Families. (2006). *The Common Assessment Framework for Children and Young People: Practitioner's guide.* London: Department for Education and Skills.

Department of Health/Department for Education and Employment/Home Office. (2000). *Framework for the Assessment of Children in Need and their Families.* London: The Stationery Office.

Gill, T. (2008). Space-oriented children's policy: creating child-friendly communities to improve children's well-being. *Children and Society*, 22, 136–42.

Health Professions Council. (2011). *Practitioner Psychologists – Threshold level of qualification for entry to the register.* Retrieved from www.hpc-uk.org/assets/documents/10002969AppendixtwoConsultationresponses.pdf.

HM Treasury. (2003). *Every Child Matters.* London: The Stationery Office.

Jack, G. (2000). Ecological influences on parenting and child development. *British Journal of Social Work,* 30, 703–20.

Jack, G. and Gill, O. (2010). The role of communities in safeguarding children and young people. *Child Abuse Review*, 19, 82–96.

Kloep, M., Hendry, L., Gardner, C. and Seage, C. (2010). Young people's views of their present and future selves in two deprived communities. *Journal of Community and Applied Social Psychology*, 20, 513–24.

Shorrock, M. (2006). *Bridging the Gap – Research and Recommendations: Therapeutic service development for NEET young people leaving local authority care.* London: Connexions.

Simpson, W., Cowie, L., Wilkinson, L., Lock, N. and Monteith, G. (2010). The effectiveness of a community intensive therapy team on young people's mental health outcomes. *Child and Adolescent Mental Health*, 15, 217–223.

Online and telephone counselling

Campbell, M. (2004). Possibilities and perils of school cybercounselling. *International Journal of PEPE Inc*, 8 (1), 19–29.

Coman, G., Burrows, G. and Evans, B. (2001). Telephone counselling in Australia: applications and considerations for use. *British Journal of Guidance and Counselling*, 29 (2), 247–58.

Hanley, T. (2004). E-motion online. *Counselling and Psychotherapy Journal*, 15 (1), 48–9.

Hanley, T. (2006). Developing youth friendly online counselling services in the United Kingdom: a small scale investigation into the views of practitioners. *Counselling and Psychotherapy Research*, 6 (3), 182–5.

Hanley, T. (2009). The working alliance in online therapy with young people: preliminary findings. *British Journal of Guidance and Counselling*, 37 (3), 257–69.

Hanley, T. (2012). Understanding the online therapeutic alliance through the eyes of adolescent service users. *Counselling and Psychotherapy Research*, 12, 35–43.

Hanley, T. and Morris, J. (2007). Real supervision in the virtual world. *Counselling Children and Young People*, December, 13–15.

Kids Helpline. (2003). Online counselling: responding to young people's feedback. *Newsletter*, November, 3–4.

Kids Helpline. (2010). *Kids Helpline: 2009 Overview.* Retrieved 07/09/2011 from www.kidshelp.com.au/upload/22862.pdf.

King, R., Spooner, D. and Reid, W. (2003). Online counselling and psychotherapy. In R. Wootton, P. Yellowlees and P. McLaren (eds). *Telepsychiatry and E-Mental Health* (pp.245–64). New York: RSM Press.

King, R., Bambling, M., Reid, W. and Thomas, I. (2006a). Telephone and online counselling for young people: a naturalistic comparison of session outcome, session impact and therapeutic alliance. *Counselling and Psychotherapy Research*, 6 (3), 175–81.

King, R., Bambling, M., Lloyd, C., Gomurra, R., Smith, S., Reid, W. and Wegner, K. (2006b). Online counselling: the motives and experiences of young people who choose the internet instead of face to face or telephone counselling. *Counselling and Psychotherapy Research*, 6 (3), 169–74.

Livingstone, S. and Bober, M. (2005). *UK Children Go Online: Final report of key project findings*. Retrieved 09/01/2008 from www.children-go-online.net.

Mehta, S. and Chalhoub, N. (2006). An email for your thoughts. *Child and Adolescent Mental Health*, 11 (3), 168–70.

Rochlen, A., Zack, J. and Speyer, C. (2004). Online therapy: review of relevant definitions, debates, and current empirical support. *Journal of Clinical Psychology*, 60 (3), 269–83.

Roy, H. and Gillett, T. (2008). E-mail: a new technique for forming a therapeutic alliance with high-risk young people failing to engage with mental health services? A case study. *Clinical Child Psychology and Psychiatry*, 13 (1), 95–103.

Sefi, A. and Hanley, T. (2012). Examining the complexities of measuring effectiveness of online counselling for young people using routine evaluation data. *Pastoral Care in Education,* 30 (1), 49–64.

Vossler, A. and Hanley, T. (2010). Online counselling: meeting the needs of young people in late-modern societies. In J. Leaman and M.Woersching (eds) *Youth in Contemporary Europe* (pp. 133–148). London: Routledge.

Xenzone. (2011). *Xenzone Annual Report*. Retrieved 07/09/2011 from www.xenzone.com/pdf/kooth_info.pdf.

Chapter 4

Allied interventions

Neil Humphrey, Emma Lindley, Kate Sapin,
Gill Parkinson, Garry Squires and Panos Vostanis

Overview

This chapter provides an overview of a range of allied interventions that may be used to complement, support or extend the therapeutic work undertaken in the course of adolescent counselling psychology. It is important to be mindful of these interventions because adolescents do not undergo counselling in a vacuum. At any one time, they may be involved with a range of agencies and professionals – for example, educational psychologists (EPs), youth workers and/or psychiatrists. If they are classed as disabled, additional support may also be available. There may also be work undertaken with the community of peers to raise awareness of mental health difficulties and reduce associated stigmatisation. Finally, they will be spending a significant proportion of their time in school (at least up to the age of 16) and will therefore be exposed to a range of strategies and approaches to support their emotional well-being – most notably the social and emotional learning (SEAL) programme. Being aware of these allied interventions – the nature of the work undertaken and its effects – helps to contribute to a more holistic picture of the influences on the young person's well-being, whilst also bringing to the fore any potential complications associated with their use alongside counselling. Effective communication between the various agencies involved is therefore encouraged.

School-based strategies to support emotional well-being – the social and emotional aspects of learning (SEAL) programme

As part of the move away from the traditional, rationalist view of education and the purpose of schooling, recent years have seen an increasing emphasis on a holistic view of learners. Much of this paradigm shift took place under New Labour, who introduced a wide range of educational initiatives, many of which had a direct focus on fostering resilience, social and emotional skills, or well-being more broadly. Examples include:

- National Healthy Schools
- Every Child Matters

- Behaviour and Attendance strategy
- SEAL
- Targeted Mental Health in Schools (TAMHS)
- Achievement for All

Schools are seen as among the most important and effective agencies for promoting the mental health of children and young people (Weare and Markham, 2005), and the introduction of the policies listed above reflects this viewpoint. Furthermore, under New Labour schools were expected to be more accountable for this aspect of their provision, with the introduction of Personal Development and Well-being as one of the strands used in school inspections by the Office for Standards in Education during the period in which these policies were rolled out. Although we have subsequently changed government in England, the early indications are that the current Coalition administration is equally focused on promoting well-being.

The enactment of policies such as those listed above has tended to reflect a model of whole-school preventive work, supported by more targeted interventions for learners at particular risk of or already experiencing social and emotional difficulties. The SEAL programme is a good example of this. SEAL is a comprehensive, whole-school approach to promoting the social and emotional skills that are thought to underpin effective learning, positive behaviour, regular attendance and emotional well-being (Department for Education and Skills, 2005). It is reported to be in use in around 90% of primary schools and 70% of secondary schools in England (Humphrey *et al.*, 2010).

SEAL is somewhat unique in relation to the broader literature on approaches to social and emotional learning in that it is envisaged as a loose enabling framework for school improvement (Weare, 2010) rather than a structured 'package' that is applied to schools. Schools are actively encouraged to explore different approaches to implementation that support identified school improvement priorities rather than following a single model, meaning that they can tailor it to their own circumstances and needs. In a sense, this means that SEAL is essentially what individual schools make of it rather than being a single, consistently definable entity. It was conceptualised in this manner to avoid the lack of ownership and sustainability that might be associated with the more 'top-down', prescribed approach that is taken in the USA.

SEAL is delivered in three 'waves of intervention' (Figure 1). The first wave of SEAL delivery centres on whole-school development work designed to create the ethos and climate within which social and emotional skills can be most effectively promoted. The second wave of SEAL involves small-group interventions for children who are thought to require additional support to develop their social and emotional skills (Department for Education and Skills, 2006). The final wave of the SEAL programme involves one-to-one intervention with children who have not benefited from the whole-school and small-group provision in a given school, and are thought to be at risk of or experiencing mental health difficulties. In many

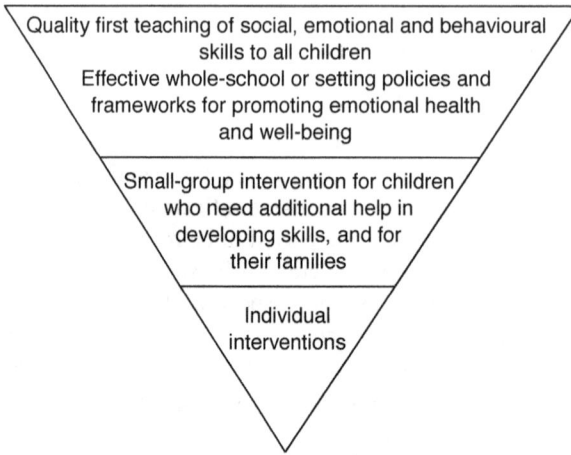

Figure 1. The wave model of social and emotional learning (SEAL) delivery.

schools this element has been delivered under the remit of the TAMHS initiative. TAMHS, like SEAL, is presented as an enabling framework rather than a 'package' of materials to be delivered. Among the key elements of the TAMHS approach are the promotion of evidence-informed practice and the facilitation of effective interagency collaboration (Department for Children, Schools and Families, 2008).

SEAL is designed to promote the development and application to learning of social and emotional skills that have been classified under the five domains proposed in Goleman's (1995) model of emotional intelligence. These are:

1. self-awareness
2. self-regulation (managing feelings)
3. motivation
4. empathy
5. social skills.

At the school level, SEAL is characterised by the following principles:

•   SEAL implementation is underpinned by clear planning focused on improving standards, behaviour and attendance.
•   SEAL aims to help build a school ethos that provides a climate and conditions to promote social and emotional skills.
•   All children are provided with planned opportunities to develop and enhance social and emotional skills.
•   Adults are provided with opportunities to enhance their own social and emotional skills.

- Staff recognise the significance of social and emotional skills to effective learning and to the well-being of pupils.
- Pupils who would benefit from additional support have access to small-group work.
- There is a strong commitment to involving pupils in all aspects of school life.
- There is a strong commitment to working positively with parents and carers.
- The school engages well with other schools, the local community, wider services and local agencies (National Strategies SEAL Priorities, 2009–2011).

Research that has been conducted into the effectiveness of the various strands of the SEAL programme has produced mixed results. The programme itself has also not been without criticism (Craig, 2007; Ecclestone and Hayes, 2008). However, despite this controversy, it has been embraced enthusiastically by schools as a framework through which to develop provision in a way that considers the personal, social and emotional growth of learners rather than just their academic prowess.

Raising awareness and reducing stigma

Life difficulties which lead to young people becoming engaged in counselling psychology only affect a minority (Meltzer *et al.*, 2003). In focusing on the particular challenges faced by young people who are having a difficult time it is easy to overlook the broader challenges of the communities which they occupy. Relationships with peers are crucially important to young people's overall well-being (Rigby, 2000) and the dangers of being stigmatised and marked out as 'different' because of being involved in counselling or using mental health services are very real (Crisp, 2004; Corrigan, 2006; Thornicroft, 2006). Therefore, there is great value in providing global mental health awareness education which aims to equip all young people with resources to negotiate emotional and mental health difficulties, whether they arise in their own lives or in those of others (Pinfold, 2003).

This short section will describe an 'inclusive dialogue' approach to mental illness education, distinct from mental health promotion, in that it does not set out to prevent the onset of mental illness. Instead, the focus is on raising awareness and understanding of how emotional distress and mental illness can affect individuals, relationships and communities. The aim is to improve understanding of emotional and mental distress among the broader community, thereby increasing solidarity amongst the peer group of those who do experience such difficulties. This approach was developed as part of an investigation into young people's sense-making on mental illness, with the development of antistigma mental illness education as a guiding stimulus. The approach facilitates dialogue between participants in small-group discussions, in which everyone is encouraged to take an active role. It is inclusive in the sense that the young people are encouraged to bring their own understandings and experiences to the discussion. It is also inclusive because it is structured to enable participants to consider emotional distress and mental illness from a diverse range of perspectives.

In this example, a group of seven year ten pupils from a mainstream secondary school in south Manchester were engaged in a series of weekly hour-long discussions led by a facilitator. These discussions began with a mind-mapping exercise, in which the young people were encouraged to write down everything that came to mind when they saw the phrase 'mental illness.' A discussion followed in which they talked about the meanings, implications and consequences of the language they had used. An example of the young people's responses is shown in Figure 2.

While much of this language appears rather negative, and some of it insulting, the discussion which accompanied it revealed that the young people were profoundly aware of the pejorative power of the words they used, and did so with sensitivity according to context.

Another exercise involved a series of photo-vignettes being introduced, which gave the young people the opportunity to consider and discuss examples of emotional difficulty in a personalised, figurative way. Figure 3 is an example of one of these photo-vignettes.

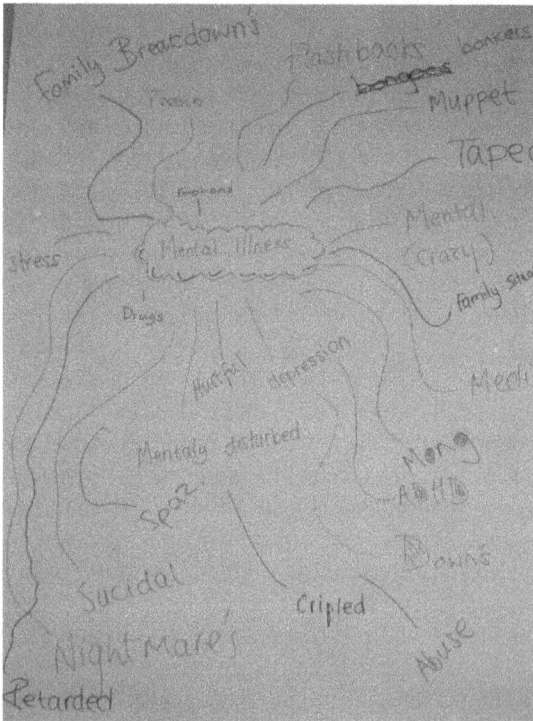

Figure 2. Young people's responses to the term 'mental illness'.

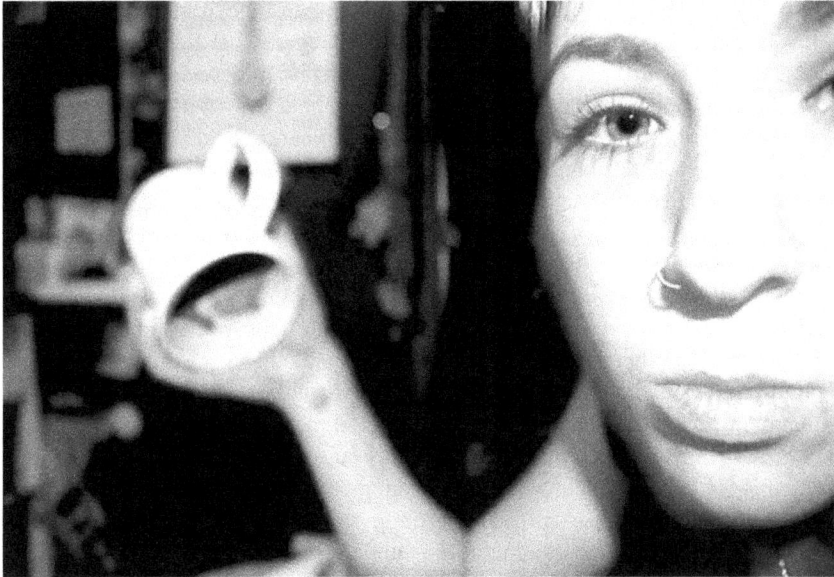

Figure 3. Example photo-vignette.

The young people came up with a range of ideas about what might be going on for Sarah and how best to respond to her. In their responses they displayed sympathy, supportiveness and concern for her.

A profile-building exercise was also carried out, in which young people were presented with descriptions of mental illness experience. They were asked to choose a person from a selection of photographs who they thought the experience might describe. They went on to build a profile for that person, selecting from collections of images to represent areas of their life. Discussion followed about the narratives they had created. Initially, the profiles young people created resulted in deficit narratives, in which people with mental illness were seen as having negative family situations, and little meaning in their lives. The profiles were then reconstructed by the facilitator, with real-life narratives being told for the people in the photographs the young people had chosen. These stories contrasted with the deficient views created by the young people in the group. Following discussions about the reconstructed profiles, the young people repeated the exercise, and the profiles they constructed this time were much less pessimistic.

Alongside these activities, the sessions were characterised by unstructured discussion, in which the young people shared their own concerns and experiences. A qualitative analysis of the young people's participation revealed that their ideas and feelings about mental illness were very diverse. They began the discussion series with considerable confusion about what mental illness is. Importantly, it became clear that the young people were well able to understand emotional distress and be empathic towards those who were, as they saw it, 'having a hard time'. The notion of 'mental illness' was more troublesome to them, and they found it less easy to empathise and be supportive towards those they regarded as being 'mentally ill' than they did towards those they viewed as having difficulties which were psychosocially explicable. Their opinions and positions about mental illness varied enormously according to context, with individual members oscillating between being sometimes quite fearful and controlling, and at other times open, supportive and empathic. Of great importance was the way in which members of the group collaborated to make meanings, pool understandings and negotiate controversial subject matter. Individuals' consideration of how they may respond to others in emotional or mental distress was influenced by how they thought their peers would behave.

The process of being engaged in the discussions appeared to influence group members in a number of ways, including that they felt they knew more, were more comfortable in talking about mental illness and that they would be more confident in knowing how to respond if they encountered mental illness in someone they knew. All of the group members said that they enjoyed the process, and that it was something they would remember. One young person commented: 'It was much more relevant and important than anything we'd normally do in life skills or whatever. We need to know about these things.'

Youth work

> 'The main objective of youth work is to provide opportunities for young people to shape their own futures' (Lauritzen, 2006, no page).

Youth work involves the development of enjoyable and educational activities that bring young people together for shared learning and opportunities to challenge and change themselves as well as the people and communities around them. The core features of youth work as defined by Davies and Merton (2009) are that participation by young people is voluntary; the starting points are set by young people; the stimulus and support provided mean that young people take themselves into personally challenging learning; engagement is through peer groups and networks; and youth workers are involved in conscious recognition and respect for young people's intrinsic power in the relationship.

The underpinning values for youth work are consistently related to a positive approach to young people, rather than a deficiency model (Davies, 2005, p.13) and to antioppressive practice. With roots in organisations providing care, welfare and leisure services and activities (Smith, 1999, 2002), youth work developed a holistic perspective to informal work with young people and, significantly, a shared understanding of a political aim to create a better society. Youth workers expect to be involved in social and political issues, for example, through challenging oppressive language and behaviour whether towards or by young people.

Youth work takes place in a wide range of organisational and physical settings, which can define the types of activities that take place. Youth work ranges from short-term projects to develop arts and drama; ongoing resources for drop-in information and/or advice with social activities; targeted support for particular groups or informal education on specific issues. The activities have the common method and purpose of facilitating and developing young people's participation not just in youth work, but also in their local and global communities. As Belton notes, 'the strength of young people is their relatively unmediated potential as a fresh and vibrant natural resource to reinvigorate and shape society' (Belton, 2010, p.x).

Youth work and mental health

Youth work addresses the mental health and well-being of young people through generic practice as well as specific issue-based work. Bolstering young people's confidence and self-esteem through enjoyable and social activities can enhance their readiness to address the issues and circumstances that could contribute to mental difficulties or undue stress. Participation in groups to plan projects provides opportunities to work with others and take leadership roles that develop friendships and relationship skills, such as assertiveness. Royal College of Psychiatrists research (2010, p.30) identified that 'problem-solving and social adjustment skills, high levels of reasons for living, optimism, participation in sporting activity, positive family and other personal relationships, and engaging with their community may modify the risks' (of suicide and self-harm). The development of young people's resilience may help to prevent stress, unhappiness or depression due to situations or circumstances or provide strengths for recovery.

A youth work approach would not be overtly therapeutic. The informal ways of working and the relationships of trust that are built between young people and youth workers mean that an environment is created where a wide range of concerns can be raised and discussed. Issue-based work may be reactive to young people's questions or revelations or proactively introduced by a youth worker. Recognising that distress can result from a range of societal factors rather than just illness, youth workers may discuss issues related to peer group and family relationships, housing, education and employment, such as body image, drug use, bullying and domestic abuse. The process could include challenging alternative perspectives to provoke new ways of thinking about situations; suggestions or shared experiences from others in similar circumstances; or action planning to make changes in situations causing difficulties. The sessions or interventions could include a range of methods to stimulate discussions, such as games, role play, informal education, creative activities or questionnaires.

The outcomes from such sessions may be raised awareness or increased knowledge about specific questions or worries that may help to circumvent anxiety, panic or other distress. Alternatively, a youth worker may take on an intermediary or mediative role where young people are facing barriers. Although consent and respect for confidentiality are dominant ethical principles, in some situations, such as severe mental trauma or illness, child protection or safeguarding, a youth worker may signpost or pass on information to other professionals.

Youth work and counselling

Youth work and counselling share many attributes. Both professions highlight the importance of voluntary relationships with young people and providing safe spaces for them to explore identity, decision making and the consequences of their actions. The young people's interests, concerns and power are considered to be central with practice depending on an awareness of 'location' and 'use' of self as well as power imbalances in relationships. Professional supervision and reflection are recognised as means of continuous professional development and ensuring ethical good practice.

The purpose and role of the two professions are quite different. An essential distinction between youth work and counselling is that having fun is one of the most important objectives of youth work. Individuals' improved mental health is more incidental outcome than a primary purpose of youth work, which would be better stated as enabling young people 'to have a voice, influence and place in their communities and society as a whole' (National Youth Agency (England)). Although young people are supported in making individual choices, youth work's principle of association underlines the significance placed on young people learning from each other. Youth workers actively seek out young people and often target this outreach work so that they can meet young people that other professions may find 'hard to reach' and who may be detached from other traditional social support structures or services. Aspiring to be 'agents of change' in society as a whole (Ewen, 1980; Sapin, 2009), youth workers' antioppressive practice includes challenging political and social structures that negatively affect young people's lives.

Joint work between youth work and counselling can be complementary. A shared understanding of roles can support appropriate signposting and useful partnerships. Examples of co-working could include targeted services and advice, such as support groups for young mothers or carers, young people's mental health organisations or sexual or general health clinics. The youth workers' role could be to reach out and welcome diverse young people and promote their equal participation in the organisation whilst counsellors could provide more focused therapy for those interested.

Educational psychology services

EPs are applied psychologists who are registered practitioner psychologists with the Health Professions Council. All EPs have a first degree in psychology and a postgraduate degree in educational psychology (since 2006, this has been at Doctorate level). As part of the training, psychologists will have some coverage of therapeutic approaches.

The majority of EPs work in an Educational Psychology Service (EPS) but some work independently in private practice. The EPSs currently operate as public services and are under the control of local government councils as part of Children's Services. In some EPSs, there may be other professionals working as part of the psychology team or alongside the team. This may include educational social workers; behaviour support teachers and teaching assistants; assistant psychologists and trainee EPs. Multiprofessional and multiagency working are common as EPs form links between schools, local authorities, health services and parents. In some services, EPs may spend some of their time attached to other organisations, such as being part of the local Child and Adolescent Mental Health Services (CAMHS) team or providing psychological services to Social Services.

Within any particular EPS, there are many tasks to do and not all EPs do all of the tasks. There is a degree of specialisation to allow the service as a whole to meet all of its commitments. Sometimes the specialisation occurs purely for pragmatic reasons – there is a job to be done and someone has to do it. More often, though, EPs are able to follow their own interests and match continuing professional development to developing skills further in one area or another. This helps the service meet its overall objectives within its position in Children's Services and the ever-changing political context in which EPs work. This has allowed some EPs to develop their skills in therapeutic approaches to a high level and some EPs will have additional accredited counselling qualifications.

The role of EPs in therapeutic work featured in the review of EP work undertaken in 2006 (Farrell et al., 2006). However, EPs are in limited supply and many respondents in the review said that EPs were highly valued but there was not enough time made available to provide all of the services that schools and parents wanted, particularly in the area of therapeutic intervention (Farrell et al., 2006). The reality is that there are only around 3,000 EPs in England and Wales to cover a wide range of tasks (at individual, group, school, systemic and local authority level). Overall individual therapeutic work was reported to take up around one to two per cent of EP time (Farrell et al., 2006). There was some hope noted by respondents that the demand on EP time to complete statutory assessments was reducing and it was thought that this could allow more EP time to be focused on therapeutic work. In some parts of the country this hope is far from reality. Time allocation models determine the level of service available to schools and a small primary school may only receive six hours of EP allocated time per year. Current cutbacks in public spending are likely to reduce the amount of EP time available further and EP time may be prioritised to address statutory duties first. Short-sighted financially driven policies may lead to less preventive work and therapeutic work being undertaken as energies and resources are directed to more reactive work around school placement decisions.

This would be a shame as schools are seen as one of the main facilitators of positive mental health in young people and National Institute for Health and Clinical Excellence guidelines frequently refer to their role (National Institute for Health and Clinical Excellence, 2004, 2005a, 2005b, 2007, 2008). The adults in schools are seen as being Tier 1 mental health workers (Health Advisory Service, 1995). Despite this, teachers have raised concerns about needing support when working with children and young people with emotional and behavioural diffi-culties throughout the history of compulsory school education. EPs can work with other professionals to support young people, such as empowering teaching assistants who work directly with pupils (Burton, 2008). This was one of the driving forces that led to the development of the profession of educational psychology at the turn of the century (Squires and Farrell, 2006).

The specific roles and duties vary from one area to another and from one psychologist to another within the same service, but generally encompass the following tasks specific to emotional well-being:

- provide psychological advice as part of Statutory Assessments undertaken by local authorities under the 1996 Education Act;
- provide psychological services to schools in the area. This would include consultation and training for teachers to help them meet the educational needs of children with special educational needs (Department for Education and Skills, 2001). Promoting inclusion of children with varied difficulties in mainstream schools in line with the *Every Child Matters* agenda (Department for Education and Skills, 2004), including those with Statements in mainstream schools (Audit Commission, 2002) and those with social, emotional and behavioural difficulties (Department for Children, Schools and Families, 2008a) or mental health difficulties (Health Advisory Service, 1995; Department of Health, 2004; Department for Children Schools and Families and Department of Health, 2008, 2009; National Institute for Health and Clinical Excellence, 2008);
- work with parents and children as part of the work to support schools. EPs tend to be involved in complex casework that often requires the input from many professionals and multiagency working. In terms of 'waves of support' they are seen as operating at the third level, referred to as School Action plus. The work might focus around individual pupils or involve group work. Parents report that the most common reason a child sees an EP is for social, emotional and behavioural reasons, with the majority of parents citing EP input as being 'helpful' or 'very helpful' in improving mental health and well-being (Squires *et al.*, 2007);
- work systemically to drive through government agendas related to inclusion, e.g. SEAL (Department for Education and Skills, 2007), TAMHS (Department for Children, Schools and Families, 2008b);
- work with organisations and agencies to develop evidence-based practice, e.g. helping a CAMHS service evaluate the effectiveness of its Tier 1 training (Squires, 2009);
- work with teaching staff to help them address their own emotional well-being so that they are more able to cope with and support the young people in their care (Stringer *et al.*, 1992; Norwich and Daniels, 1997; Squires, 2007; Maag, 2008);
- train teachers and help them introduce school-based emotional and social curricula such as Promoting Alternative Thinking Strategies (PATHS: Kusche and Greenberg, 1993) or FRIENDS (Barrett, 1996).

EPs can engage in direct work with individual children and young people or with groups. They may use the theoretical models derived from a range of therapeutic approaches to help in discussions with key adults such as teachers and parents. The types of therapeutic work undertaken by EPs draw upon different models. A few examples are given below (this is not an exhaustive list and there are many other examples in the literature):

- behavioural therapies, including the use of contingencies and functional behavioural analysis;
- person-centred counselling approaches (Rogers, 1951);
- cognitive approaches based on cognitive-behavioural therapy (CBT) (Beck and Emery, 1979; Beck *et al.*, 1979, 1985, 2004) and rational emotive behaviour therapy (Ellis and Dryden, 1999). Successes have been reported using small-group work to improve pupils' self-control and teacher reports of pupil behaviour (Squires, 2001); reducing examination stress and anxiety (Gregor, 2005); helping young people with Asperger's syndrome (Greig and MacKay, 2005); improving children's reading by retraining their attributions of success and failure (Toland and Boyle, 2008); and reducing exclusions (Burton, 2006; Humphrey and Brooks, 2006). Examples from individual casework include improving handwriting (Ahrens-Eipper and Hoyer, 2006) and improving classroom behaviour and compliance (McNamara, 1998). The implications of these approaches for EP practice have been discussed elsewhere (Rait *et al.*, 2010);
- solution-focused approaches, based on solution-focused brief therapy (SFBT) (De Shazer, 1985). The techniques from SFBT are increasingly applied in consultation with teachers to help them reflect on 'working out what works' and this has been applied to whole-classroom management and behaviour improvement (Kelly and Bluestone-Miller, 2009);
- personal construct psychology, based on personal construct therapy (Kelly, 1955);
- neurolinguistic programming (Bandler and Grinder, 1975; Grinder and Bandler, 1976);
- narrative therapy;
- other non-specific therapeutic approaches such as circle time (Mosley, 1993; Lown, 2010); social skills groups; anger management groups (Faupel *et al.*, 1988) and self-esteem groups (Burton, 2004).

There is a range of potential evidence-based practice that EPs have to offer in relation to counselling approaches used in schools. However, the differing initial and postqualification training of EPs and the varied time allocation models used across different EPSs mean that there is unevenness in what EPs can deliver in practice.

Support for disabled young people

So far in this chapter we have been encouraged to draw on the resources of allied professions such as EPs , to work in a collegiate manner, and to include relevant professionals when counselling young people. But how do we or should we react when faced with the referral of a young person who is described simply as having special educational needs, or who is described as 'disabled'? What concept of that individual springs to mind when we read terms such as 'intellectually impaired' or 'has communication difficulties' or 'has a chronic medical condition'? Is our first reaction to reach for documentary evidence or seek informal verbal advice from teachers and/or parents about this aspect of the referral so we can 'know' what we are taking on? Or should we disregard this aspect and view the young person as a client in his or her own right? Are we being discriminatory by acknowledging that here is a student with a label (seemingly) already attached before he or she has even set foot in the counselling room?

There is a question therefore about whose interests are best served in the way in which young people are represented, and this is particularly true when being asked to counsel a disabled young person.

Certainly the climate of counselling has changed radically in recent times, reflecting the general move in service delivery away from adherence to the medical model of disability (Reeve, 2000; 2002; Alexander, 2003; for further discussion of the different models of disability, see Chapters 1–4 of Barnes and Mercer's (2010) *Exploring Disability*). However, as Reeve (2000) states, while the presenting problem of the client may be ameliorated, its resolution does not necessarily provide that person with the desired power or control needed to improve his or her quality of life. Although this may read uncomfortably, this may in part be due to the attitude of the counsellor. Research carried out by Parkinson (2006) with counsellors in training encouraged trainees to explore their own attitude towards people with disabilities, resolve potential conflict of interest and thus promote a positive, antidiscriminatory stance within the counsellor–client relationship from the outset. This was felt by trainees (some of whom were already working in a counselling environment) to be beneficial in the formation of a relationship, where one was then able to avoid developing a preconception of the client as someone psychoemotionally troubled by his or her disability. Such an approach avoids the presumption that the disability per se was not the primary driver for the initial referral to the counselling service.

Wilson (2003) describes a case of a wheelchair-user who was referred by her mother to the counselling service. Although Lynn (the client described by Wilson) was an adult, this case serves as a suitable example of how we might make unsupported assumptions that could be detrimental to the therapy on offer. Although her mother made the referral, Lynn was encouraged to make, and thus take responsibility for, the appointment herself. When Lynn arrived for her first session (with her mother), the counsellor gave Lynn the opportunity to enter the counselling room alone, while knowing that her mother, waiting outside, could be called on (by Lynn) if needed. As Wilson says, the counsellor now has the choice, at an agreed point, of letting the parent join the therapy session utilising a systemic family perspective, yet maintaining a person-centred approach by maintaining and supporting Lynn as the main decision-maker regarding who should be involved and share information arising from therapy.

Let us extend this scenario further. Suppose, on meeting Lynn, the counsellor found that she was virtually unable to understand what Lynn was trying to say to her. Should she terminate the session and arrange for support and advice from a speech and language therapist or signed speech interpreter? Should she investigate the support Lynn uses in everyday situations – either in the form of technical support such as an assistive communication device, or through the aid of a support worker or teaching assistant (if still in education)? Two issues need to be considered here.

First, how much information should be sought beforehand? Medical information, for example, might be required for health and safety reasons. However, one could argue that the possession of such information could potentially cloud the counsellor's judgement. Potentially, this might change the focus of the counselling session before the relationship between counsellor and client has even started to develop (see Downer, 2001, on counselling deaf clients). Yet, shouldn't we have information about what might put the client at risk – such as what stressor might provoke an asthma attack, a seizure or an irretrievable breakdown in communication? Therefore, while we want to start the session with an open mind, there is a justifiable need to gather information for the purposes of a risk assessment. The risk assessment should focus on the accessibility and nature of the counselling room, moving to a more suitable one if there are problems with physical access and level of ambient noise (in the case of a deaf client) or to a distraction-free location (if this is likely to impinge on the client's behaviour or mood state), for example. Working at the individual's home should be avoided as a first choice because of the inevitable lack of neutrality that this may carry with it.

The second issue concerns whether the client should be accompanied, and if so, what role that third party should play in the therapeutic relationship. Should that person act simply as a facilitator/communicator on the client's behalf, or take the role of an active participant within the counselling framework? If the decision is made to include a third party, then the counsellor needs to consider the following questions. How does this affect the power relationship within the therapeutic context? Is it likely to enhance or restrict the client's ability to communicate easily with the counsellor? Also, does it impinge on the client's ability to disclose information that is either sensitive or intimate in nature, or that might lead to incrimination of someone known to the third party?

There are no neat or right answers to these issues and questions. However, when planning to take on a young disabled person for counselling, or for a longer-term more therapeutic relationship, it is advisable to think and plan ahead and thus be prepared to deal with issues that would not necessarily be included in other types of counsellor–client relationship. Such a list might include:

- selecting essential information that will have the least impact on your perceptions of and attitudes towards a disabled person while still providing him or her with a conducive therapeutic environment for the session;
- the location of the sessions;
- who (if anyone) should accompany the young person for the first and subsequent sessions, and how best such choices can be made by the young person without undue pressure from parents or carers;
- planning the nature of the communicative environment – which does not necessarily have to be a verbal one;
- remember not to presume that because the young person is disabled or impaired in some way his or her reason for seeking help is automatically or even tangentially related to that aspect of the person's life.

Specialist CAMHS, psychiatry and medication

Psychiatry is a professional discipline operating within specialist CAMHS. Different branches of psychiatry cover the lifespan, from childhood to old age. In most services for young people, psychiatrists work with both children and adolescents, usually up to the age of 18 years. Some specialise in problems and disorders of adolescence, and are based in community or inpatient settings.

It is thus important to contextualise their role by placing it in a service and multidisciplinary perspective, with CAMHS teams consisting of other disciplines, most commonly nursing, psychology and therapies, broadly of psychodynamic, cognitive-behavioural and family/systemic frameworks. As services have evolved, because of expanding resources, available evidence and training opportunities, the CAMHS workforce has developed more specific and eclectic skills and expertise, in contrast with 10–20 years ago, when small teams adopted a more generic function. Psychiatry has not been an exception to this trend.

Adolescent psychiatry encompasses assessment, treatment, consultative, training and organizational roles, which are usually interlinked with those of other disciplines. Psychiatric assessments involve emergencies such as deliberate self-harm or acute presentations that might indicate the onset of mental illness and diagnostic assessment of potential depressive, psychotic, eating or neurodevelopmental disorders, mainly autism spectrum and attention deficit-hyperactivity disorders (ADHD). Young people may present at different times and through different referral routes, often with more than one type of concern.

Treatment skills are not exclusive to any particular professional discipline, as the new generation of CAMHS practitioners, including psychiatrists, should have an awareness of different therapeutic modalities, in terms of their indications, objectives and limitations. Pharmacological treatment for adolescents is almost always initiated and monitored by psychiatrists of medical background, but even this field is undergoing change, with nurse practitioners continuously expanding their skills in the use of psychiatric medication, at least in the UK. The use of medication depends on the underlying disorder, and is rarely the only treatment modality. Overall, this is not used as much as with adults, predominantly because psychotic conditions are less prevalent in the younger age group, and the more common but less severe forms of depression respond well to psychotherapeutic interventions like CBT. Below, the main indications for pharmacological treatment are summarised.

The incidence rate of psychotic disorders is around 15 per 100,000. These include schizophrenia, drug-induced psychosis and bipolar affective disorders (manic depression). Antipsychotic medication is prescribed when a diagnosis has been made; it can be difficult to establish a firm diagnosis with adolescents, as the onset at this age can be gradual or insidious, rather than acute. This can take the form of social withdrawal, declining school performance and unusual behaviours before the onset of florid symptoms such as delusions (abnormal beliefs) or hallucinations (abnormal perceptions). For this reason, designated early intervention psychosis teams have been established in recent years to cross over into adulthood, thus providing continuity of care. Medication should always be complemented by psychosocial interventions and education, as well as family support.

Depression happens more frequently, between one per cent in early adolescence (no gender differences) and four per cent in later adolescence (higher in girls). The key features are similar to those experienced by adults, that is, depressed mood (persistent for at least two weeks), irritability, poor or excessive sleep, change in appetite (usually decrease), weight changes (usually loss), self-harm thoughts, impaired concentration, loss of interest in previously enjoyable activities, fatigue, and negative cognitions (feeling useless, inadequate, ugly, guilty, hopeless). Young people with depression often have concurrent anxiety, behavioural or eating problems. The severity varies from mild to severe. Medication is not indicated for the milder forms of depression, where psychological interventions such as CBT and dealing with the underlying issues such as family or school difficulties take precedence. Even in the moderate and severe presentations, antidepressant medication is not necessarily the first line of treatment, as modalities like CBT and interpersonal therapy have been found to be as effective. A number of factors need to be taken into consideration before adopting a pharmacological approach, including poor response to psychological kinds of help, the young person's and parents' wishes and risk factors such as deliberate self-harm. It is important to note that medication and psychological interventions like counselling are not mutually exclusive, but can work well in conjunction or sequentially, as long as there is clear communication of objectives and expectations.

ADHD should have been diagnosed much earlier during childhood, although there are an increasing number of adolescents who remain on medication if they benefit from it. Starting with the diagnosis, this is more subjective during adolescence, that is, impaired attention/concentration and restlessness, rather than physical overactivity, which is seen in younger children, hence the condition is even more difficult to diagnose. As the diagnosis and treatment of ADHD can still cause debate, despite the large body of research evidence, it is important that this is assessed thoroughly, with close co-operation with the family and teachers, and that everybody is clear on what medication is meant to achieve, or not. Psychological (cognitive) assessment of the young person's concentration can be particularly useful in making a diagnosis with adolescents, as one relies less on direct observations. Like in depression, mild forms do not require the use of medication, but rather school support systems in place, psychological techniques and parenting work. These remain complementary and effective when stimulant medication is used in more severe forms of ADHD. Its likely impact should be clear to all involved from the outset, as this targets attention and activity levels, but not challenging behaviours, as is often misperceived. Sometimes breaking the cycle can be useful in improving academic attainment and behaviours, but these are indirect rather than direct effects of pharmacological treatment. Close monitoring with the family and the school is essential in establishing these outcomes.

These are the three main conditions related to the use of medication in adolescence. Other indications may include severe obsessive-compulsive symptoms, sleep disturbance (insomnia) or acute anxiety (panic attacks). These situations should be rare, and only for brief periods and under close supervision, as behavioural techniques are usually more effective.

Conclusion

This chapter has provided a brief overview of a range of allied interventions that may take place in parallel to therapeutic counselling as part of a comprehensive package of support to improve a young person's emotional well-being. Although they are all underpinned by a common aim – to help the young person – they are each unique in the approaches they take, the background and training of the professionals involved and the stage at which they may come into play in the young person's life. From the point of view of the adolescent counselling psychologist, developing an understanding of what allied interventions a young person may be exposed to is obviously a crucial consideration. This is not just because it helps to provide a more holistic picture; it also helps in highlighting any potential complications associated with multiple interventions carried out in parallel to one another. Effective communication between the various agencies involved is therefore crucial. In this sense, tools such as the Common Assessment Framework, which allow a more 'integrated' approach to the assessment of a young person's needs (and deciding how they should be met), are to be recommended.

Summary

- As schools begin to adopt a more holistic approach to learning, numerous strategies to improve student well-being are incorporated into the day-to-day activities. A major programme of this kind within England is SEAL, based on Goleman's (1995) model of emotional intelligence.
- Young people can have a difficult relationship with the language that surrounds mental health. Encouraging engagement and discourse around commonplace terminology can help to break down myths and misunderstandings.

- Youth work plays an important role in supporting young people to shape their own futures. It often utilises creative approaches to engage young people in discussions around complex issues such as mental health.
- EPs offer a wide range of services within educational settings. These include undertaking statutory assessments, consultation and training, and therapeutic interventions.
- Engagement with issues around disability can easily be ignored or avoided within counselling relationships. Decisions around working with young people with disabilities can therefore be complex and should be considered with appropriate sensitivity.
- Psychiatrists work with individuals with a wide variety of complex presenting issues. Such professionals work alongside other professionals and, where necessary, they are likely to oversee pharmacological treatment.

Further reading

As with Chapter 3, further reading is not directly suggested here as the sources referred to by the contributing authors provide numerous directions for consideration.

References

School-based strategies to support emotional well-being – the social and emotional aspects of learning (SEAL) programme

Craig, C. (2007). *The Potential Dangers of a Systematic, Explicit Approach to Teaching Social and Emotional Skills (SEAL)*. Glasgow: Centre for Confidence and Wellbeing.

Department for Children, Schools and Families (2008). *Targeted Mental Health in Schools*. Nottingham: DCSF Publications.

Department for Education and Skills. (2005). *Excellence and Enjoyment: Social and emotional aspects of learning (guidance)*. Nottingham: DfES Publications.

Department for Education and Skills. (2006). *Excellence and Enjoyment: Social and emotional aspects of learning: key stage 2 small group activities*. Nottingham: DfES Publications.

Ecclestone, K. and Hayes, D. (2008). *The Dangerous Rise of Therapeutic Education*. London: Routledge.

Goleman, D. (1995). *Emotional Intelligence*. New York, NY: Bantam Books.

Humphrey, N., Lendrum, A. and Wigelsworth, M. (2010). *Secondary Social and Emotional Aspects of Learning (SEAL): National evaluation*. Nottingham: DFE Publications.

Weare, K. (2010). Mental health and social and emotional learning: evidence, principles, tensions, balances. *Advances in School Mental Health Promotion*, 3, 5–17.

Weare, K. and Markham, M. (2005). What do we know about promoting mental health through schools? *Promotion and Education*, 3–4, 118–22.

Raising awareness and reducing stigma

Corrigan, P. (2006). *On the Stigma of Mental Illness: Practical strategies for research and social change.* Washington: American Psychological Association.

Crisp, A. (2004). *Every Family in the Land: Understanding prejudice and discrimination against people with mental illness.* London: Royal Society of Medicine Press.

Meltzer, H. Gatward, R., Goodman R. and Ford T. (2003). Mental health of children and adolescents in Great Britain. *International Review of Psychiatry,* 15 (1), 185–7.

Pinfold, V. (2003). Awareness in Action: changing discriminatory and negative attitudes to mental illness should start at school. *Mental Health Today,* July/August, 24–7.

Rigby, K. (2000). Effects of peer victimization in schools and perceived social support on adolescent well-being. *Journal of Adolescence,* 23 (1), 57–68.

Thornicroft, G. (2006). *Shunned: Discrimination against people with mental illness.* Oxford: Oxford University Press.

Youth work

Belton, B. A. (2010). *Radical Youth Work: Developing critical perspectives and professional judgement.* Lyme Regis: Russell House Publishing.

Davies, B. (2005). Youth work: a manifesto for our times. *Youth and Policy* 88, summer.

Davies, B. and Merton, B. (2009). *Squaring the Circle? Findings of a 'modest inquiry' into the state of youth work practice in a changing policy environment.* Leicester: De Montfort University.

Ewen, J. (1980). Crisps and Coca-Cola or agents of change. In F. Booton and A. Dearling (eds) *The Changing Scene of Youth and Community Work.* Leicester: National Youth Bureau (cited in Smith, 1999, 2002).

Lauritzen, P. (2006). *Defining youth work. Nonformality.* Weblog accessed 2.9.2011 from www.nonformality.org/2006/06/defining-youth-work/.

National Youth Agency. (undated). *The NYA Guide to Youth Work in England.* Retrieved 2.9.2011 from nya.org.uk/catalogue/workforce-1/nya-guide-to-youth-work-and-youth-services.

Royal College of Psychiatrists. (2010). *Self-harm, Suicide and Risk: Helping people who self-harm. Final report of a working group.* College Report CR158. Retrieved from www.rcpsych.ac.uk/files/pdfversion/CR158.pdf.

Sapin, K. (2009). *Essential Skills for Youth Work Practice.* London: Sage Publications.

Smith, M. K. (1999, 2002). Youth work: an introduction. etrieved 02/09/2011 from www.infed.org/youthwork/b-yw.htm.

Educational psychology services

Ahrens-Eipper, S. and Hoyer, J. (2006). Applying the Clark–Wells model of social phobia to children: the case of a 'dictation phobia'. *Behavioural and Cognitive Psychotherapy,* 34 (1), 103–6.

Audit Commission. (2002). *Special Educational Needs: A Mainstream Issue.* Wetherby: Audit Commission Publications.

Bandler, R. W. and Grinder, J. T. (1975). *The Structure of Magic.* Palo Alto, California: Science and Behaviour Books.

Barrett, P. (1996). *Friends for Life.* Bowen Hills: Australian Academic Press.

Beck, A. T. and Emery, G. (1979). *Cognitive Therapy of Anxiety and Phobic Disorders*. Philadelphia: Center for Cognitive Therapy.

Beck, A. T., Rush, A., Shaw, B. and Emery, G. (1979). *Cognitive Therapy of Depression*. New York: The Guilford Press.

Beck, A. T., Emery, G. and Greenberg, R. (1985). *Anxiety Disorders and Phobias: A cognitive perspective*. New York: Basic Books.

Beck, A. T., Freeman, E., Davis, D. and Associates. (2004). *Cognitive Therapy of Personality Disorders* (2nd edition). London: The Guilford Press.

Burton, S. (2004). Self-esteem groups for secondary pupils with dyslexia. *Educational Psychology in Practice, 20* (1), 55–73.

Burton, S. (2006). 'Over to you': group work to help pupils avoid school exclusion. *Educational Psychology in Practice, 22* (3), 215–36.

Burton, S. (2008). Empowering learning support assistants to enhance the emotional wellbeing of children in school. *Educational and Child Psychology, 25* (2), 40–56.

De Shazer, S. (1985). *Keys to Solutions in Brief Therapy*. New York: Norton.

Department for Children, Schools and Families. (2008a). *The Education of Children and Young People with Behavioural, Emotional and Social Difficulties as a Special Educational Need*. London: Department for Children, Schools and Families.

Department for Children, Schools and Families. (2008b). *Targeted Mental Health in Schools Project. Using the evidence to inform your approach: a practical guide for headteachers and commissioners*. Nottingham: DCSF Publications.

Department for Children, Schools and Families, and Department of Health. (2008). *Improving the Mental Health and Psychological Well-Being of Children and Young People. National CAMHS Review: Interim report*. London: DCSF and DH.

Department for Children, Schools and Families, and Department of Health. (2009). *Healthy Lives, Brighter Futures. The strategy for children and young people's health*. London: Central Office of Information for the Department of Health and the Department for Children, Schools and Families.

Department for Education and Skills. (2001). *Special Educational Needs Code of Practice*. Nottingham: DfES Publications.

Department for Education and Skills. (2004). *Every Child Matters: Change for children*. Nottingham: Department for Education and Skills Publications.

Department for Education and Skills. (2007). *Social and Emotional Aspects of Learning. . . Improving Behaviour. . . Improving Learning*. Nottingham: DfES.

Department of Health. (2004). *CAMHS Standard, National Service Framework for Children, Young People and Maternity Services: The mental health and psychological well-being of children and young people*. London: Department of Health Publications.

Ellis, A. and Dryden, W. (1999). *The Practice of Rational Emotive Behavioural Therapy*. London: Free Association Books.

Farrell, P., Woods, K., Lewis, S., Rooney, S., Squires, G. and O'Connor, M. (2006). *A Review of the Functions and Contribution of Educational Psychologists in England and Wales in Light of 'Every Child Matters: Change for Children'*. Research report RR792. Nottingham: Department for Education and Skills.

Faupel, A., Herrick, E. and Sharp, P. (1988). *Anger Management: A practical guide*. London: David Fulton Publishers.

Gregor, A. (2005). Examination anxiety: live with it, control it, or make it work for you? *School Psychology International, 26* (5), 617–35.

Greig, A. and MacKay, T. (2005). Asperger's syndrome and cognitive behaviour therapy: new applications for educational psychologists. *Educational and Child Psychology,* 22 (4), 4–15.

Grinder, J. T. and Bandler, R. W. (1976). *The Structure of Magic II.* Palo Alto, California: Science and Behaviour Books.

Health Advisory Service. (1995). *Together We Stand: The commissioning, role and management of Child and Adolescent Mental Health Services.* London: The Stationery Office.

Humphrey, N. and Brooks, A. G. (2006). An evaluation of a short cognitive-behavioural anger management intervention for pupils at risk of exclusion. *Emotional and Behavioural Difficulties,* 11 (1), 5–23.

Kelly, G. A. (1955). *The Psychology of Personal Constructs.* New York: Norton.

Kelly, M. S. and Bluestone-Miller, R. (2009). Working out what works (woww): coaching teachers to do more of what's working. *Children and Schools,* 31 (1), 35–8.

Kusche, C. A. and Greenberg, M. T. (1993). *The Paths (Promoting Alternative Thinking Strategies) Curriculum.* Deerfield, MA: Channing-Bete.

Lown, J. (2010). Circle time: the perceptions of teachers and pupil. *Educational Psychology in Practice,* 18 (2), 93–102.

Maag, J. W. (2008). Rational emotive therapy to help teachers control their emotions and behavior when dealing with disagreeable students. *Intervention in School and Clinic,* 44 (52), 52–7.

McNamara, E. (1998). The role of thinking and feeling: extending assessment beyond behaviour. *Pastoral Care,* 16, 10–19.

Mosley, J. (1993). *Turn Your School Around.* Wisbech: LDA.

National Institute for Health and Clinical Excellence. (2004). *Self-Harm. The short-term physical and psychological management and secondary prevention of self-harm in primary and secondary care.* London: National Institute for Health and Clinical Excellence.

National Institute for Health and Clinical Excellence. (2005a). *Depression in Children and Young People: Identification and management in primary, community and secondary care.* National clinical practice guideline number 28. Nottingham: National Collaborating Centre for Mental Health, Royal College of Psychiatrists' Research and Training Unit, National Institute for Health and Clinical Excellence and The British Psychological Society.

National Institute for Health and Clinical Excellence. (2005b). *Final Appraisal Determination: Computerised cognitive behaviour therapy for depression and anxiety.* London: National Institute for Health and Clinical Excellence.

National Institute for Health and Clinical Excellence. (2007). *Depression (Amended): Management of depression in primary and secondary care.* London: National Institute for Health and Clinical Excellence.

National Institute for Health and Clinical Excellence. (2008). *Promoting Children's Social and Emotional Wellbeing in Primary Education.* London: National Institute for Health and Clinical Excellence.

Norwich, B. and Daniels, H. (1997). Teacher support teams for special educational needs in primary schools: evaluating a teacher-focused support scheme. *Educational Studies,* 23 (1), 5–24.

Rait, S., Monsen, J. J. and Squires, G. (2010). Cognitive behaviour therapies and their implications for applied educational psychology practice. *Educational Psychology in Practice,* 26, 105–22.

Rogers, C. (1951). *Client Centred Therapy: Its current practice, implications and theory.* Boston: Houghton Mifflin.

Squires, G. (2001). Using cognitive behavioural psychology with groups of pupils to improve self-control of behaviour. *Educational Psychology in Practice,* 17 (4), 317–35.

Squires, G. (2007). *Community Psychology: 'Capacity building' by meeting the needs of the adults in schools.* Paper presented at the International School Psychology Association 29th Annual Colloquium. Retrieved 01/08/2007 from www.ispaweb.org/Colloquia/ Tampere/Presentations/Squires_Community_Psychologypdf.pdf.

Squires, G. (2009). *Helping the Children's Workforce Feel Confident in Meeting Children's Mental Health Needs.* Paper presented at the International School Psychology Association 31st Annual Colloquium.

Squires, G. and Farrell, P. (2006). Educational psychology in England and Wales. In S. R. Jimerson, T. D. Oakland and P. T. Farrell (eds) *The Handbook of International School Psychology,* Thousand Oaks: California Sage Publications.

Squires, G., Farrell, P., Woods, K., Lewis, S., Rooney, S. and O'Connor, M. (2007). Educational psychologists' contribution to the Every Child Matters agenda: the parents' view. *Educational Psychology in Practice,* 23 (4), 343–61.

Stringer, P., Stow, L., Hibbert, K., Powell, J. and Louw, E. (1992). Establishing staff consultation groups in schools. *Educational Psychology in Practice,* 8 (2), 87–96.

Toland, J. and Boyle, C. (2008). Applying cognitive behavioural methods to retrain children's attributions for success and failure in learning. *School Psychology International,* 29, 286–302.

Support for disabled young people

Alexander P. (2003). Inclusion: a reality for all? *Counselling and Psychotherapy Journal,* September, 5–9.

Barnes, C. and Mercer, G. (2010). *Exploring Disability* (2nd edition) Cambridge: Polity Press.

Downer, B. (2001). Counselling deafened clients. *Counselling Psychotherapy Journal,* July, 21–23.

Parkinson, G. (2006). Counsellors' attitudes towards disability equality training (DET). *British Journal of Guidance and Counselling,* 34 (1), 93–105.

Reeve, D. (2000). Oppression within the counselling room. *Disability and Society,* 15 (4), 669–82.

Reeve, D. (2002). Oppression within the counselling room. *Counselling and Psychotherapy Research,* 2, 11–19.

Wilson, S. (2003). *Disability Counselling and Psychotherapy: Challenges and opportunities.* London: Palgrave Macmillan.

Specialist CAMHS, psychiatry and medication

As the author has not made use of references within this section, the following are a list of recommendations for further reading on the subject matter.

Bhangoo, R. and Carter, C. (2009). Very early interventions in psychotic disorders. *Psychiatric Clinics of North America,* 32, 81–94.

Dogra, N., Vostanis, P. and Karnik, N. (2007). Child and adolescent psychiatric disorders. In D. Bhugra and K. Bhui (eds) *Textbook of Cultural Psychiatry* (pp.301–313). Cambridge: Cambridge University Press.

Dogra, N., Parkin, A., Gale., F. and Frake, C. (eds) (2008). *A Multidisciplinary Handbook of Child and Adolescent Mental health for Front-line Professionals* (2nd edition). London: Jessica Kingsley.

Fonagy, P., Target, M., Cottrell, D., Phillips, J. and Kurtz, Z. (2002). *What Works for Whom? A critical review of treatments for children and adolescents.* New York: Guilford.

Goodman, R. and Scott, S. (2005). *Child Psychiatry* (2nd edition). Oxford: Blackwell.

Goodyer, I., Dubicka, B., Wilkinson, P., Kelvin, R., Roberts, C., Byford, S., Breen, S., Ford, C., Barrett, B., Leech, A., Rothwell, J., White, L. and Harrington, R. (2007). Selective serotonin reuptake inhibitors (SSRIs) and routine specialist care with and without cognitive behaviour therapy in adolescents with major depression: randomised controlled trial. *British Medical Journal*, 335, 142–6.

Green, H., Mc Ginnity, A., Meltzer, H., Ford, T. and Goodman, R. (2005). *Mental Health of Children and Young People in Great Britain.* London: Palgrave MacMillan.

National Institute for Health and Clinical Excellence. (2005). *Depression in Children and Young People: Identification and Management in Primary, Community and Secondary care.* Quick reference guide. London: NICE.National Institute for Health and Clinical Excellence. (2008). *Attention Deficit-Hyperactivity Disorder: Diagnosis and management of ADHD in children, young people and adults.* London: NICE.

Vostanis, P. (2007). Mental health and mental disorders. In Coleman, J. and Hagell, A. (eds) *Adolescence, Risk and Resilience: Against the odds* (pp.89–106). Chichester: Wiley.

Watanabe, N., Churchill, R., Hunot V. and Furukawa, T. (2006). Psychotherapy for depression in children and adolescents. *Cochrane Systematic Review*, 3.

Wolpert, M., Fuggle, P., Cottrell, D., Fonagy, P., Phillips, J., Pilling, S., Stein, S. and Taggert, M. (2006). *Drawing on the Evidence: Advice for mental health professionals working with children and adolescents* (2nd edition). London: CAMHS Evidence Based Practice Unit.

Part 2

Psychological change for young people

Chapter 5

Adolescence in context

Clare Lennie and Terry Hanley

Overview

The emphasis of this book is on working with a particular client group, therefore the aim of this chapter is to give a psychological underpinning as to what we mean by the term 'adolescence'. The part begins by explaining that the term is a relatively recent creation but its roots can be traced back to the writings of Plato 2000 years ago. Cultural and gender variations are discussed. We then move on to look at the main theoretical explanations for understanding the transitions that occur in adolescence, looking firstly at evolutionary explanations before moving on to psychoanalytic and cognitive perspectives. Although each of these perspectives varies in the emphases that it takes, there is a common element that runs through all of them in their emphasis on this being a 'tricky' time of life. Due to this 'trickiness' we then move on to discuss some of the hazards that young people might come across as they navigate their journey through this period, looking specifically at the overlapping areas of social roles and drug use before finally moving on to explore therapeutic approaches that might be employed with this client group. We begin this final part by exploring purist approaches, giving an overview of the main behavioural/cognitive-behavioural, psychodynamic and person-centred paradigms before finishing by exploring what more pluralistic approaches to therapy might offer to this client group.

What is adolescence?

When were your years as an 'adolescent'? Why do you choose these years?

This section will explain the emergence of adolescence as a concept and associated cross-cultural variations, before attempting to define this stage of development.

The term 'adolescence' is relatively new, coming originally from the Latin *adolescere,* meaning to grow to maturity. The ways in which it is marked and recognised vary greatly from culture to culture and across time but there is a general consensus that it is undoubtedly a period of much transition and change, both psychologically and physically.

Adolescence, as we know it, was barely recognised before the end of the nineteenth century. Demos and Demos (1969) noted that in examining various written materials from the period from 1800 to 1875 there was almost no usage of the word and only a limited degree of concern with the stage and its characteristic behaviour. It was only with the work of G Stanley Hall that adolescence was made the focus of a new current of psychological study. This developing interest is often associated with changes in western culture, societal and family values and structures. In western society the lengthy period of adolescence is often criticised as a luxury, a delay in taking on adult business which can result in complications of being an adult and child at the same time. Indeed, Furstenberg (2000) defines it as a life stage which emerged as full-time education took over from full-time employment as the primary activity of young people. However, despite sometimes being viewed as a modern phenomenon, the potential for the young to 'shake things up' and reshape existing social orders can be seen in the writings of Plato 2000 years ago and, in terms of cultural variation, despite the differences in age cross-culturally, periods of some form of significant transition and change are observed in most societies (Coleman, 1995).

Often the period is associated with marker events or initiation rites associated with adulthood, for example leaving home or starting work or college. In western cultures this stage of development spans a relatively long period, between the ages of 11 and 25 or beginning at puberty, the period when sexual maturation begins. Girls often reach puberty before boys and therefore even within one culture there is considerable variation regarding the time that we can say this stage has been reached. It is therefore difficult to pin a definitive age to adolescence and we may often refer to it as the 'teenage years', associating it with rebellion and angst. Downey (2003) highlights the main features of adolescence as:

- defining the self in unique terms
- capability to locate self as 'object' in an abstracted personal history and interpersonal context
- emergence of global self-awareness is associated with increased preoccupation with self and sensitivity to the perceptions of others
- capability to maintain mood state through active rumination but also capable of concealing affective state, even when in distress, whilst maintaining general functioning
- an ambivalent view of adults as a helpful social resource.

The psychology of adolescence

How might psychology explain what was happening to you as you found your way through the wilderness years of adolescence?

As outlined above, the first major theory of adolescence came from the evolutionist G. Stanley Hall (1844–1924) and it was this that sparked further interest in research and theory related to its study. Broadly, classical theories of adolescence propose three main components: (1) storm and stress; (2) identity crisis; and (3) the generation gap. Further theories have, in their own way, developed each of these components and will be grouped under the broad headings of evolutionary, psychoanalytic and cognitive theories.

Evolutionary theories – adolescence as a recapitulation of the human species' stormy past

G. Stanley Hall's theory of adolescence drew on the work of Charles Darwin and his thoughts regarding evolution. Hall believed that a person's psychological development in some way recaptures or recapitulates the evolution of the human species, both physically and culturally. He believed the turbulence, often viewed as part of adolescence, mirrored the volatile history of the human race over the last 2000 years and he called this turbulence *Sturm und Drang* (storm and stress). The term comes originally from the writings of Schiller and Goethe in German literature, a literary style which is concerned with idealism, commitment to a goal, revolution against the old, expression of personal feelings, passion and suffering – all attributes that Hall believed to be reflected in the psychological characteristics of adolescence. So, for Hall, the individual relives the developmental stages of the human race, from early animal-like primitivism through a period of savagery, to the more recent 'civilised' ways of life that characterise maturity. For Hall, adolescence is a new birth from which high-order traits emerge, a stage of maturity that echoes developing civilisation and in this sense for maturity is not fixed but is ever-developing.

Anecdotally there is considerable evidence to support Hall's notion of storm and stress in this stage of development. Parents can often be heard saying that their offspring are hard to handle, moody, slamming doors, being temperamental and hormonal. Indeed, this is often a hard time for parents too as they are viewed with ambivalence in terms of their being a 'helpful resource' (Downey, 2003). Further emotional and behavioural ambivalence is reflected in Hall's writing, with oscillating and contradictory energy levels and need for solitude but becoming entangled in powerful peer groups and romantic crushes.

With regard to more empirical research, the turbulence that Hall reports is thought to relate more to the reactions in the young person being more intense, rather than it being a time of storm and stress per se. In two classic studies, Bandura and Walters (1959) found that adolescence was in itself no more of a stressful stage than childhood or adulthood, whereas Rutter *et al.* (1976) only found a small increase in psychological disturbance between 10-year-olds, 14-year-olds and adults. Often where disturbance did exist it had been in existence from childhood and its onset was associated with stress, for example, marital discord. So this might not be so turbulent a time for most. More typically, young adults possess an ego which is strong enough to sustain them through difficult life experiences and they are supported by stable-enough relationships to be protected from the turmoil of the disturbed adolescent. However, for some, without this emotional support it can indeed be a troublesome time. We will return to this later.

Psychodynamic theories of adolescence – the roles of urges, crises, exploration and will

Sigmund Freud

Freud's theory of psychosexual development paid little attention to the stage of adolescence specifically; indeed, his developmental stages stopped at 18 years, which marked the onset of 'adulthood'. For Freud, the stages of development (oral 0–1 years, anal 1–3 years, phallic 3–6 years, latent 6–12 years and genital 12–18 years) were genetically determined and little influenced by environmental factors. In terms of adolescence, Freud believed that the behavioural, social and emotional changes that occur and the relationships between the physiological and psychological transition influenced the young person's self-image, often resulting in an increase in negative emotions, such as moodiness, anxiety, loathing, tension and other forms of behaviour observed in the young person.

Anna Freud

Further writings that come from the psychodynamic field are those of Anna Freud (1896–1982), who believed that puberty is a major influencing factor on later character formation. The biological changes occurring at this stage of life reawaken the id (the part of personality structure proposed by Freud which is full of basic instinctual urges, waiting for immediate gratification and pleasure), creating a disequilibrium from the harmony that had been achieved during the latency or resting psychosexual stage. This, she believed, resulted in individuals engaging in behaviours where they actively try to re-establish equilibrium. The two main defence mechanisms typical of the adolescent striving for equilibrium are asceticism and intellectualisation. Asceticism is due to a generalised mistrust of all instinctual wishes and associated abstinence of behaviours that give pleasure, not only in relation to sex but also including eating, sleeping and dressing habits. Intellectual activities might be used as a defence mechanism against urges of the libido.

Otto Rank

Otto Rank (1884–1939) was a follower of the psychoanalytic school but then criticised Freud's emphasis on the unconscious, believing it only to be of importance if it impacts on present behaviours. Otto was interested in the role of will in determining behaviour, rather than being beholden to the impulses of the id and the associated shift from dependence to independence that is central to transition in adolescence.

Erik Erikson

Probably the main writer that needs to concern us from the psychodynamic world is Erikson. In developing Freud's writing, Erikson was one of the first to challenge the idea that personality development stops in childhood. He maintained that social and psychological change is driven by a genetic structure which is common to us all: we all pass through stages and in this sense they are thought to be both universal and psychosocial. However, Erikson believed that there was complexity as to how we come through each of the stages, suggesting that each centres around a particular crisis for which there is a struggle between positive (adaptive) and negative (maladaptive) outcomes. He did not see the outcome of each stage as 'either/or', rather more which outweighed the other. Healthy personality development is one where the adaptive outweighs the maladaptive.

Erikson's eight stages are:

1. Trust versus mistrust. From ages birth to one year, children begin to learn the ability to trust others, based upon the consistency of availability of their caregiver(s), resulting adaptively in confidence and security in the world around the child. Unsuccessful completion of this stage can result in an inability to trust and a resulting sense of fear about the inconsistent world.
2. Autonomy versus shame and doubt. Between the ages of one and three years, children begin to assert their independence in terms of increased mobility and choice. If children are encouraged and supported in this increased independence, they become more confident and secure in their own ability to survive in the world. With criticism or excessive control they begin to feel inadequate in their ability to survive.
3. Initiative versus guilt. Around age three to six years, children increasingly assert themselves, so developing a sense of initiative. If this tendency is overly controlled or the child's actions are criticised, the child could remain a follower, lacking in self-initiative.
4. Industry versus inferiority. At age six years to puberty, children begin to develop a sense of pride in their accomplishments. If their initiative is not encouraged, children begin to feel inferior, doubting their own abilities and therefore possibly not reaching their potential.
5. Identity versus role confusion. This is the stage which is central to adolescence and is discussed below.
6. Intimacy versus isolation. In young adulthood, we share ourselves increasingly with others in an intimate way leading toward longer-term commitments, resulting in comfortable relationships and a sense of commitment, safety and care. Avoiding intimacy and fearing commitment and relationships can lead to isolation, loneliness and sometimes depression.
7. Generativity versus stagnation. In middle adulthood we establish our career, settle down within a relationship, rear our own families and develop a sense of being a part of the bigger picture and giving back to society. By failing to achieve these objectives, we become stagnant and feel unproductive.

8. Ego integrity versus despair. As we grow older and become senior citizens, we tend to slow down our productivity, and explore life as a retired person contemplating our accomplishments. We are able to develop integrity if we see ourselves as leading a successful life. If we evaluate our life as unproductive, or we feel guilt about events in the past, we become dissatisfied with life, despairing and hopeless.

For Erikson the stage which is central to adolescence is the fifth, the major task of which is establishing a strong sense of personal identity. The confusions of puberty and the biological and physical changes that ensue, alongside their developing intellectual ability, often result in painful evaluations of personal strengths and weaknesses in finding their own place in an adult society. A personal sense of identity is achieved through effort and this is often a painful process. As outlined above, in a western society adolescence is often referred to as a moratorium – a delay in taking up the full responsibilities of adulthood in order for young people to take more time in finding their sense of self in an adult society. This can however lead to its own confusions in the mixed messages regarding role and status that society gives. For example, the age at which one becomes 'adult' will differ across contexts so leading to confusions – we are able to become a parent at 16 yet cannot vote until 18. Which is the weightier duty?

The adolescent has to juggle concepts of past, present and future in considering the central questions of Who am I? and also Who will I be? Considering older generations can be helpful in establishing identity but often these role models are felt to have little to do with the uniqueness of the young person's situation. Adults are in a tricky position of fluctuating from supporting young people in developing their own autonomous thinking on the one hand and condemning them for their self-centredness on the other. It is in this sense that peer groups become central as a frame of reference, giving important feedback to young people as to how they present themselves to the world. Answers related to self-identity are also often associated with career choice or role in life but more centrally are to do with the feedback from peers. Erikson observed that adolescents are sometimes morbidly preoccupied with what they appear to be in the eyes of others (Erikson, 1963). We return to peer groups and gangs as a key issue later in this chapter.

The positive outcome of this stage for Erikson is a strong sense of ego identity, knowing what one stands for and remaining true to these ideals, a sense of self that will carry the individual through hard times. Indeed, much of Erikson's work was with psychiatrically disturbed soldiers from World War II: Erikson believed much of their trauma had been caused by their lack of personal identity and sense of self. A failure to develop a coherent sense of self results in role confusion and this can manifest itself in many ways, for example aimlessly drifting through social and occupational roles or engaging in abnormal or delinquent behaviours. Adolescents may often take on roles that set them aside from others in terms of risky behaviour or appearance; for Erikson this type of role confusion is referred to as negative identity. Such an extreme position is preferable to failing to find a position in an adult world and the loneliness and failure that might ensue.

Although inherently attractive in terms of everyday observations of young adults, Erikson's theory has been criticised mainly for its gender bias, his observations all coming from a male sample. Gilligan (1982) argues the theory is androcentric in that males might want to forge independent separate identities, whilst females might be more concerned with nurturing relationships and less concerned with separateness.

James Marcia

Marcia defines identity as an internal, self-constructed, dynamic organisation of drives, abilities, beliefs and individual history. He believes that the better developed this structure is, the more aware individuals appear to be of their own uniqueness and similarity to others. They also become aware of their strengths and weaknesses in making their way in the world. According to Marcia, the criteria for the attainment of a mature identity are based on two essential variables: crisis and commitment. Crisis refers to times during adolescence when the individual is involved in choosing among alternative occupations and beliefs, whereas commitment refers to the degree of personal investment the individual expresses in an occupation or belief (Marcia, 1980).

Marcia interviewed students aged 18–22 years about their occupational choices, religious and political beliefs and values – all central aspects of identity. He classified students into four categories of identity status based on first, whether they had gone through an 'identity crisis', as described by Erikson, and second, the degree to which they were now committed to an occupational choice and to a set of values and beliefs.

The four categories of identity status as defined by Marcia are as follows:

1. Identity diffusion: The individual is in crisis and is unable to formulate clear self-definition, goals and commitments – in summary, an inability to take on adult identity.
2. Identity foreclosure: The individual has avoided the uncertainties and anxieties of crisis by committing rapidly to safe and conventional goals without exploring options.
3. Moratorium: Decisions regarding identity are postponed while the individual tries out alternative identities without committing to any particular one.
4. Identity achieved: The individual has experienced a crisis but has emerged successfully with firm commitments, goals and ideologies.

Marcia believes that moratorium and the associated activities of experimentation are central to identity achievement but he does not see the stages as sequential, although some research suggests that they might be age-related (Kroger, 1996). Modern schooling has been criticised for the extent to which it encourages foreclosure in emphasising testing and knowledge-based domains of learning rather than creativity and exploration. Once again the theory rests, however, on observations from male samples.

Margaret Mead

Striving for a meaningful identity is central too to Margaret Mead's work on anthropological and cultural considerations on adolescence. She believes this is a more complicated task in modern democratic societies where role models come from the mass media rather than those which are more familial and local. Those that come from the family may be viewed as outdated compared with images we see on television and our computers. Mead also believed that a period of experimentation is important for successful transition through this stage, without any expectation of demonstrating 'success'.

Cognitive views – changes in thinking and morality

The theories presented so far emphasise the social and biological aspects of development. Cognitive theories focus on the organisation of intelligence and how it changes as children grow.

Jean Piaget

Piaget (1896–1980) believed that children's thinking develops sequentially and that, through a process of accommodation and assimilation, children's' schemas or building blocks of intelligent behaviour develop and change, so resulting in learning. Assimilation is where new information is fitted into existing schemas, resulting in a state of equilibrium. Where existing schemas cannot cope with new information, a state of disequilibrium occurs where the child is motivated to restore equilibrium and needing to accommodate or modify his or her schema. For Piaget, the stages of cognitive development are sensorimotor (birth to 2 years), pre-operational (2–7 years), concrete operational (7–11 years) and formal operational (11 years onwards). As children progress to the final stage, their thinking becomes more abstract and they are able to manipulate thoughts as they might do physical objects in the preceding stages. Central too to Piaget's work is the concept of egocentrism; that is, the ability only to see the world from one's own standpoint. There are various shifts in egocentric thinking as the child develops, the final one being at the shift between concrete operational and formal operational thinking. The young person at this stage is able to hypothesise and consider reshaping reality and possibilities by carrying out manipulation of symbols in his or her mind. This is abstract thought and, as many parents will report, young people who are at this stage spend a lot of time lost in their own thoughts.

Lawrence Kohlberg

In a similar way to Erikson, who developed Freud's stage theory into adulthood, Lawrence Kohlberg extended Piaget's theory into adulthood, believing that cognitive development preceded moral development. Kohlberg distinguishes three basic levels of moral development: (1) the preconvention or premoral level; (2) the conventional level; and (3) the postconventional or autonomous level. Morality is an idea of justice that is primitive, undifferentiated and egocentric in young children, and becomes more sophisticated and social as the adolescent moves through specific stages of moral thinking.

The hazards of adolescence

What were your adolescent years like? Honestly?

The sections above have highlighted differing views on the concept of adolescence as a developmental stage, all of which reflect challenges of transition which are faced at this stage. How these challenges manifest themselves for the young person are varied. Downey (2003) notes that young people either internalise the problem, for example, by anxiously ruminating, or externalise the problem, for example, by becoming aggressive with others. Without a doubt these activities vary greatly in severity but there are an increasing number of reports outlining how commonplace some of the more extreme manifestations of psychological difficulties may be. For instance, conclusions have been drawn stating that 'Roughly 1 in 10 children have at least one DSM-IV disorder, involving a level of distress or social impairment likely to warrant treatment' (Ford et al., 2003, p.1203), one in three young people have contemplated suicide (Steinberg, 1996) and 24,000 potentially self-harmed in 1999 (Oxford Centre for Suicide Research, 1998).

Questions of 'who am I?' and 'who will I become?' are profound and complex. Relationships with parents, peers and self are complicated too but, for most, negotiating this stage is possible due to the protection that these relationships bring. For others, the transition is not so straightforward. The sections above suggest ways in which young people might navigate their way in a less productive manner, for example, Erikson's understanding of the negative identity. Although the dangers of foreclosure and the need for creativity and free experimentation that a moratorium offers in developing identity achievement are central to the work of Marcia and Mead, the potential for this experimentation to become excessive and risky is clear. Young people might often view themselves as indestructible. We go on to look briefly at two potential and overlapping hazards in more detail below. These are social roles and drugs.

Social roles

Who did you hang around with? Why?

Adolescence is inherently about developing independence and therefore the role that parents take on in supporting this process is tricky. Research suggests that positive, rational and interactive communication is key, alongside firm and consistent discipline (Baumrind, 1991) with clear boundaries (Gaoni *et al.,* 1994) in order to support young people in dealing with hazardous life events. However, there will almost inevitably be tensions between the expectations of peer groups with whom the young person might be hanging around and parents. The oscillations and contradictions that Hall notes reflect this: young people are trying to assert their independence whilst still needing social approval and this often results in their withdrawal from family and increased reliance on peer groups, which might present opportunity of hazardous or undesirable activities. The foundations that family interactions have put in place are vital in order for young people to gain emotional support from their peers, whilst not necessarily conforming to group pressures to indulge in group activities. Young people who have a more chaotic family background might be more seduced by conforming to group pressures, and all that this entails (Shulman *et al.,* 1995).

The tendency to join with peers and form groups is usually viewed as healthy and adaptive, happening throughout life. However, for adolescents their peer group might easily be viewed as a 'gang' by wider society. Often emerging in urban areas, such groups may exert undesirable influences on impressionable young people (Sigler, 1995). Despite their undeniable negative consequences, gangs can sometimes serve a purpose for the young person; for example, for minority groups they might remind them of their cultural heritage, although at the same time this may make assimilation with the majority culture more difficult (Calabrese and Noboa, 1995).

Drug use

What were you doing as you hung around with them? Why?

If experimentation and exploration are important facets of a healthy development of self-identity, then the availability of drugs to the young person presents a particular type of hazard. Perhaps the most widely available drug, and that which is often most influenced by peer pressure, is smoking. However, Michell and West (1996) suggest that even though peer pressures are powerful in terms of starting to smoke, the decision also contains strong elements of active self-determination, indicating that fitting in is important but so is the development of a personal identity. If adolescence is associated with a need for sensation-seeking, and risk-taking – 'shaking up the norm', which Plato recognised 2000 years ago – research strongly suggests that in the case of stronger drugs peer pressures become more powerful, not least because socialising with others who take such drugs makes them more available. Indeed, Swahn *et al.* (2010) found that gang members were significantly more likely than non-gang members to have initiated alcohol early and to have engaged in alcohol-related physical fighting, drug use and drug selling within their neighbourhood.

Counselling adolescents

The purist approaches

Having looked at the psychology of adolescence and considered some of the hazards that might ensue, we now look towards what psychology might offer in terms of support. In answer to this, the arena of counselling and therapy offers a complex and confusing array of potential; it is currently estimated that there are over 500 different types of therapy related to work with children and young people (Kazdin, 2000). In choosing an appropriate intervention, a variety of factors need to be considered and the young person's developmental stage and social context are vital in reaching any therapeutic decision. In undertaking therapeutic work it is important to understand the young person's cognitive, self-reflective and social capacities which are each drawn upon, to a greater and lesser extent, in different modalities of working. For example, very young children are limited in their ability to self-reflect, or indeed to use language to describe and discuss their reflections and experience, so impacting on the work undertaken. In a similar way, theories of adolescence might argue that young people at this stage find it difficult to decentre themselves in order to see the world from opposing viewpoints, so impacting on the use that they might make in therapy at all.

In adopting any approach to working therapeutically, the young person's social context is central; individuals may be tied into their immediate grouping or family and in no position to 'leave'. This will be an important filter through which experience is construed (Downey, 2003). Even where they do have the independence to leave, the process of this transition might be likened to the young baby's experience of the strange situation where leaving a secure base can result in high levels of anxiety. The family is an important dynamic in the young person's life and some would argue that counselling the child individually detracts from understanding the important influences and dynamics that are exerted on the child by the family. Such a view would espouse a family therapy approach. Others would suggest that working with the family dilutes the potential for personal issues to be explored fully and worked with.

In the sections below, we outline the three major paradigms of therapeutic practice that might be utilised when working with a young person individually. Following on from this we discuss practical ways of integrating approaches of therapy in working with a client at this developmental stage.

Behavioural and cognitive approaches

Behavioural approaches concentrate on behaviour and the consequences of action, rather than what is going on in the head in terms of thought process. Based on the work of Pavlov, the basic premise of a behaviourist position is that if a stimulus such as food is paired often enough with a neutral stimulus, for example a bell, then an animal or human will eventually respond to the bell by salivating. This new response, learned through association, might generalise to other sounds outside the laboratory and can find its application in work with issues such as phobias, where usually neutral stimuli become associated with a stressful experience.

Following from this work, eminent psychologists such as Skinner and Watson proposed that the consequences of our actions are important in determining the likelihood of them reappearing. Put simply, if something pleasant happens after we have behaved in a certain way, we are likely to do it again. We will also repeat our behaviours if we have avoided something unpleasant happening and if something unpleasant does happen our behaviour will cease. A 'rebellious teenager' could, in this way, be maintained through the attention that he receives from those around him, thus reinforcing and maintaining his actions. Although there is no need for particular insight in this intervention, the model does require for the young person to be motivated to engage in therapy with a level of self-control and awareness of his presenting behaviour. Due to its emphasis on measurable behaviour, there is more empirical research on these approaches. For example, systematic desensitisation, where clients are gradually exposed to their feared stimulus whilst pairing it with relaxation, has generally been found to be helpful with simple phobias in young children (Ollendick and King, 1998).

In cognitive-behavioural therapy (CBT) there is still the emphasis on behavioural components, as outlined above, but with a further focus on the cognitions associated with maintaining behaviours. CBT is not just concerned with fixing problems but also with the achievement of a happier life with discrete and meaningful goals, rather than broad-based 'therapy'. The here-and-now is emphasised rather than the past, with a realistic and positive reframing of negative thoughts to reduce negative emotions.

This approach is perhaps better suited to older children as their cognitive and linguistic skills are more sophisticated. CBT has been seen to be helpful with a number of child psychological problems such as generalised anxiety (Silverman et al., 1999) and social phobias (Spence et al., 2000). CBT for such disorders has five components:

1. psychoeducational – providing corrective information about anxiety and feared stimuli
2. somatic management skills training – targeting autonomic arousal and physiological responses
3. cognitive restructuring skills focusing on identifying maladaptive thoughts and teaching coping focused thinking

4. exposure methods, involving graduated and controlled exposure to feared situations
5. relapse prevention plans, focusing on consolidating and generalising treatment gains (Albano and Kendall, 2002).

Additionally, there are specialised manuals that offer resources for practitioners in relation to some of the core concepts of CBT with young people (Stallard, 2007).

Psychodynamic approaches

Psychodynamic approaches are based on the importance of the relationship in therapy, viewing this as the primary instrument for change in terms of interpretation, personal insight and awareness. Due to its focus on relationships, where these have been damaged early in life, it is likely that the young person will have to have a number of sessions at least at the start of therapy in order to develop an enduring and transportable sense of the relationship (Downey, 2003).

The roots of psychodynamic therapy lie in the work of Sigmund Freud and the psychosexual stages of development and theory of personality. Underlying each of these are Freud's ideas of ego functions, defence mechanisms and superego formulation; indeed, adults may sometimes find themselves regressing back to adolescent-type behaviours, which may reflect itself in the therapeutic process of an inability to commit or 'acting out'. With its emphasis once again on higher-level cognitive and linguistic skills, it is unlikely that this way of working would be appropriate for younger children but it can be of use to older children. The attributes of those who may benefit from psychodynamic psychotherapy include the following:

- conflict-free areas of functioning
- relate to and communicate well with others at an age-appropriate level
- demonstrates interest in school or hobbies
- awareness of symptoms and wish for change
- ability to use metaphor
- affect stability with some capacity for ambivalence (Delgado, 2008).

In working psychodynamically with young people, therapists need to be aware of issues of transference where the child might respond to the counsellor as if she were the child's mother or some other significant person. Such transference can be worked through in session by bringing it to the child's awareness. Countertransference occurs where the counsellor responds to the child's transference unconsciously, as if the counsellor were that significant other, and this needs to be owned and worked through by the therapist.

It is unusual for long-term 'pure' psychodynamic work to be offered in a school, largely due to practical limitations of the setting. For instance, immediately being returned to the school environment postsession may not be appropriate, thus mediating the necessary boundaries needed in this type of work is important. Broader psychodynamic interventions offered are likely to help in understanding the dynamics that arise between pupils, family, school staff and issues of parenting. Dysfunctional attachment and relationship patterns in the family can arise in the school setting and are able to be worked through by bringing them into conscious awareness through deep understanding, so impacting on the new relationships the child enters into (Lanyado and Horne, 2009).

Person-centred approaches

The main founder of this position was Carl Rogers who, disenchanted with more mainstream approaches to psychology and the objectivist stance of behaviourism, believed that human beings had an innate need for respect and understanding. His ideas are still central to professional work where human growth is seen as central and his core principles can be summarised as follows:

- emphasising the central role and importance of the counselling relationship as a significant factor in promoting change
- describing 'the person' as resourceful and tending towards actualisation of potential
- emphasising and developing the central role of listening and empathy in counselling and other relationships
- using the term 'client' rather than 'patient' to signify respect for the person coming for help and to acknowledge his or her dignity
- making sound recordings of counselling interviews and using them to learn about the counselling process
- engaging in scientific research and encouraging others to do so
- making the counselling process more democratic and encouraging non-psychologists and non-medical people to become counsellors (Cain, 2002).

Essentially, this approach to helping is concerned with the counsellor or helper becoming the best kind of companion in facilitating the client in accessing his or her own wisdom in a way that acknowledges that the client knows best. For this reason, this approach is often referred to as client-centred or non-directive counselling. In work particularly with young people, the counsellor–child relationship is fundamental and provides a link between the child's inner world and that of the counsellor. It must therefore be exclusive, safe, authentic, confidential (subject to limits), non-intrusive and purposeful (Geldard and Geldard, 2010); we refer to these points later in this chapter.

Taking an integrated approach – one size doesn't fit all

Given that the research findings indicate there is little difference in the effectiveness of different types of therapeutic intervention (Wampold, 2001), alternative ideas of working with young people comes from integrative, eclectic or pluralistic approaches. The first two terms are often confused or amalgamated together. Commonly, however, integrative approaches often refer to approaches that are formally combined into a new theoretical conceptualisation of therapy, while an eclectic practitioner often pays less regard to theoretical consistency (for an informative discussion on this, see Hollanders, 2003). As pluralism is discussed within the following chapter, we choose not to mention this further for the time being.

One popular integrative model of working with young people is Geldard and Geldard's (2010) proactive approach. This model emphasises that, if counselling is to be successful with this age group, it needs to be tailored to the young person's need. They argue for a proactive approach to working with a young person in the period of adolescence which is based on four foundations:

1. an existentialist philosophy – that is, trying to make sense of life. This fits well with working with this client group as this is precisely what they are struggling to do;
2. constructivist thinking – where constructs are formed to explain the world we live in and these are changed and developed in the light of human experience. Again, this echoes the development of thinking and changes in ideas that young people come across as they go through this stage of transition;
3. personal qualities of the counsellor – emphasising the counsellor's understanding of developmental processes, his or her ability to connect with the counsellor's own inner adolescent, an ability to symbolise and model individuation and in so doing be celebratory of uniqueness. Rogerian qualities of congruence and unconditional positive regard are seen as central, with an ability to relate easily and with empathy to adolescents;
4. the particular qualities of the adolescent–counsellor relationship – as outlined above, the relationship in counselling is seen to be the most important predictor of a positive outcome: it is of vital importance in working with this client group.

Such a stance may therefore draw on a number of models as appropriate to the young person's need. Concepts from person-centred counselling may be drawn upon as the young person tells his or her story and later ideas from CBT might be used in working with maladaptive thoughts, options and choices. Finally, as the young person experiments with new behaviours, these are evaluated in their use from a behavioural perspective. All in all, these methods promote a different model of change, drawing on different types of intervention in the ultimate goal of making the young person feel better.

Conclusion

There seems to be common agreement across different psychological paradigms that adolescence is a complex and challenging time, although the importance of strong and consistent relationships around the person is central if there is to be a calm navigation through this period. Drives to explore and experiment in developing self-identity equally form important components to all theories but the extent to which this is facilitated and supported by stable relationships around the young person is central if the young person is not to fall into the 'wrong hands'. The oscillations of adolescents and their ambivalence in relation to the adults around them can result in their being particularly dependent on peers for support, and this has both positive and negative connotations.

Psychological theories offer a diverse way of responding to the young person's needs therapeutically. Each of the major therapeutic paradigms – psychodynamic, cognitive-behavioural and person-centred – has been utilised for work with this age group. Likewise, integrative models have been created for specific use with young people. In the next chapter we consider how they may be brought together using the met-theory proposed within the movement towards pluralistic therapeutic approaches.

Summary

- The period of adolescence is difficult to pin down to a specific age due to cultural and gender variations.
- The first major theory of adolescence had its roots in evolution, suggesting that the turbulence, contradictions and oscillations often observed in this age group reflected the evolutionary past of the human species (Hall).
- Psychodynamic theories of adolescence all emphasise, to a greater or lesser extent, the control of urges and impulse. However, Erikson's theory is best detailed in outlining the crises that we face during adolescence and the ways that these are navigated in developing our sense of identity and role in society.
- In developing Erikson's work, Marcia emphasised the need for exploration as a moratorium before making definite commitment in developing a sense of identity in terms of the choices we make for ourselves. The lack of this type of 'space' is viewed as a potential criticism of current educational practices which emphasise knowledge testing as opposed to creativity.
- The ambivalence towards authority figures, increased need for independence but alongside it the need for social acceptance, paired with a desire for exploration and experience make adolescents vulnerable to risky behaviours and unhelpful peer relationships. However, positive communication and interaction with the young person setting boundaries and imposing consistently firm discipline are both helpful in young people bonding with group members, whilst having the psychological maturity to be able to resist maladaptive group behaviours.

- There are numerous brands of therapy that are transferred to work with young people. These include those that align themselves with purist psychological approaches such as psychodynamic, cognitive-behavioural and person-centred approaches. Furthermore, more distinct models of integrative practice have also appeared, such as Geldard and Geldard's (2010) proactive approach to working with adolescents.

Further reading

Numerous texts regarding adolescence may be useful in continuing learning within this area. One text that we recommend is John Coleman's (2010) book, *The Nature of Adolescence* (London: Routledge). Additionally, useful overviews of the theories of adolescence are given in most human development textbooks (e.g. Bee and Boyd, 2006, is a very digestible text to begin further reading in this area).

Within the therapeutic arena numerous texts may also be useful. There are texts reflecting upon the psychodynamic approach:

Lanyado, M. and Horne, A. (eds) (2009). *The Handbook of Child and Adolescent Psychotherapy. Psychoanalytic approaches* (2nd edition). London: Routledge.

The person-centred approach:

Prever, M. (2010). *Counselling and Supporting Children and Young People: A person-centred approach.* London: Sage.

And numerous helpful workbooks focusing upon cognitive-behavioural techniques:

Seiler, L. (2008). *Cool Connections with Cognitive Behavioural Therapy: Encouraging self-esteem, resilience and well-being in children and young people using CBT approaches.* London: Jessica Kingsley.

Stallard, P. (2007). *Think Good – Feel Good. A cognitive behaviour therapy workbook for children and young people.* West Sussex: Wiley.

As indicated within the chapter, people may find the proactive approach of counselling adolescents advocated by Geldard and Geldard very helpful:

Geldard, K. and Geldard, D. (2010). *Counselling Adolescents: The proactive approach for young people* (3rd edition). London: Sage.

References

Albano, A.M. and Kendall, P.C. (2002). Cognitive behavioural therapy for children and adolescents with anxiety disorders: clinical research advances. *International Review of Psychiatry*, 14, 128–33.

Bandura, A. and Walters, R. H. (1959). *Adolescent Aggression*. New York: Ronald Press.

Baumrind, D. (1991). Parenting styles and adolescent development. In R.Lerner, A. C. Peterson and J. Brooks-Gunn (eds) *The Encyclopaedia of Adolescence*. New York: Garland.

Bee, H. and Boyd, D. (2006). *The Developing Child* (11th edition). Boston: Pearson Education (US).

Cain, D. (2002). *Classics in the Person-centred Approach*. Ross-on-Wye, UK: PCCS Books.

Calabrese, R. L. and Noboa, J. (1995). The choice for gang membership by Mexican American adolescents. *High School Journal, 78*, 226–35.

Coleman, J. C. (1995). Adolescence. In P. E. Bryant and A. M. Coleman (eds) *Developmental Psychology*. London: Longman.

Coleman, J. (2010). *The Nature of Adolescence* (4th edition). London: Routledge.

Delgado, S.V. (2008). Psychodynamic therapy for children and adolescents: an old friend revisited. *Psychiatry (Edgmont)* 5 (5), 67–72.

Demos, J. and Demos, V. (1969). Adolescence in a historical perspective. *Journal of Marriage and Family, 31* (4), 632–8.

Downey, J. (2003). Psychological counselling of children and young people. In R. Woolfe, S. Strawbridge, B. Douglas and W. Dryden (eds) *Handbook of Counselling Psychology* (3rd edition) (pp.322–42). London: Sage.

Erikson, E. (1963). *Childhood and Society* (2nd edition). New York: Norton.

Ford, T., Goodman, R. and Meltzer, H. (2003). The British Child and Adolescent Mental Health Survey 1999: the prevalence of DSM-IV disorders. *Journal of the American Academy of Child and Adolescent Psychiatry, 42* (10), 1203–11.

Furstenberg, F. (2000). The sociology of adolescence and youth in the 1990s: a critical commentary. *Journal of Marriage and the Family, 62*, 896–910.

Gaoni, B., Kronenberg, J. and Kaysar, N. (1994). Boundaries during adolescence. *Israeli Journal of Psychiatry and Related Sciences, 31*, 19–27.

Geldard, K. and Geldard, D. (2010). *Counselling Adolescents: The proactive approach for young people* (3rd edition). London: Sage.

Gilligan, C. (1982). *In a Different Voice: Psychological theory and women's development*. Cambridge, MA: Harvard University Press.

Hollanders, H. (2003). The eclectic and integrative approach. In R. Woolfe, W. Dryden and S. Strawbridge (eds) *Handbook of Counselling Psychology*. London: Sage.

Kazdin, A. E. (2000). Psychotherapy for children and adolescents. In A. E. Bergin and S. L. Garfield (eds) *Handbook of Play Therapy and Behaviour Change* (4th edition). New York: Wiley.

Kroger, J. (1996). *Identity in Adolescence: The balance between self and other* (2nd edition). London: Routledge.

Lanyado, M. and Horne, A. (eds) (2009). *The Handbook of Child and Adolescent Psychotherapy. Psychoanalytic approaches* (2nd edition). London: Routledge.

Marcia, J. E. (1980). Identity in adolescence. In J. Andelson (ed.) *Handbook of Adolescent Psychology*. New York: Wiley.

Michell. L. and West, P. (1996). Peer pressure to smoke: the means depends on the method. *Health Education and Research, 11*, 39–49.

Ollendick, T. and King, N. (1998). Empirically supported treatments for children with phobic and anxiety disorders. *Journal of Clinical and Child Psychology, 61* (2), 235–47.

Oxford Centre for Suicide Research. (1998). *Annual Report on Suicide Statistics*. Oxford: University of Oxford.

Rutter M., Graham, P., Chadwick, D. F. D. and Yule, W. (1976). Adolescent turmoil: fact or fiction? *Journal of Child Psychology and Psychiatry, 17*, 35–56.

Shulman, S., Seiffge-Krenke, I., Levy-Shiff, R. and Fabian, B. (1995). Peer group and family relationships in early adolescence. *International Journal of Psychology, 30*, 573–90.

Sigler, R.T. (1995). Gang violence. *Journal of Health Care for the Poor and Undeserved* 6, 198–203.

Silverman, W. K., Kurtines, W. M., Ginsburg, G. S., Weems, C. F., Lumpkin, P. W. and Carmichael, D. H. (1999). Treating anxiety disorders in children with group cognitive behaviour therapy: a randomised clinical trial. *Journal of Consulting and Clinical Psychology,* 67, 995–1003.

Spence, S., Donovan, C. and Brechman-Toussaint, M. (2000). The treatment of childhood social phobia: the effectiveness of a social skills training-based cognitive behavioural intervention with and without parental involvement. *Journal of Child Psychology and Psychiatry,* 41, 713–26.

Stallard, P. (2007). *Think Good – Feel Good. A cognitive behaviour therapy workbook for children and young people.* West Sussex: Wiley.

Steinberg, L. (1996). *Beyond the Classroom: Why school reform has failed and what parents need to do.* New York: Simon Schuster.

Swahn, M. H., Bossarte, R. M. and West B. (2010). Alcohol and drug use among gang members: experiences of adolescents who attend school. *Journal of School Health,* 80 (7), 353–60.

Wampold, B. E. (2001). *The Great Psychotherapy Debate: Models, methods and findings.* Mahwah, NJ: Erlbaum.

Chapter 6

Research into youth counselling

A rationale for research-informed pluralistic practice

Terry Hanley, Aaron Sefi, Laura Cutts and Sue Pattison

Overview

Within this chapter we begin to reflect upon the research related to therapeutic practice with young people. We start by introducing the literature regarding therapeutic outcomes with this client group before moving on to consider the therapeutic alliance within the relationship between counsellor and young person. This initial section culminates in a discussion about what young people themselves want from therapy. In the second section of this chapter we then consider how research findings can be harnessed into research-informed practice. Specifically we reflect upon the way in which research may be used by practitioners, before moving on to consider a pluralistic framework, emphasising the collaborative nature of therapy and the use of practice-based evidence.

Evaluating youth counselling

In the following sections we summarise key literature related to how individuals conceptualise the success of youth counselling. This begins by briefly discussing the empirical evidence reflecting the effectiveness of youth counselling before focusing in on the issue of the therapeutic alliance with young people. To end this section we reflect upon the literature examining what young people actually want when approaching therapeutic services.

The effectiveness of youth counselling

In the past there has been a tradition of applying the findings of studies conducted with adults to work with adolescents. This view is now commonly challenged and individuals have become more sensitive to the specific nature of the adolescent–therapist relationship (Shirk and Saiz, 1992; DiGiuseppe *et al.*, 1996; Weisz and Kazdin, 2010). This appears to be a particularly appropriate shift given earlier discussions in this text which reflect some of the developmental challenges that adolescents face and the alternative methods and theoretical conceptualisations that therapists make when working with this client group (see Chapter 5).

There have now been at least 1,500 clinical trials examining whether therapeutic interventions work with young people (Durlak *et al.*, 1995; Kazdin, 2000) and a majority of this work focuses on the more technical therapies such as cognitive-behavioural therapy. These studies have led to four important meta-analyses, all of which suggest clinical parity to adult counterparts (see Weisz *et al.*, 2005, for a brief summary of these studies). From this work it can be concluded that those individuals within therapy were more likely to be functioning better after treatment than 75% of those in control groups (Weisz *et al.*, 2005). Such a finding acts as a useful indicator of the general helpfulness of therapy with this client group.

Just as adult psychotherapy research has evolved through a variety of generations (Barkham, 2003), research into child and adolescent services has begun to change focus. It has started to move away from the general question of whether therapy works with young people, to beginning to consider which treatment types work with which clients. A number of empirically supported treatments have been identified by undertaking this process and clinical problems, including anxiety, depression, oppositional and conduct disorders, and attention deficit-hyperactivity disorders have been attributed best-practice responses (Lonigan *et al.*, 1998; Carr, 2000; Christophersen and Mortweet, 2001; Fonagy *et al.*, 2002; Weisz and Kazdin, 2010; see www.effectivechildtherapy.com). Conclusions from such work highlight the lack of a clear empirical basis for many treatments and thus note that the efficacy of such work is inconclusive. This is compounded by the complexities of the research methods that such trials utilise. For instance, the work of Spielmans *et al.* (2010) highlights that where usual care is appropriately defined and implemented within trials there is often similar effectiveness as empirically supported treatments.

A systematic review conducted for the British Association for Counselling and Psychotherapy also examined whether counselling proves to be effective with children and young people (Harris and Pattison, 2004; also see Pattison and Harris, 2006, for an overview of the review). The review specifically aimed to examine the impact that a variety of therapeutic approaches (cognitive-behavioural, psycho-analytic, humanistic and creative therapies) had upon young people in relation to a broad range of issues. As with the findings of other studies the review concluded that the four therapeutic approaches appear to be effective in providing appropriate support for some of the difficulties investigated. They also note that, unfortunately, the evidence base still proves to be extremely limited and the absence of studies therefore made it difficult to specify what approaches work with what problems:

Although the findings show that there is little or no evidence for the effectiveness of some therapies for particular issues, this may not reflect the lived experience of children and young people engaged in counselling in a range of community or institutional settings (Pattison and Harris, 2006, p.233).

This summary echoes the conclusions of the earlier reviews presented above. However, it should be noted that it does so in a way which proves much more cautious, and reflects a stance that proves more accepting of a broad range of therapeutic approaches. Notably, it appears to advocate the sentiments of many practitioners who feel that the absence of evidence does not necessarily reflect ineffective or inferior treatment.

There has been a surge of interest in school-based therapeutic interventions in recent years. For instance, a meta-analysis of a range of therapeutic interventions delivered in the USA (predominantly cognitive-behavioural therapies) showed a moderate positive effect (Baskin *et al.*, 2010: a mean weighted effect size = 0.45). Additionally, within the UK, a comprehensive review of 30 evaluation studies in youth provision carried out by Cooper (2009) identified that 'counselling was associated with large improvements in mental health (mean weighted effect size = 0.81)' (p.137). Such an effect size can be interpreted as 'large'. Nevertheless, there are perhaps more unanswered questions resulting from limitations in the data collection of the studies utilised in the work, for instance, a lack of comparison groups to limit external factors as a confounding variable, many incomplete questionnaires and a lack of follow-up scores to determine that change was maintained. Following on from this review paper, work has been undertaken to examine therapy in more controlled settings (Cooper *et al.*, 2010) or to collect data more systematically within naturalistic settings (Hanley *et al.*, 2011). These have provided mixed results and highlighted the complicated nature of evaluating youth counselling services. Most specifically, the limitations identified within the Cooper paper were behind the motivation for a recent feasibility study for a randomised control trial (RCT) in school-based counselling (Cooper *et al.*, 2010). Utilising a range of outcome measures, and randomising young people to a waitlist or humanistic counselling, the results were mixed and inconclusive and indicated little difference between these two phases. Therefore, the research was unable to recommend counselling as an alternative to cognitive-behavioural therapy for treatment of depression in young people, as laid out in the National Institute for Health and Clinical Excellence (NICE) guidelines (NICE, 2005). However, a more recent RCT performed under similar conditions, but with slight variations in its methodology, has shown counselling to have a significant effect size after three months (McArthur *et al.*, 2011). At this point, it is fair to say that trials have been inconclusive about the efficacy of school counselling, though it is showing promising signs that this might be established at some point.

In bringing together views about the outcomes of therapy with children and young people there are more unanswered questions than answered ones. It is a field that is in major development and this is displayed by the disparate nature of the existing research. Numerous studies have been conducted which suggest that therapy is a useful activity for adolescents experiencing difficulties; however, our understanding of the active ingredients of therapy within such settings is still incredibly limited (Kazdin and Nock, 2003). This leads individuals from both quantitative and qualitative research camps to conclude that more attention needs to be focused upon understanding the therapeutic process itself (see for example, Kazdin and Nock, 2003, and Paulson *et al.*, 2001, respectively).

The therapeutic alliance in youth counselling

The therapeutic alliance is a concept that has received a great deal of attention within the world of counselling and psychotherapy. However, when considering its importance when working with young people, it is an area that has received little attention despite the omission from the literature being noted at regular intervals over recent decades (Kazdin *et al.*, 1990; Shirk and Saiz, 1992; Bickman *et al.*, 2004; Green, 2006). In a meta-analysis examining the importance of relational factors in determining the outcome of therapy with young people, only 23 studies (18 published and five unpublished) were found of an appropriate quality between the years 1973 and 2000 (Shirk and Karver, 2003); this contrasts with approximately 2,000 studies that have been examined within adult therapy (Horvath and Bedi, 2002). Such a sparseness of the literature even leads some to conclude that the therapeutic alliance has been a 'neglected' variable within adolescent mental health (Green, 2006). Hence the contents of this section discuss the implications of the work conducted by a limited few and reflect upon the gaps that presently exist when compared to the adult literature on the subject matter.

Theoretically it has been suggested that the therapeutic alliance between young clients and their therapists is more important than within adult therapy (DiGuiseppe *et al.*, 1996; Green, 2006). Such thoughts also appear to be deeply entrenched within the minds of practitioners working with young people. This is evident in a survey of child and adolescent therapists in which 90% of respondents reported the quality of the therapeutic relationship to be one of the most important variables to influence change (Kazdin *et al.*, 1990). With such consensus on the importance of the relationship being reported such a long time ago, it is therefore surprising that it has still received so little attention.

In considering the therapeutic alliance with young people, individuals working in this area have to be mindful of outside influences or developmentally different perceptions of therapy:

> The facts that (a) children are most often not self-referred and (b) frequently come to therapy in a resistant, precontemplative stage of change are presented as the major obstacles to forming effective alliances with children and adolescents (DiGiuseppe *et al.*, 1996, p.85).

In particular young people are often guided or even forced into therapy, a factor that can prove to be a detrimental starting position for developing an alliance (French *et al.*, 2003). Such conflicts of power may even lead to young people questioning the motivations behind adult referrals (DiGiuseppe *et al.*, 1996) or highlight that some adolescent clients may not have a sufficient understanding behind the purposes of therapy to make use of the space provided (Shirk and Saiz, 1992). With such challenges being immediately faced by individuals working in this area, the issue of developing youth-friendly services which utilise appropriate therapeutic approaches becomes increasingly important.

As mentioned above, relatively few studies have been conducted examining the therapeutic alliance in youth counselling. The work of Shirk and Karver (2003) provided the first comprehensive review of quantitative studies conducted within this area. The review examined 23 studies and compared alliance scores with outcome reports. In doing so a modest effect size (0.24) was reported, a mean correlation which proves almost identical to those reported within adult samples. In contrast to the findings of adult studies it was noted that therapist and parent ratings of the alliance were more accurately associated with successful outcome. It is suggested that this may be partially due to the high alliance scores reported by adolescents. Such scores may produce a ceiling effect and consequently lead to a decrease in the predictive value of the self-report questionnaire (Kendall *et al.*, 1997). Another factor of interest, which again contrasts with studies with adult clients, is that alliance measures collected later in therapy proved more accurate predictors than those reported during the early stages of therapy. Such findings alongside the limited data available therefore led Shirk and Karver (2003) to draw the appropriately cautious conclusion from their findings:

> On the basis of current findings, there is very little support for a *predictive* association between relationship variables and outcomes (p.461).

One of the major limitations to the meta-analysis conducted by Shirk and Karver (2003) is that the studies involved are very disparate in nature. For instance, the papers collated utilised a multitude of measures and alliance scores came from numerous different perspectives. Such inconsistencies prove problematic when drawing conclusions about the predicative nature of the alliance with young people. In more recent studies this confusion has been compounded with alliance scores continually varying significantly between respondents (Bickman *et al.*, 2004; Green, 2006; Hogue *et al.*, 2006; Kazdin *et al.*, 2006). In particular Kazdin *et al.* (2006) found that both positive child–therapist and parent–therapist alliance scores were related to positive therapeutic change. However, the findings also indicated that the parent–therapist rating was a more accurate predictor, a finding which contradicts studies with adult clients. Anomalies identified by studies such as this highlight the limited understanding of the phenomenon in question.

Two more recent meta-analyses add a little clarity to this developing field of research, but not much. The first examined the effect of alliance on the outcome of therapy (McLeod, 2011). In this review of 38 suitable studies, the findings indicated that the alliance has a variable effect on outcome, a factor which appeared dependent upon substantial theoretical (i.e. child age, problem type, referral source and mode of treatment) and methodological factors (i.e. source and timing of alliance assessment; domain, technology and source of outcome assessment; single versus multiple informants). Overall, the link between outcome and alliance proved small; however it is suggested that the varied nature of the data may be partly responsible for these results. The second meta-analysis to mention here is that of Shirk *et al.* (2011 – a follow-up to the Shirk and Karver, 2003, paper introduced above). This study contradicts McLeod's findings to some degree and indicates a moderate relationship between the alliance and outcome. This study identified 16 studies which met rigorous criteria akin to work used to examine adult therapy, and found a moderate relationship between the alliance and outcome. In contrast to their earlier conclusion noted above, the authors now conclude more positively, noting that the '[a]lliance is an important predictor of youth therapy outcomes and may very well be an essential ingredient that makes diverse child and adolescent therapies work' (Shirk *et al.*, 2011, p.22). Both studies, once again, highlight the need for continued examination of this area.

As with the literature specifically examining the adult therapeutic alliance, there is also limited qualitative research that has been conducted with young people. Work in this area tends to focus upon more specific elements of the encounter such as the qualities of the counselling agency or those of counsellors themselves and they do not generally explicitly link findings to the concept of the alliance. Two studies that do make useful references to the alliance are those conducted by French *et al.* (2003) and Everall and Paulson (2002). These are briefly outlined below.

French *et al.* (2003) examined what aspects of service delivery influenced young people's engagement with counselling services. From interviewing 16 clients they found that 'the accessibility of the service', 'the attractiveness of what the service can offer', and 'an assertive personal follow-up from the point of referral' were important factors in getting young people into counselling and developing an alliance with a therapist. This work identifies that there are numerous factors that can impact upon young clients' decisions to access therapeutic services and challenges any notion that adolescents are passive consumers. In placing young people at the hub of the alliance, they consider problem awareness, and their motivations for, and perceptions of, counselling as critical when considering what they may ultimately bring to therapy. These perceptions then meet with the reality of the service during the initial engagement with the service. In relation accessibility, it is argued that services for the client group in question need to be free at the point of delivery, have extended opening hours, be based in the community and offer some outreach. In relation to why young people find services attractive, the respondents appreciated the confidential aspect, the space for one-on-one interaction and the information and understanding that derive from their contact with the service. Finally, the key factors in assertive follow-up were identified as maintaining personal contact and ensuring there is a minimal waitlist, if any. These were all seen as important to the young person's initial experience of a service. Thus, without adequate attention to the engagement phase of therapy, the development of an alliance may not be possible. Interestingly, such an emphasis upon initial engagement has also been outlined within studies exploring the development of the alliance in online youth therapeutic services (Hanley, 2012).

Everall and Paulson (2002) pay particular attention to the way in which young people perceive the therapeutic alliance. Their qualitative study examines the views of 18 young people and outlines three major themes that this client group reports to be important when developing a therapeutic alliance. These were the therapeutic

Table 1. Key themes identified when consulting young people about their experiences of the therapeutic alliance

Theme	Description
Therapeutic environment	'the climate or "ambience" within which the therapist and client functioned' (p.81). This was influenced by preconceived ideas and stereotypes derived from television programmes
The uniqueness of the therapeutic relationship	'it provided a level of understanding and freedom that they had not experienced through other support systems' (p.82). This contrasts with negative therapeutic relationships in which the counsellor was viewed as a powerful authoritative figure who took on the role of 'expert'
Therapist characteristics	'A positive relationship was associated with a sense that the therapist was authentic, open, and sincerely cared' (p.83). These traits helped to facilitate trust and eventual indepth disclosure. They also highlighted the preference for counsellors 'who are flexible and open minded, adjusting therapeutic interventions to address developmental variability' (p.84)

Themes derived from Everall and Paulson (2002).

environment, the uniqueness of the therapeutic relationship and therapist charac-teristics. Table 1 briefly outlines what is meant by each of these themes.

These themes prove relatively intuitive and act as a useful reminder of the youth perspective of the alliance. They also resonate with studies reflecting upon what young people want from therapy (see below). Importantly, this study reports the importance of being aware of the power imbalance between adults and young people as central to each theme. Additionally, it provides a sobering reminder that, as with qualitative work examining adult clients' perceptions of the alliance (Bachelor, 1995), it should be noted that the findings of this study do not fit neatly into theoretical formulations of the alliance.

What do young people want from therapy?

In Cooper's (2009) review of evaluation data from school-based counselling, several key factors that young people identified as being most helpful in therapy were identified. Using seven studies with sufficient qualitative data, Cooper was able to quantify which factors the respondents considered most important. By far the most frequently cited factor (over three times more frequent than any other) was 'talking to someone and being listened to'. Other factors included: an opportunity to get feelings out; talking as practice for 'real-life' situations; and the friendliness of the counsellor. Such sentiments reflect the need for therapists to pay careful attention to relational factors within the therapeutic alliance, with young people reporting the need for trusted counsellors who they felt confident enough to talk to.

The quality of the relationship was not the only component reported by young people to be helpful within the Cooper study noted above (Cooper, 2009). Young people also discussed the need for counsellors to utilise therapeutic techniques. Key cited factors which could be considered as involving active therapist interventions included: problem-solving activities; guidance – the advice and suggestions of the counsellor; insight – developing more awareness and understanding of self and others; asking questions; advice and strategies for dealing with problems; teaching the clients particular techniques, such as relaxation exercises; and finally, feeling understood, empathised with and accepted by the counsellor.

A final area to consider is the environment in which young people attend therapy. Cited factors which relate to practical or environmental conditions included: confidentiality – the privacy of the counselling work; and, independence – the counsellor was not a family member or teacher (Cooper, 2009). Another recommendation for the environment to be conducive to young people is that it is embedded within the school context, to avoid stigmatising the part it plays in the daily routine of school life (Pattison *et al.*, 2009). In accounting for the relational, technical and environmental components of therapeutic relationships with young people it would appear that the most important part of the process for young people is the fundamental act of talking and being listened to in a space where they feel safe. With all the potential for different interventions based on theoretical supposition, perhaps it is telling that the most crucial cited factor relates to the most simple act of being present and available (although it is worth remembering that a majority of the studies which reflect the voices of young clients have recruited individuals who have attended humanistic counselling services). The subsequent factors relate to the inner workings of therapy, the active interventions of the therapist and how the client experiences contact with the therapist. Some relate to the environmental and practical conditions that can be helpful when present and consequently unhelpful when they are not.

The information collated from studies that actively consult with young people about the positives and negatives that youth therapeutic services have to offer is an incredibly important part of the therapeutic picture. Qualitative studies examining youth counselling services have acknowledged the importance of listening to young service users for ways to develop (Everall and Paulson, 2002; Hanley, 2012). Such a recommendation is often counter to the norm, with services being regularly examined from a top-down perspective and research being conducted 'on' young people. Although we recognise that this model proves inevitable within the current political climate, which focuses upon therapeutic outcomes which are linked to models of psychopathology, where possible studies that work 'with' young people should complement such findings and potentially provide a steer to future research. Considerations regarding how people go about researching youth therapy are continued in Chapter 9. In the following section we move to considering how the research findings may be harnessed within practice.

Developing a research-informed approach

Within this section, we first hope to outline the need for counselling practice to be research-informed. Following this, we aim to set out the way in which pluralistic models of therapy such as the recent framework by Cooper and McLeod (2007, 2011) can be useful in harnessing research-informed counselling psychology practice.

The notion that therapeutic approaches are related to research findings and 'evidence' is not a concept that proves ground-breaking. Indeed, the counselling psychology profession adopts a 'scientist-practitioner model' whereby research and practice should interact and inform each other (Lane and Corrie, 2006; Jones and Mehr, 2007; Blair, 2010). Indeed, '[s]cientist-practitioner psychologists embody a research orientation in their practice and a practice relevance in their research' (Belar and Perry, 1992, p.72). Based on this, it could be argued that looking to the research literature to inform our practice proves part and parcel of the work of counselling psychology professionals. Nevertheless there is discussion within the field around to what extent we should really direct our practice based on research findings.

For many therapists, the research literature is not something that impacts their day-to-day working practice. In fact, many practitioners have acknowledged that research does not play a major part in their practice (Morrow-Bradley and Elliott, 1986). (An aside to this is that one may then ask: if nobody is reading the research or learning from it, why conduct research in the first place (West and Byrne, 2009)?). Hage (2003) suggests that in adopting an 'evidence-based model' where practice is wholly directed by research findings, counselling psychology would be moving away from its roots as a profession. Indeed, one could argue that the scientific notions of research and evidence are at odds with the ideas and philosophies contained within counselling psychology. Additional to these issues, some practitioners may be so dominated by the literature that was presented to them within their core therapeutic training that they dogmatically adhere to it as if it were doctrine throughout their career, despite the potential for new and more informed ways of working coming to the fore. In this case, practitioners would not be using the research literature effectively to inform their practice. Here it is noteworthy that we do not mean to undermine core therapeutic approaches with this statement (theoretical consistency is an important harnessing component for therapy), but we would challenge those who ignore discussion about contemporary debates and discussion.

At the other extreme of the spectrum to those who do not see the value of using research to inform practice are those who believe that all therapeutic practice should be wholly directed by research. Such models of health care are well evidenced within institutions such as the UK NHS. Hierarchies of evidence are produced upon research findings (often prioritising RCTs) which lead to the commissioning of specific services. Some proponents of this position would argue that to ignore or dismiss research findings in any case would be irresponsible at best and unethical at worst. Such an approach on face value makes a lot of common sense; however this end of the spectrum is also not without challenge. In particular, many dispute, or at least question, the philosophical stance of the hierarchies of evidence that have been created (McLeod, 2000) while others use empirical methods to challenge the basis of many of the claims (Westen *et al.*, 2004).

Within the realms of youth counselling, one meta-analysis goes as far as to challenge the very notion of evidence-based treatments (EBTs), concluding that the 'superior efficacy of EBTs for youths may be an artefact of confounded research designs' (Spielmans *et al.*, 2010, p.234). This comprehensive study demands at least a certain level of caution, when attempting to draw conclusions about what constitutes an evidence-based practice (EBP). However, in the interest of not being drawn into conflict between EBP on the one hand, and 'practice wisdom' on the other, it is arguably in everyone's interest to find common ground between the opposing arguments and employing research methods that integrate the need for evidence with this wisdom of experience (Mitchell, 2011).

In terms of finding an appropriate balance on the issue of integrating research and practice, we advocate here the notion of 'research-informed practice' as opposed to 'research-directed practice' (Bohart, 2005). Such an approach acknowledges the importance of research as just one factor in the decision-making process of therapists. In addition, numerous other factors such as personal experience, supervisory influence and psychological theory are important considerations. As noted within Mick Cooper's *Essential Research Findings in Counselling and Psychotherapy*:

Such a position may seem wishy-washy when compared to harder nosed, scientifically orientated approach, but it is worth noting that it is entirely consistent with the American Psychological Association's latest definition of 'evidence-based psychological practice': 'the integration of best available research *with clinical expertise in the context of patient characteristics, culture, and preferences*' (APA, 2006: 273, italics added) (Cooper, 2008, p.5).

Thus, from our perspective, although being research-informed may seem relatively logical, it is not always the case that therapeutic practice evolves with research findings in mind.

Here, we have attempted to set out briefly the important distinction between being 'research-informed' and 'research-directed' in order to shed light on the question of to what extent research should influence our practice. Moving on from this, a second important question to address is: how can research inform practice? How do we helpfully harness and make use of such a vast body of research literature, alongside our clinical judgement and personal experience?

A pluralistic framework

As set out above, being research-informed involves practitioners drawing on the research literature alongside clinical judgement amongst other things. Mick Cooper and John McLeod (2007, 2011) have suggested that an appropriate response to the problem of how to integrate such factors when deciding what interventions to use in therapy is to look toward a pluralistic framework for counselling. Indeed, individuals of all ages may require different approaches at different times in therapy, and the pluralistic framework gives practitioners this flexibility, whilst harnessing all of the above influences on decisions in counselling.

In the rest of this chapter, we look at the pluralistic framework in greater detail, in order to harness a research-informed approach. First, we discuss the influences and background to the framework, then we go on to consider the collaborative nature of the relationship, followed by discussing the idea of negotiated goals, tasks and methods in therapeutic work. Finally we look at the potential for outcome-informed therapy. As we outline these ideas, we make reference to literature related to work with young people. This section can be contrasted more explicitly with the content of Chapter 8, which will reflect upon each of the sections in a more applied fashion, notably providing composite case examples from the authors' therapeutic work with young people to bring the concepts to life.

Background and key influences

At its core, the framework holds the philosophical and ethical position of pluralism. That is, in contrast to the research-driven approaches discussed above, it acknowledges that a multiplicity of models of therapy and approaches to working with clients may be helpful.

Different explanations will be true for different people at different points in time and therefore different therapeutic methods will be most helpful for different clients at different moments (Cooper and McLeod, 2007, p.137).

At the core of Cooper and McLeod's work is the notion that the relationship needs to consist of fundamental values not unlike the necessary and sufficient conditions for therapeutic change originally conceived by Carl Rogers and outlined in his seminal 1957 paper. Cooper and McLeod (2007) note, however, that to be truly client-centred in practice, models of therapy potentially need to be driven by the clients' goals rather than the therapists' theoretical orientation. Within this point of view, it could be argued that Rogers' core conditions cannot be both necessary and sufficient for all clients.

The framework also builds upon Edward Bordin's original conception of the therapeutic alliance, which outlined that a strong alliance in therapeutic work consists of three important things: goals, tasks and a bond (Bordin, 1979, 1994). Within this conceptualisation of therapy, in the instance that there is agreement between therapist and client on the goals and tasks of therapeutic work, and there is a strong sense of bond between the two individuals, then successful therapy is likely to occur.

This concept of the therapeutic alliance has been subject to a great deal of scrutiny within adult literature. Within the seminal text, *Psychotherapy Relationships that Work* (Norcross, 2002, 2011), in which an American Psychological Association Task Force looked at the vast body of literature with a view to gaining a greater sense of what it suggested was helpful within therapy, the therapeutic alliance was hailed as one of the four demonstrably effective factors in therapy, along with empathy, goal consensus, and collaboration and cohesion in group therapy.

In addition, further conditions were suggested as promising and probably effective. These were:

- positive regard
- congruence/genuineness
- repair of alliance ruptures
- self-disclosure
- management of countertransference
- quality of relational interpretations.

Such sentiments therefore provide a useful starting point for considering what the active ingredients of successful therapy may be, and potentially prove useful when considering how to integrate research and practice. Unfortunately, such a selection of findings has been based upon the abundance of literature regarding therapy with adult clients, and many of these areas have yet to receive a great deal of attention when considering work with younger clients. For instance, as noted earlier in this chapter, exploration of the therapeutic alliance in work with young people has been a relatively 'neglected' territory (Green, 2006), and yet there are suggestions that the relationship may in actual fact be more complex in adolescent therapeutic work due to the power differentials within adult–adolescent relationships (DiGiuseppe *et al.*, 1996). Recent years have seen an increase in research in this area, with a chapter summarising much of the high-quality work in this area being published in the new edition of *Psychotherapy Relationships that Work* (Shirk and Karver, 2011; Shirk *et al.*, 2011) being a major landmark. Nevertheless, research on the therapeutic alliance in work with young people remains relatively newly charted waters.

As with adult therapy, we do however see a groundswell of literature focusing upon psychopathology models of support for young people. Once again, as noted in the earlier sections of this chapter, edited texts such as Weisz and Kazdin's *Evidence Based Psychotherapies for Children and Adolescents* (2010) and Fonagy *et al.*'s *What Works for Whom: A critical review of treatments for children and adolescents* (2003) provide comprehensive summaries of therapeutic interventions that have displayed themselves to be effective with specific difficulties. Although such content can be incredibly useful when considering therapeutic interventions, it is not felt that this is the only decision-making pathway within adolescent mental health care. As discussed above, we would suggest counselling psychologists should look to become research-informed rather than research-driven.

Collaboration and the relationship

Within the literature surrounding the therapeutic relationship, the notion of collaboration is extremely important, and is something that is emphasised within this pluralistic way of working. The pluralistic framework acknowledges that the client's view of what is helpful in therapy is just as valid an opinion as that of the therapist. Cooper and McLeod note that: 'at the heart of the present pluralistic framework is a collaborative relationship between therapist and client' (Cooper and McLeod, 2007, p.139).

The process of therapy is conceptualised as co-constructed, as opposed to prescribed by the therapist for the client.

Such a collaborative approach views clients as active self-healing agents, who do not have something done to them in therapy, but rather do something themselves. Bohart (2000) has suggested that the client is the common factor in therapy: the therapist supplies the chair, whilst the client takes the therapist input and uses it to achieve his or her own ends. Contrary to approaches which view the client as passive, whilst the heroic counsellor 'fixes' the client, this places the client wholly back in the fore of therapy and suggests that collaboration is of utmost importance for successful outcome. Along a similar vein, David Rennie (2001) has used the method of interpersonal process recall, where clients listen to or watch a tape of the counselling session to stimulate their recollection of the process, to demonstrate clients' self-awareness during therapeutic work. Clients responded to what a therapist had said based on what they desired and what they felt safe to say: they were not passive receivers of therapist input and responded with a level of control and agency. Consistent with the literature on collaboration, in a recent meta-analysis of research published between 2000 and 2009, Tyron and Winograd (2011) found a medium effect size between collaboration and therapeutic outcome.

In order to foster a collaborative and understanding relationship, it has been suggested that therapists may look to 'metacommunication' as a tool for being transparent and open about processes in therapy. Metacommunication can at base level be described as communicating about communicating. In therapy, Rennie (2007) describes four types of metacommunication which can be used by counsellor and client: (1) disclosing the intention behind what they are saying/have said; (2) disclosing the reaction to what the other has said; (3) inviting the other to reveal their intentions behind what was said; and (4) inviting the other to reveal their reactions to what was said. Such metacommunication on the part of both the therapist and the client has been suggested to be consistent with an enhanced therapeutic relationship (Hill and Knox, 2009). Indeed, resolving ruptures in the relationship involves a process of metacommunication (Safran and Muran, 2000).

Goals, tasks and methods

Similar to Bordin's goals, tasks and bonds, Cooper and McLeod (2007, p.137) suggest that therapeutic work can be divided into three overlapping 'domains', in this case being conceptualised as goals, tasks and methods. As mentioned above, the 'bond' in this case is seen as the underlying concept, at the heart of the framework. As a way of conceptualising this framework, it is maybe helpful to perceive it in terms of a journey – the goals being the destination, the tasks being the routes or roads you want to take and the methods being the vehicles you choose for this journey (a metaphor attributed to the qualitative research of Nicky Forsythe in Cooper and McLeod, 2011).

Goals of counselling are individual to clients and are looked at as what a client wants, not what a client needs, as judged by an independent professional. For example, within the pluralistic framework, it isn't possible to say that two people experiencing 'depression' should both follow the same therapeutic path as their 'goal' is the same. Instead, their goals may be conflicting, they may be multiple and they are likely to change the course of therapy. Each client is likely to have many goals: both low-level, specific goals which may involve the negation of a problem, as well as higher-level, broader goals in relation to their life and their person as a whole (Cooper and McLeod, 2007). As mentioned above, research shows that goal consensus is demonstrably effective in therapy. In brief, goal consensus means that both client and counsellor agree on the goals of the therapeutic work. Tryon and Winograd (2002) suggest that goal consensus at intake may mean that clients are more likely to be engaged in the process of therapy.

Tasks can be seen as more concrete than the higher-order goals: a task relates to the 'doing' of therapeutic work. For each goal there may be numerous tasks, and these are once again transtheoretical. Tasks arise at different points of the therapeutic process: an initial goal of 'to come to terms with things' may be explored by the client and therapist and discrete tasks may emerge which can structure the therapeutic work. Cooper and McLeod (2007, p.138) give examples of 'talking openly and meaningfully about current problems in living', 'changing behaviour' and 'problem-solving, planning and decision making'. They note that tasks are 'central to the aim of demystifying therapy' (p. 138).

Each task may be achieved using a variety of methods. Methods of counselling can be viewed as the specific activities undertaken in therapy, either carried out by the therapist or the client. These activities can be attributed to specific theoretical models: a method used in cognitive-behavioural therapy might be to keep a log of negative automatic thoughts, in psychodynamic therapy it may be exploring early childhood experience and in gestalt therapy two-chair work might be used as a possible method.

Within the pluralistic framework, Cooper and McLeod (2011, p.93) encourage therapists to disregard the 'brand names' of cognitive-behavioural therapy, gestalt therapy and psychodynamic therapy for example, and instead consider the 'multiplicity of methods' provided by the wealth of counselling and psychotherapy literature. Furthermore, not only can methods come from traditional therapeutic models such as the ones mentioned above; a pluralistic framework encourages counsellors and clients to draw from cultural and societal resources such as playing music, art, walking, reading and sport, amongst others, as well as idiosyncratic practices and personal resources ('existential touchstones'). When viewed in this way, the methods making up the practice of therapy are vast and can be tailored to the individual client in a multitude of ways.

Of great importance to working with goals, tasks and methods is the need for collaboration, as detailed above. Goals, tasks and methods are not ascribed to the client by the therapist; instead the process is co-created and responsive. Indeed, similar to the discussion above around metacommunication, Cooper and McLeod (2011) encourage a dialogue around therapeutic work.

Outcome-informed therapy and practice-based evidence

A final piece of the jigsaw is the notion that therapy can be informed by the ongoing evaluation of the work. As opposed to providing a client with an evidence-based approach and in this way being research-directed, as discussed above, this approach suggests that counsellors instead use practice-based evidence to tailor therapy to the individual client. Such an idea has been convincingly put forward to the therapeutic community by the likes of Miller *et al.* (2005), who advocate that the therapist routinely monitors the progress of therapy with clients using techniques that are easily implemented within everyday practice. The outcome-informed approach detailed by these authors suggests that, rather than needing to know what particular therapeutic approach or technique to use, therapists need to know whether the relationship is working with a particular client. Referring to the work on the therapeutic alliance and collaboration discussed above, Miller *et al.* (2005) point out that the client should be put back in the driver's seat in therapy. For them, the shared goals, consensus on methods or tasks and the therapeutic bond or alliance are all held together by the client's theory of change.

In relation to the above approach advocated by Miller *et al.* (2005), the authors recommend incorporating a number of short rating scales into clinical practice in order to collect ongoing information from the client, such as the Session Rating Scale (SRS: Johnson *et al.*, 2000). This short form can be filled in by the client at the end of each session to monitor the client's views of how the work is progressing. It is a very brief four-item measure and takes less than a minute to complete, therefore not taking up too much of the therapeutic time. Examples of questions include rating the following statements: 'We worked on my goals during the session' and 'My therapist understood me and my feelings'. The idea behind this scale is that it encourages a dialogue about the work between the therapist and client at each session. The authors also suggest using the Outcome Rating Scale (ORS: Miller and Duncan, 2000), which is again a short four-item measure, which can be used at the beginning of each session with the client. This looks at gathering data on the client's experience of change in four areas: individually, interpersonally, socially and overall.

In the UK, psychometric questionnaires, such the use of a Young Person's Clinical Outcome Measures in Routine Evaluation (YP-CORE), which emerged out of an adult version of the psychometric measure (Twigg *et al.*, 2009), or specifically modified versions of the ORS and SRS are being increasingly adopted by services as an easy-to-use self-report questionnaire distinguishing levels of distress (see Chapter 9 for more discussion on such tools). However, used on their own they can potentially be 'blunt instruments' and should be treated with some caution. The emergence of goal-based outcome measures can arguably allow for greater collaborative practitioner–client involvement in routine evaluation, and lead to more research-informed practice. Such measures are being piloted within the Child and Adolescent Mental Health Services and could have a significant contribution to offer this level of evidence gathering (Sefi and Hanley, 2012).

As mentioned above, gathering data such as this has been classed as 'practice-based evidence', which can be seen as a response to the ideas of being research-driven and using only 'evidence-based' models of practice. Instead, practice-based evidence allows the counselling psychologist to monitor how the client sees the work is progressing and adapt future work. This links directly to the idea that the therapist should, at times, discuss explicitly with the client how therapy is progressing for the client and therefore is consistent with the pluralistic framework and the idea of metacommunication, developed above.

Conclusion

Therapy for young people is a developing area for counselling psychologists and in recent years there has been an increase of literature reflecting the potential positive effects of such provision. Alongside this, however, is also a growing body of literature reflecting the complexity of evaluating the efficacy and effectiveness of such work. Similarly, exploration of the therapeutic alliance has raised plenty of interesting questions, but few answers. In contrast, qualitative exploration of young people's view of such provision has provided a rich insight into what this group wants from therapy and should ultimately help steer the development of such service delivery.

Alongside personal experience, supervisory influence and psychological theory, research findings are an important consideration with regard to therapeutic work. Research-informed practice with young people can be harnessed around a pluralistic framework which emphasises the importance of a strong therapeutic relationship and advocates collaboration between therapist and client on the goals, tasks and methods of therapy. Such an approach may look to utilise practice-based research and goal-based outcome measures to inform therapeutic work.

Summary

- In relation to the outcome of therapeutic work with young people, research indicates that a majority of those young people who access therapy services improve in some way. Research agendas are now progressing to look at what treatments work for whom, with a view to developing empirically supported treatments. To date, results in this area primarily reflect cognitive-behavioural therapies; however more relational approaches are also being examined.

Continued exploration in this area displays the complexity and challenge of undertaking evaluative work in this field.

- The therapeutic alliance between counsellor and client has received a limited amount of attention within the field of youth counselling. Although there are suggestions that the links between alliance and successful therapeutic outcomes are equivalent to those within adult therapy, individuals are presently cautious to draw conclusions to this effect. As is evident within the adult literature on the therapeutic alliance, it is important to acknowledge that conceptualisations of the alliance can vary. This is evidenced in how young people themselves report the nature of the alliance.

- Research exploring what young people actually want from their therapeutic services has confirmed the importance of relational aspects of the work. In addition, therapeutic techniques used by the practitioner and the therapeutic environment in which counselling takes place are incredibly important. Such research can be used to inform the way in which services are run, thereby giving young people a greater role in directing the services they receive.

- As opposed to an inflexible research-based approach to therapeutic work, this text encourages a research-informed approach to therapy. Practitioners are encouraged to engage actively with the research literature; however, it is also acknowledged that other factors are likely to provide important indicators as to the direction of therapy (e.g. psychological theory, therapist skills).

- Frameworks of pluralistic counselling psychology can provide a useful metatheory for holding theoretical tensions that exist between psychological models of therapy. The framework proposed by Cooper and McLeod (2007; 2011) is utilised in this text. This emphasises the collaborative nature of the relationship and focuses the reader upon the consensus between client and therapist about the goals of therapy, and the tasks and methods undertaken within therapy.

- Outcome-informed therapy utilises practice-based evidence to communicate with clients about how therapeutic work is progressing, and can inform future work. Goal-based outcome measures specifically to be used with young people are currently being piloted and may contribute to this outcome-informed, collaborative way of working.

Further reading

In keeping with the research-informed nature of the approach described in this chapter, we recommend readers to follow up their reading by going to the original sources noted in the text (and listed below). In particular we recommend reading the meta-analyses and summaries of literature in the first instance.

In relation to research-informed practice we recommend reading Mick Cooper and John McLeod's (2011; London: Sage) text *Pluralistic Counselling and Psychotherapy* as a starting point. Texts such as *The Heroic Client* (Duncan, B., Miller, S. and Sparks, J. 2004; San Francisco: Jossey Bass) and *Developing and*

Delivering Practice-Based Evidence (Barkham, M., Hardy, G. and Mellor-Clark, J. 2010; Chichester: Wiley-Blackwell) also add to this area of interest. Finally, introductory research texts such as Mick Cooper's (2008) *Essential Research Findings in Counselling and Psychotherapy* (London: Sage) and Terry Hanley, Clare Lennie and William West's (2012) *Introducing Counselling and Psychotherapy Research* (London: Sage) will also prove useful.

References

Bachelor, A. (1995). Clients' perception of the therapeutic alliance: a qualitative analysis. *Journal of Counseling Psychology*, 42 (3), 323–37.

Barkham, M. (2003). Quantitative research on psychotherapeutic interventions: methods and findings across four research generations. In R. Woolfe, W. Dryden and S. Strawbridge (eds) *Handbook of Counselling Psychology* (2nd edition). London: Sage.

Baskin, T. W., Slaten, C. D., Crosby, N. R., Pufahl, T., Schneller, C. L. and Ladell, M. (2010). Efficacy of counseling and psychotherapy in schools: a meta-analytic review of treatment outcome studies. *The Counseling Psychologist, 38* (7), 878–90.

Belar, C. D. and Perry, N. W. (1992). National conference on scientist-practitioner education and training for the professional practice of psychology. *American Scientist,* 47 (1), 71–5.

Bickman, L., Vidas de Andrade, A., Lambert, E., Doucette, A., Sapyta, J., Boyd, A., Rumberger, D., Moore-Kurnot, J., McDonough, L. and Rauktis, M. (2004). Youth therapeutic alliance in intensive treatment settings. *Journal of Behavioral Health Services and Research*, 31 (2), 134–48.

Blair, L. (2010). A critical review of the scientist-practitioner model for counselling psychology. *Counselling Psychology Review, 25* (4), 19–30.

Bohart, A. C. (2000). The client is the most important common factor: clients' self-healing capacities and psychotherapy. *Journal of Psychotherapy Integration, 10* (2), 127–49.

Bohart, A. C. (2005). Evidence-based psychotherapy means evidence-informed, not evidence-driven. *Journal of Contemporary Psychotherapy, 35* (1), 39–53.

Bordin, E. (1979). The generalizability of the psychoanalytic concept of the working alliance. *Psychotherapy: Theory, Research and Practice*, 16, 252–60.

Bordin, E. (1994). Theory and research on the therapeutic working alliance: new directions. In A. Horvath and L. Greenberg (eds) *The Working Alliance: Theory, research, and practice* (pp.13–37). New York: Wiley.

Carr, A. (2000). *What Works with Children and Adolescents? A critical review of psychological interventions with children, adolescents and their families.* London: Routledge.

Christophersen, E. and Mortweet, S. (2001). *Treatments That Work with Children: Empirically supported strategies for managing childhood problems.* New York: American Psychological Association.

Cooper, M. (2008). *Essential Research Findings in Counselling and Psychotherapy: The facts are friendly.* London: Sage.

Cooper, M. (2009). Counselling in UK secondary schools: a comprehensive review of audit and evaluation data. *Counselling and Psychotherapy Research*, 9 (3), 137–50.

Cooper, M. and McLeod, J. (2007). A pluralistic framework for counselling and psychotherapy: implications for research. *Counselling and Psychotherapy Research, 7* (3), 135–43.

Cooper, M. and McLeod, J. (2011). *Pluralistic Counselling and Psychotherapy.* Sage: London.

Cooper, M., Rowland, N., McArthur, K., Pattison, S., Cromarty, K., Richards, K. (2010). Randomised controlled trial of school-based humanistic counselling for emotional distress in young people: feasibility study and preliminary indications of efficacy. *Child and Adolescent Psychiatry and Mental Health,* 4, 12.

DiGiuseppe, R., Linscott, J. and Jilton, R. (1996). Developing the therapeutic alliance in child-adolescent psychotherapy. *Applied and Preventive Psychology*, 5, 85–100.

Durlak, J. A., Wells, A. M., Cotton, J. K. and Johnson, S. (1995). Analysis of selected methodological issues in child psychotherapy research. Unpublished thesis, Loyola University Chicago. Cited in Weisz, J., Sandler, I., Durlak J. and Anton, B. Promoting and protecting youth mental health through evidence-based prevention and treatment. *American Psychologist,* 60 (6), 628–48.

Everall, R. and Paulson, B. (2002). The therapeutic alliance: adolescent perspectives. *Counselling and Psychotherapy Research,* 2 (2), 78–87.

Fonagy, P., Target, M., Cottrell, D., Philips, J. and Kurtz, Z. (2003). *What Works for Whom? A critical review of treatments for children and adolescents.* New York: Guilford Press.

French, R., Reardon, M. and Smith, P. (2003). Engaging with a mental health service: perspectives of at-risk youth. *Child and Adolescent Social Work Journal*, 20 (6), 529–48.

Green, J. (2006). Annotation: The therapeutic alliance – a significant but neglected variable in child mental health treatment studies. *Journal of Child Psychology and Psychiatry*, 47 (5), 425–35.

Hage, S. M. (2003). Reaffirming the unique identity of counseling psychology: opting for 'the road less traveled by'. *Counseling Psychologist,* 31 (5), 555–63.

Hanley, T. (2012) Understanding the online therapeutic alliance through the eyes of adolescent service users. *Counselling and Psychotherapy Research*, 12 (1), 35–43.

Hanley, T., Sefi, A., and Lennie, C. (2011) Practice-based evidence in school-based counselling. *Counselling and Psychotherapy Research*, 11 (3), 300–9.

Harris, B. and Pattison, S. (2004). *Research on Counselling Children and Young People: A systematic scoping review.* Rugby: BACP.

Hill, C. E. and Knox, S. (2009). Processing the therapeutic relationship. *Psychotherapy Research,* 19 (1), 13–29.

Hogue, A., Dauber, S., Stambaugh, L., Cecero, J. and Liddle, H. (2006). Early therapeutic alliance and treatment outcome in individual and family therapy for adolescent behavior problems. *Journal of Consulting and Clinical Psychology*, 74 (1), 121–9.

Horvath, A. and Bedi, R. (2002). The alliance. In J. Norcross (ed.) *Psychotherapy Relationships that Work: Therapist contributions responsiveness to patients.* New York: Oxford University Press.

Johnson, L. D., Miler, S.D. and Duncan, B. L. (2000). *The Session Rating Scale* 3.0. Chicago: Authors.

Jones, J. L. and Mehr, S. L. (2007). Foundations and assumptions of the scientist-practitioner model. *American Behavioural Scientist,* 50 (6), 766–71.

Kazdin, A. (2000). *Psychotherapy for Children and Adolescents: Directions for research and practice.* Oxford: Oxford University Press.

Kazdin, A. and Nock, M. (2003). Delineating mechanisms of change in child and adolescent therapy: methodological issues. *Journal of Child Psychology and Psychiatry*, 44 (8), 1116–29.

Kazdin, A., Siegel, T. and Bass, D. (1990). Drawing on clinical practice to inform research on child and adolescent psychotherapy: survey of practitioners. *Professional Psychology: Research and Practice*, 21, 189–98.

Kazdin, A., Whitley, M. and Marciano, P. (2006). Child–therapist and parent–therapist alliance and therapeutic change in the treatment of children referred for oppositional, aggressive and antisocial behavior. *Journal of Child Psychology and Psychiatry*, 47 (5), 436–45.

Kendall, P., Flannery-Schroeder, E., Panichelli-Mindell, S., Southam-Gerow, M., Henin, A. and Warman, M. (1997). Therapy for youths with anxiety disorders: a second randomized clinical trial. *Journal of Consulting and Clinical Psychology*, 65, 366–80.

Lane, D. A. and Corrie, S. (2006). *The Modern Scientist-Practitioner: A guide to practice in psychology.* London: Psychology Press.

Lonigan, C., Elbert, J. and Johnson, S. (1998). Empirically supported psychosocial interventions for children: an overview. *Journal of Clinical Child Psychology*, 27, 138–45.

McArthur, K., Cooper, M. and Berdondini, L. (2011). A pilot randomised controlled trial to assess the impact of school-based counselling on young people's wellbeing, using pastoral care referral. Paper presented at the British Association for Counselling and Psychotherapy Research Conference, Liverpool.

McLeod, J. (2000). The contribution of qualitative research to evidence based counselling and psychotherapy. In S. Goss and N. Rowland (eds) *Evidence-based Counselling and Psychological Therapies: Research and applications* (pp.11–126). London: Sage.

McLeod, B.D. (2011) Relation of the alliance with outcomes in youth psychotherapy: a meta-analysis, *Clinical Psychology Review,* 31 (4), 603–16.

Miller, S. D. and Duncan, B. L. (2000). *The Outcome Rating Scale.* Chicago: Authors.

Miller, S. D., Duncan, B. L. and Hubble, M. A. (2005) Outcome-informed clinical work. In J. C. Norcross and M. R. Goldfried (eds) *Handbook of Psychotherapy Integration* (2nd edition) (pp.84–102). Oxford: Oxford University Press.

Mitchell, P. F. (2011). Evidence-based practice in real-world services for young people with complex needs: new opportunities suggested by recent implementation science. *Children and Youth Services Review,* 33, 207–16.

Morrow-Bradley, C. and Elliott, R (1986). Utilization of psychotherapy research by practicing psychotherapists. *American Psychologist*, 41, 188–97.

National Institute for Health and Clinical Excellence (2005). *Depression in Children and Young People: Identification and management in primary, community and secondary care.* Retrieved 20/04/11 from www.nice.org.uk/nicemedia/live/10970/29859/29859 .pdf.

Norcross, J. (2002). (ed.) *Psychotherapy Relationships that Work: Therapists' contributions and responsiveness to patients.* New York: Oxford University Press.

Norcross, J. (2011). (ed.) *Psychotherapy Relationships that Work: Evidence-based responsiveness* (2nd edition). New York: Oxford University Press.

Pattison, S. and Harris, B. (2006). Counselling children and young people: a review of the evidence for its effectiveness. *Counselling and Psychotherapy Research*, 6 (4), 233–7.

Pattison, S., Rowland, N., Richards, K., Cromarty, K., Jenkins, P. and Polat, F. (2009). School counselling in Wales: recommendations for good practice. *Counselling and Psychotherapy Research*, 9 (3), 169–73.

Paulson, B., Everall, R. and Stuart, J. (2001). Client perceptions of hindering experience in counselling. *Counselling and Psychotherapy Research*, 1 (1), 53–61.

Rennie, D. L. (2001). The client as a self-aware agent in counselling and psychotherapy. *Counselling and Psychotherapy Research,* 1 (2), 82–9.

Rennie, D. L. (2007). Reflexivity and its radical form: implications for the practice of humanistic psychotherapies. *Journal of Contemporary Psychotherapy,* 37, 53–8.

Rogers, C. (1957). The necessary and sufficient conditions of therapeutic personality change. *Journal of Consulting Psychology,* 21, 9–103.

Safran, J. D. and Muran, J. C. (2000). *Negotiating the Therapeutic Alliance: A relational treatment guide.* New York: Guilford.

Sefi, A. and Hanley, T. (2012). Examining the complexities of measuring effectiveness of online counselling for young people using routine evaluation data. *Pastoral Care in Education,* 30 (1), 49–64.

Shirk, S. and Karver, M. (2003). Prediction of treatment outcome from relationship variables in child and adolescent therapy: a meta analytic review. *Journal of Consulting and Clinical Psychology,* 71 (3), 452–64.

Shirk, S.R. and Karver, M. (2011). The alliance in child and adolescent psychotherapy. In J. Norcross (ed.) *Psychotherapy Relationships that Work: Evidence-based responsiveness* (2nd edition) (pp.70–91). New York: Oxford University Press.

Shirk, S. and Saiz, C. (1992). Clinical, empirical, and developmental perspectives on the relationship in child psychotherapy. *Development and Psychopathology,* 4, 713–28.

Shirk, S.R., Karver, M. and Brown, R. (2011). The alliance in child and adolescent psychotherapy. *Psychotherapy,* 48 (1), 17–24.

Spielmans, G.I., Gatlin, E. T. and McFall, J. P. (2010). The efficacy of evidence-based psychotherapies versus usual care for youths: controlling confounds in a meta-reanalysis. *Psychotherapy Research,* 20 (2), 234–46.

Twigg, E., Barkham, M., Bewick, B., Mulhern, B., Connell, J. and Cooper, M. (2009). The young person's CORE: development of a brief outcome measure for young people. *Counselling and Psychotherapy Research,* 9 (3), 160–8.

Tyron, G. S. and Winograd, G. (2011). Goal consensus and collaboration. *Psychotherapy: Theory, Research and Practice,* 48 (1), 50–7.

Weisz, J. and Kazdin, A. (eds) (2010) *Evidence Based Psychotherapies for Children and Adolescents* (2nd edition). New York: The Guildford Press.

Weisz, J., Sandler, I., Durlak, J. and Anton, B. (2005). Promoting and protecting youth mental health through evidence-based prevention and treatment. *American Psychologist,* 60 (6), 628–48.

West, W. and Byrne, J. (2009). Some ethical concerns about counselling research. *Counselling Psychology Quarterly,* 22 (3), 309–18.

Westen, D., Novotny, C. and Thompson-Brenner, H. (2004). The empirical status of empirically supported psychotherapies: assumptions, findings, and reporting in controlled clinical trials. *Psychological Bulletin,* 130 (4), 631–63.

Part 3

Counselling young people in action

Chapter 7

The counselling infrastructure

Terry Hanley, Peter Jenkins, Sue Pattison,
Maggie Robson and Gareth Williams

Overview

This chapter provides an exploration of some of the infrastructure with which counselling psychologists engage when working with young people. It begins by introducing key issues that relate to ethics and law in this work before moving on to consider the policies and procedures which emerge out of such judgements. Following on from this, the chapter then focuses upon more specific issues that surround therapeutic contracts with this age group and the supervisory relationships that practitioners may look for. Although it is acknowledged that there are numerous other components that impact upon the counselling infrastructure, these are viewed as some of those pertinent to all settings.

Ethics and the law

This section will look at the relevance for counselling psychologists of ethics and the law. Ethics may be seen as being somewhat high-flown, abstract and philosophical, but ethical models actually relate to very concrete and specific behaviours on the part of a counselling psychologist, such as checking that a client fully understands and consents to a proposed course of action. An understanding of ethics can also be a very practical resource, in helping to identify different choices when faced with a pressing dilemma, such as whether to respect, or to breach, a young client's right to confidentiality. Similarly, the law may seem to be rather rigid, impersonal and remote from everyday professional practice. In fact, the law provides an overarching framework for professional decision making, which, in turn, is based on ethical principles and an array of fascinating cases which have been decided in court. Rather than being fixed for all time, the law is currently undergoing rapid change, with significant amendments in terms of recognising the rights of children and young people in recent years.

This section will provide a brief outline of ethical frameworks and the law in the UK, with particular reference to the key concepts of competence and confidentiality. Ethics is defined as 'a generic term for various ways of understanding and examining the moral life' (Beauchamp and Childress, 2008, p.1). It provides ways of distinguishing between what is good and bad, acceptable or unacceptable, within society. There are different frameworks for understanding ethics, particularly professional ethics, which it is useful to understand. One major approach is based on a deontological, or rule-following, approach, arguably as used by the Health Professions Council (2008). Another follows more of a teleological, or outcomes-based, approach, such as the British Psychological Society *Code of Ethics and Conduct* (2009). Other approaches emphasise the importance of acknowledging rights, such as the rights of children and young people (Jenkins, 2003).

Legal framework

The law refers to all systems of civil and criminal law, including statute (Acts of Parliament), common law and case law. There are different jurisdictions within the UK, including Scotland, Northern Ireland, Wales and England. Most of the examples given in this section will relate to the law in England and Wales. Broad legal principles will apply within the UK as a whole, but may be expressed in terms specific to that jurisdiction, for example, as in the Social Work (Scotland) Act 1995. There are key pieces of statute (i.e. Acts of Parliament) which have particular relevance for counselling psychologists working with children and young people, such as the Children Acts of 1989 and 2004, and the Mental Health Act 1983 (revised in 2007). While the Acts are important documents, easily available online (www.opsi.gov.uk), there is usually available operational guidance which will often be more immediately relevant for the practitioner. Such guidance includes, for example, the *Special Educational Needs Code of Practice*, deriving from the Education Act 1996 (Department for Education and Skills, 2001). Working with children and young people, it is also important to have a grasp of quasi-legal documents, such as the *United Nations Convention on the Rights of the Child*, ratified by the UK in 1991 (UNICEF, 1989). This sets out children's rights to provision, protection and participation, and has increasing relevance as a template for childcare legislation being considered by the Welsh Assembly. It has been influential in key decisions made by the courts in England and Wales, in cases relating to children and young people, such as the *Axon* case [2006].

Agency practice

At a practical level, much of what a counselling psychologist is required to do on a day-to-day basis may derive ultimately from the law, but is actually 'filtered' through a set of agency protocols. NHS agencies, for example, place a premium on the ethical principles of welfare and avoidance of harm, particularly in working with children and young people. Voluntary agencies, or practitioners working on a private basis, may at times prefer to place a higher value on promoting adolescent autonomy. Agency protocols are a clear reference and important point for decision making, but may be no more than an expression, or interpretation, of the law, rather than being the final word, for example, in working with young people who are judged to be at risk of self-harm.

In some cases, legal terms may be used slightly out of context, which may be somewhat confusing or misleading as a result. For example, within many voluntary agencies, schools and the NHS, counselling psychologists will often refer to the use of 'contracts' with clients. In reality, these are more likely to be a form of working agreement with clients than a legally enforceable contract as such, unless they authorise the exchange of a specified counselling service for an agreed fee (Jenkins, 2006).

Duty of care

The law does play a very necessary and valuable role in providing protection for clients, via recourse to legal action where a service has fallen below the expected standard. The term 'duty of care' may have entered the everyday language of therapy, but not always in a sense which is properly understood. A counselling psychologist owes a duty of care to each client, namely to work to accepted professional standards. Here, the employment context of practice is important, as a private practitioner will be personally liable for errors or malpractice. Alternatively, one that is employed will be protected, to some extent, by the employer holding vicarious liability for its employees. In both cases, the standard applied by the courts in a case of litigation, say for professional negligence, will be the *Bolam* test, derived from medical case law. This requires that a practitioner works within the accepted standards of a normally competent practitioner. In essence, this is a form of peer defence, largely reliant on the judgement of expert witnesses. Case law relating to therapy is rare. However, in the case of *Phelps* v *Hillingdon Borough* [1997], a local educational authority educational psychologist was found to be negligent for failing to carry out an assessment for dyslexia for a pupil experiencing severe difficulties in her schooling (Jenkins, 2007).

The term 'competence' is of key importance in working with children, young people, and, for that matter, adults. The notion of competence is, in turn, closely linked to the concept of capacity. Capacity is defined in the Mental Health Act 1983 Code of Practice as 'the ability to make a decision at the time the decision needs to be made' (Departmentof Health, 2008, p.356). Following the Family Law Reform Act 1969, it has been established that 16–17-year-olds have capacity to make their own decisions regarding confidential medical treatment. Under the *Gillick* case, it was decided by the House of Lords that young people under the age of 16 years were also entitled to confidential medical treatment, dependent upon their demonstrating 'sufficient understanding' of the alternatives to, and consequences of, their decision. Subsequent case law has restricted the rights of children and young people, however, to refuse medical treatment, particularly in the case of life-threatening conditions, such as anorexia.

Confidentiality

The *Gillick* case was directly challenged via judicial review in 2006, but was upheld, with the judge expressing the view that '*Gillick* remains good law'. The *Gillick* and *Axon* cases have major implications for the provision of confidential counselling to young people in a wide range of settings. There is a widely accepted practice of requiring evidence of parental permission before a young person can access confidential counselling. This applies, for example, in many secondary school settings (Jenkins and Polat, 2006, p.8). However, this stands in direct conflict with the young client's entitlements under established case law, such as *Gillick* in England and Wales, and statute in Scotland, under the Age of Legal Capacity Act (Scotland) Act 1991.

Children and young people have substantial rights to confidentiality under case law (*Gillick, Axon*), and under statute (Data Protection Act 1998). Article 8 of the Human Rights Act 1998 also affords all citizens, regardless of age, the right to respect for privacy and to family life. This was successfully used by the model, Naomi Campbell, to protect her right to access therapy as a privacy matter (*Campbell* v *MGN* [2004]). Arguably, the same principle could be used by children and young people in a similar manner (Daniels and Jenkins, 2010, p.162).

Information sharing and disclosure

Counselling psychologists will often be working in multidisciplinary teams, where the assumption is that key information about children and young people will be shared with other professionals, on a 'need to know' basis. This approach may be underpinned by established agency practice, plus an ethical perspective prioritising the child's welfare and one which is ultimately legitimated by the authority of 'implied consent'. Patient consent which has been given to one health practitioner is thus able to be extended on this basis, in order to share information with the wider team. This approach is widely practised, for example, in NHS settings, where information is shared in the patient's best interests.

However, there are limits to the appropriateness of information sharing. A young person may readily disclose information to one practitioner, which is not necessarily to be shared with others, for example, about bullying, or sexual health matters. Disclosure of sensitive personal information should be carefully negotiated and agreed with the child or young person on a step-by-step basis, rather than taken to be automatically suitable for passing on to interested others. Parents do not necessarily have a 'right to know' about the detailed content of therapeutic work, although they may be quite insistent on this point at times. However, in the case of a child or young person, it is likely that the law will support a breach of confidentiality as being 'in the public interest' in situations involving a risk of significant harm (Her Majesty's Government, 2010, pp.140–1).

Policies and procedures

As a counselling psychologist, you will be working within a wide range of settings which provide services for children and young people. As your experience broadens, you may notice that different agencies have differing policies and procedures. While there may be underlying consistencies, there may also be appreciable differences. There may well be more scope for professional discretion in terms of decision making, for example, in private practice or in the third sector, as compared with the statutory sector, such as the NHS. Policies and procedures may derive their ultimate authority from the law and from key ethical principles, but are often filtered and shaped by the specific organisational setting in which practitioners work. This section will consider some of the main organisational settings for counselling psychologists working with children and young people and some of the key policies and procedures, relating to referral systems, assessment and data protection.

Organisational contexts for practice

The agency context provides the immediate environment for counselling psychology practice with children, in terms of its aims and goals, strategies, resources and organisational culture. Your work as a counselling psychologist may be central to the remit of the agency, as in the case of therapeutic work provided within the NHS, or more ancillary, in the case of work within an educational setting, such as a local education authority. Within the statutory sector, counselling psychology provision can be found within education, children's services, criminal justice and the health service. In the education sector, counselling psychologists work in and have contact with schools, both mainstream and specialist, sixth form colleges and further education settings. Within the criminal justice system, counselling psychologists may have a role within youth offending teams and within youth custody settings. Counselling psychology services are also provided to Children's Social Care (or Children's Services in Wales), to more specialist safeguarding units, as part of local children safeguarding boards, and to court welfare services for families and children.

   Within the NHS, counselling psychology is centred within Child and Adolescent Mental Health Services (CAMHS), but also makes a contribution to primary care services, including Improving Access to Psychological Therapies programmes, and to specialist outpatient and inpatient services. Much contemporary counselling for children and young people is to be found in the voluntary or third sector (sometimes referred to as 'third-sector CAMHS'), with a wide range of agencies providing psychological support in the community. Finally, some counselling psychologists work predominantly in the private sector, providing consultancy, therapeutic services, assessments and reports under contract to other agencies and to families.

   The organisational context may have a direct influence on working practice, for example with regard to 'gatekeeping', or how children and young people can access the service. For example, many schools require evidence of parental permission before offering children under 16 access to confidential counselling (Jenkins and Polat, 2006, p.8). Within CAMHS, children under 16 may not be able to access therapeutic services independently, whereas the principle of independent access by adolescents may be a well-established norm for many voluntary agencies.

Referral systems

Counselling psychology operates within a matrix of systems for access and onward referral for more specialist services. Within education, primary care and CAMHS, there is a hierarchy of services, dependent on onward referral for access to more specialist and resource-intensive services, such as psychiatric care, or inpatient provision for young people with eating disorders. Services are organised in terms of steps, or, more commonly, 'tiers', whereby generic or self-help services are provided at initial levels, and individuals needing more complex services, provided by a team of professionals, are referred on via an assessment and selection process (Box 1).

Box 1. Tiered provision of counselling psychology services for children and young people

Tier 1

Primary level of service, including interventions by general practitioners, health visitors, school nurses, social services, voluntary agencies and teachers. These are usually non-specialists in mental health, who are able to identify mental health issues at an early stage and offer advice and treatment at an initial level.

Tier 2

This level of service is provided by specific professional workers, operating on the basis of liaison, via referral networks, rather than as members of a multidisciplinary team. They could include clinical child psychologists, community paediatricians, educational psychologists, child psychiatrists, community psychiatric nurses and counsellors in school settings.

Tier 3

This provides a specialist service for working with more complex, severe and persistent mental health problems, via multiprofessional teams, often based in a community or outpatient setting. The team can include child and

---

adolescent psychiatrists, social workers, clinical psychologists, community psychiatric nurses, child psychotherapists, occupational therapists, art, music and drama therapists.

Tier 4

These are tertiary-level services of a highly specialised nature, working via outpatient teams and inpatient units, with children and young people who are severely mentally ill or at risk of suicide. These teams or units often serve a district or region or take referrals from other parts of the country. Examples would include adolescent inpatient units, secure adolescent forensic units, eating disorder units and specialist teams for sexual abuse or for neuro-psychiatric problems.

(Modified from Jenkins & Polat, 2006, p.13.)

Assessment

Clearly, counselling psychologists are involved in a wide range of assessment processes relating to children and young people. These can include assessment of a child's level of competence or capacity to consent to an intervention. It may include a contribution towards a formal assessment of a child's special educational needs, under statutory procedures. It may also involve an assessment of the degree of risk posed by a child towards self, in the form of self-harm or risk of suicide, or to others, via aggression, bullying or arson. Assessment of a child's needs may also entail consideration of the extent to which he or she is exposed to a risk of significant harm, whether physical or psychological in nature, and therefore require referral to Children's Social Care (Daniels and Jenkins, 2010).

As outlined above, access to specialised mental health services, such as CAMHS, is made via a complex process of assessment and onward referral. Under the parallel, but largely separate, systems provided with Children's Social Care, children and young people seen to be 'in need' or at risk of 'significant harm' can gain access to specialist services provided by the local authority. This is also based on a hierarchy, ranging from levels 1 to 4, following the principle of holistic assessment of the child's needs, initially via the Common Assessment Framework (Department of Health/Department for Education and Employment/Home Office, 2000, p.89 – see Table 2 for a summary of these levels).

In practice, the levels of intervention for accessing services under Children's Social Care and the tiers of provision for accessing CAMHS support may overlap. However, practitioners need to have a good working grasp of the principles of referral operating for whatever system they are working within, in order to understand the specific language, criteria and priorities which drive that particular system. Often, the operation of Children's Social Care will have significant local

Table 2. Levels of intervention for children assessed as being 'in need' or 'at risk'.

Assessment of child's needs	Relevant criteria	Outcome of assessment and action required
Level 1 Universal needs	Child in need of mainstream resources only	Single-agency assessment, e.g. via school, through completion of Common Assessment Framework (CAF)
Level 2 Need for support	Child living with parents or carers, subject to stress or adverse circumstances, e.g. severe disability	Additional services to be provided via relevant agency, as determined by CAF
Level 3 Need for prevention	Child's health and development adversely affected by family circumstances, e.g. domestic violence, mental health problems	Multiagency assessment, chaired by Children's Social Care
Level 4 Need for protection	Child experiencing, or likely to experience, significant harm (e.g. physical or sexual abuse) unless circumstances change	Referral to Children's Social Care for Core Assessment, under s.47, Children Act 1989

policy influences or emphases, despite originating from a broadly based model. Again, a successful assessment and referral of a child or young person as meeting 'level 4' criteria will then need, in turn, to follow a separate set of timescales and priorities for completion of a Core Assessment and any ensuing legal intervention via the courts (Her Majesty's Government, 2010, pp.173–8).

Data protection and recording

While different agencies may have distinct policies and procedures, all will require strict compliance with their own model of data protection, recording and confidentiality. Data protection includes any form of capture and processing of personal data relating to living individuals, whether in handwritten or electronic format. This can include, for example, DVD, video and audio recordings of sessions, where the recording is deemed to constitute part of a child's (or adult's) file. There are key data protection principles, set out in the Data Protection Act 1998, requiring that data processing be carried out fairly, accurately and with the consent of the individual concerned (Jenkins, 2007; Bond and Mitchels, 2008). The Act also provides for rights of access to records by 'data subjects', in accordance with the principles of transparent and accountable recording, which are also required by the British Psychological Society as a professional association and by the Health Professions Council, as the statutory regulating body (British Psychological Society/Professional Practice Board, 2008, pp.12–15; Health Professions Council, 2008). Detailed guidance is provided by the Information

Commissioner in published form (Information Commissioner's Office, 2001, 2009) and is also available via the internet (www.ico.gov.uk).

The contract

This section will focus on the need for the counselling psychologist to create an appropriate working contract with adolescent clients. Links will be made with other sections in this chapter, including ethics and the law, and policies and procedures. This section will examine the nature of contracts in counselling psychology, reasons for contracting with adolescent clients, the types of contracts, how contracts are negotiated and agreed and the contextual nature of contracts. The type of contracts that may be agreed will be looked at in relation to ethics, legislation, policy, research and good practice.

What are counselling psychology contracts?

As suggested earlier in this chapter, the term 'contract' in counselling psychology normally refers to a working agreement rather than a legally enforceable contract. The nature of contracts and agreements varies between professions and organisations. For example, in the business and other contexts, contracts are often drawn up to be legally binding. In the counselling profession, the types of contracts most widely used are not always intended to have legal powers; they are an agreement between the counselling psychologists, their client and the service provider. Voluntary agencies, schools and the NHS are most likely to refer to these working agreements as contracts (Jenkins, 2006). In the context of counselling psychology, Sills (2006) states that: 'A contract is an agreement made between two or more people concerning the type of activity or relationship they will have with each other' (p.3).

Contracts and agreements have their roots in ethics, the law, policies and procedures, as outlined in previous sections of this chapter. The British Association for Counselling and Psychotherapy (2010) suggests that therapists should: 'engage in explicit contracting in advance of any commitment by the client' (p.3).

The major reason for contracting is to make sure that each party to the agreement (the psychologist and the client and, in certain cases, the agency) is clear about what is being offered. For example, a voluntary counselling agency providing services to adolescents may discuss the limits of confidentiality at the beginning of counselling in order to give choice regarding disclosure. This allows each the opportunity to give informed consent and also makes apparent, as far as is possible, the limits to the relationship and the responsibilities each party is expected to hold.

In order to explore this further, it may be useful to look at the major concepts that are likely to be included in contracts, particularly around the type of activity or relationship to be agreed. There is wide diversity in terms of the exact nature of counselling psychology contracts in relation to adolescents in terms of organisational context and service provider. This can lead to confusion over what constitutes a contract, whether the contract should be verbal or written, and arrangements regarding recontracting. Horton (2000) suggests that: 'Therapists approach contracting with clients with varying degrees of formality, clarity and explicitness ... The nature of the therapeutic contract and whether it is stated explicitly and even written down will depend very much on the therapist's theoretical orientation' (p.117).

However, the major issues commonly addressed in counselling contracts are confidentiality, time, place, goals, contact and boundaries and fees, if applicable (Sills, 2006). These can be categorised into 'administrative details' and 'therapist and process relationship issues'.

Administrative details include time, place, fees (if applicable) and duration of the sessions and series of sessions. These are included so that both the psychologist and the client can predict what is planned to happen and also to allow boundaries to be set. Boundaries are important because, as Bayne *et al.* (1994) argue: 'Boundaries are a part of being clear with yourself and with clients, and being trustworthy. They offer stability, and apply the idea (and existential fact) that there are limits to relationships, including counselling relationships' (p.15).

Boundaries around sessions also mean that the concept of 'justice' can be addressed in terms of fairness of service provision. For example, if a client does not attend for a session on several occasions without prior notice or agreement, this is a resource that is being denied to other adolescents. There may be many reasons for non-attendance, but this can be addressed in an overt, upfront manner when the contract or agreement is negotiated at the beginning of therapy.

The therapist and process relationship issues refer to the structure of sessions, negotiation of goals, contact and boundaries, nature of relationship, review and recontracting, risk and safety, confidentiality and endings.

The therapeutic environment, relationship and therapist characteristics are found to be key to the process of therapy with adolescents (Everall and Paulson, 2002). In terms of the uniqueness of the therapeutic relationship, this can be contrasted with other support relationships where the helper is a more powerful authoritative figure, in the role of 'expert'. This is significant when considering the nature of a counselling contract. Worrall (2006) argues that:

> The contracts we make, and the way we make them, arise out of and make manifest our views of human nature. Once manifest, they define the relationship within which we work, and limit or enhance the nature and quality of our work
>
> (p.52)

Negotiation and a joint contracting process seem most appropriate especially as adolescents' rights to participation are made explicit in the *United Nations Convention on the Rights of the Child* (UNICEF, 1989). The nature of the contract can be informed by research such as the Welsh Assembly Government's evaluation of counselling in schools (Pattison *et al.*, 2009) and information from the Children's Legal Centre (2006; www.childrenslegalcentre.com).

Why do we have contracts?

It is useful to have an idea of what we value as 'healthy' and so an idea of what may be worked towards in our work with clients (Wibberley, 1988). Depending on the agency context, different ethical values may be prioritised. For example, if you are working for the NHS, you are more likely to prioritise welfare and risk, but if you work in the voluntary sector, you are likely to put a higher value on adolescent autonomy. Several factors are generally regarded as healthy in relation to ethics, one of which is having a sense of our own personal rights and boundaries:

> We should be assertive enough to claim and protect our own rights, whilst respecting the rights of others. We need to be able to distinguish between self and others in thought, feelings, behaviour and responsibility . . . In making our own life choices, or asserting our sense of boundaries, an ability to say 'Yes' and 'No' is extremely useful
>
> (Wibberley, 1988, p.66)

Having a clear contract allows us to do this. Moreover, as discussed earlier in this chapter, the counselling contract can operationalise ethical models, for example, by checking that a client fully understands and consents to the proposed course of action. Boundaries can be made explicit in terms of the counselling relationship by making it evident that the counselling psychologist is providing a specialist service as a professional and this is not to be confused with friendship. You may also want to make the nature and boundaries of confidentiality clear. Some organisations assume the nature of confidentiality, as mentioned earlier in this chapter. For example, if you work as a counselling psychologist in the NHS, information is likely to be shared within teams of professionals on a 'need to know' basis in the perceived best interest of the client. This institutional interpretation of 'confidential' may not be made explicit to the client, and sharing of a client's information in this way may be assumed when the nature of confidentiality is discussed as part of the contract.

One of the motivations for counselling psychologists to have a contract with a client is to try to prepare for 'when things get difficult'. The main concern of counselling psychologists, as has been discussed previously in this chapter, is to try and ensure they practise ethically and lawfully. Ethical principles may conflict when clients suggest that they may harm themselves or others or disclose sexual abuse of themselves or of other young people. Sometimes the law or the agency policy is clear and leaves the psychologist with a clear choice, for example, if the client intends to break the law. However, other situations may be more ambiguous. Thus, contracts need to address these issues and usually do by outlining the limits to confidentiality. These normally include an agreement to break confidentiality if there is a perceived risk to 'self or others'. Through this, clients are then put in a position where they can choose what to disclose and are aware of potential courses of action that you might take as counselling psychologist if they do disclose. However, when a situation occurs where the counselling psychologist perceives a risk, it may not always be clear to the psychologist as to the appropriate action to be taken. The competing demands of the ethical principles of autonomy, beneficence and non-maleficence may suggest different and contradictory actions. It is imperative that counselling psychologists think about and plan for these situations before they occur and make sure they can discuss these issues with a supervisor.

Some counselling psychologists, in an attempt to guarantee that clients will not harm themselves, have 'no self-injury contracts'. However, the evidence suggests these rarely work and Sutton (2005) claims they may lead to shame and dishonesty. There is a sense in which it can be argued that these kinds of contract are generally made to meet the needs or fears of the therapist (Alderman, 1997). Yet, in practice, as evidenced through the authors' supervision work, particularly in the voluntary sector, this type of agreement is frequently made with the best interests of the client in mind and to help avoid escalating the client's care to other, often statutory or medical agencies for crisis care when this may be unnecessary and/or harmful to the client.

While counselling psychologists are naturally concerned about such issues as clients committing suicide, harming themselves or disclosing abuse, it is not illegal in Britain to keep confidentiality and not disclose to outside agencies or other professionals (Bond, 2000). Mitchels and Bond (2010) go on to say:

With the exception of a situation where the law requires disclosure, e.g. terrorism, therapists may use their discretion in making decisions about breaching confidentiality, for example in situations of child protection, self harm or certain suspected less serious criminal activity (pp.12–13).

However, they go on to caution that such decisions may be open to questioning and may have to be justified if there is a legal challenge.

Counselling psychology: contracts in practice

As a counselling psychologist or psychological therapist working with adolescents you may be guided through the contracting process as an employee or volunteer of an agency or organisation with strong, clear policies and guidance on this matter. Alternatively, you may have to work more autonomously and proactively to ensure that that you and your young client have negotiated a workable and ethically sound contract or agreement to support the counselling process. The information contained in this section can help to inform your thinking and practice, and in turn stimulate further reading and exploration of issues around contracting for counselling work with adolescents. Practice is never perfect, in spite of the traditional saying, and different types of counselling work, diverse contexts and organisational issues can all impact on your work with adolescents. By continuing your professional development postqualification, familiarising yourself with the relevant legislation, Code of Ethics, professional guidance, organisational policies and registering or accrediting with a professional body, you are more likely to negotiate intelligent, well-thought-out contracts that are operational in practice and provide a high degree of safety for client and counsellor.

Supervision of youth-friendly counselling

For a practitioner providing therapeutic support to young people, not having a supervisor with a shared understanding of the particular complexities and challenges of working with this age group is likely to slow things down. It is taken as a given that practitioners will recognise the importance of supervision; here we explore some of the benefits of working with a supervisor who has experience and awareness of the field of adolescent counselling psychology. Before moving on, for those who are unfamiliar with the literature around supervision, it is noteworthy that there are several models of supervision (Carroll, 1996; Tudor and Worrall, 2004; Hawkins and Shohet, 2007). There are also several formats for supervision, including groups and with peers. This section focuses on individual supervision between therapist/supervisee and supervisor. In doing so it outlines some key issues that individuals might wish to consider when choosing to work with this client group.

Common features of therapy with young people

At this point it seems appropriate to present a brief summary of some common features that set therapeutic work with youth apart from generic adult counselling.

- Young people are often 'sent' to therapy by teachers, parents, social workers or other adults. Thus, a significant proportion of young clients tend to have an ambivalent, 'precontemplative' (Prochaska *et al.*, 1994) attitude to therapy.
- The traditional 'two chairs and a box of tissues in a room' approach found in adult counselling is often incompatible with the style and needs of young people (Miller *et al.*, 2007). Uncomfortable silences can be detrimental to the forming of a therapeutic alliance and youth-friendly facilitators usually need to take a flexible 'proactive' approach (Geldard and Geldard, 2010). This calls for an accessible, down-to-earth, creative way of interacting on the part of the therapist (see Chapter 8 for more details).
- Young people tend to have less autonomy than adults and are therefore more dependent upon their families or other social systems, such as schools. In many cases, the most effective help for young people can involve family therapy, advocacy, involvement of other support agencies or to provide support directly to parents/carers (Dishion and Kavanagh, 2003; Selekman, 2005; Hughes, 2007; Sanders, 2008).
- Legally, there are extra considerations when clients are children and this has important implications for the limits of confidentiality and clients' rights to make their own decisions (Hess, 2008; see the section on ethics and the law earlier in this chapter for more information). Therapists working within organisations and/or school settings are required to observe policies and procedures regarding safeguarding the well-being of children. Many organisations require supervisors of their employees to familiarise themselves with these protocols.

Supervisors without an understanding of these characteristic features may be resistant or even antagonistic to therapists operating outside the traditional boundaries of adult therapy. For example, there is a widespread acceptance of the so-called therapeutic hour. Without a supervisor with awareness of the difficulty some young people have in being in a one-to-one meeting with an adult, a school therapist who offers clients shorter, 25–30-minute sessions might receive criticism for not following appropriate procedures. With young people engagement is key (Castro-Blanco and Karver, 2010), therefore it is vital to tailor support to the needs and style of each young person.

A space to explore dilemmas

Supervision offers space to explore dilemmas, both those found in generic counselling and those particular to work with youth. For example, how does one balance the needs of a therapeutic alliance with a young person and an alliance with the parent/carer who brings the young person to therapy (Hess, 2008; Shirk et al., 2011)? Research has shown that a positive relationship between parent/carer(s) and therapist is a predictor of attendance (Shirk et al., 2011) and of positive therapeutic outcome (Robbins et al., 2006). Some research has indicated that imbalances in alliance can predict poor outcome (Robbins et al., 2008). If parent/carer(s) want to know how therapy is proceeding, what is appropriate to disclose?

Is breaking confidentiality in the client's best interests?

Jess is a 15-year-old girl. She has been meeting with Rob, her school counsellor, once a week for four weeks. She has repeatedly mentioned her interest in taking recreational drugs and in the last session she told Rob that she and her friends were smoking high levels of cannabis every day, sometimes coming to school 'well stoned'. Rob has expressed his concern about this but Jess only laughed and said there was no need to worry. Jess has GCSE exams coming up and the school learning mentor has approached Rob to ask if he has any ideas about why Jess' grades are not as high as they were a few months ago.

Confidentiality is generally a vital ingredient of counselling. However, when working with people legally considered children, safeguarding and child protection take precedence. It is important to clarify this when establishing a contract (formally or informally) and it may be appropriate to give reminders throughout counselling. If we consider the case of Jess above, we might ask numerous questions. For instance, if we are to break confidentiality, who will we tell? Does the agency we work for have requirements or guidelines? What about the school we work in? If we breach confidentiality, will it undermine or destroy the alliance?

Will it really be of benefit to the client? Are we acting out of a wish to 'cover our back'? Can we get the client's consent and can we proceed with transparency? These are all questions we can address in supervision.

Self-disclosure

> Joe (14-year-old client): Oh man, that's gay, that is!
> Tony (school counsellor): I notice I get uncomfortable when you say that. It upsets me when people use the word 'gay' as a put-down.
> Joe: Why? Are you gay?

How is Tony to respond to this? There are, of course, a variety of possibilities. Was it appropriate for Tony to challenge the remark? Irrespective of our ethical stance, the fact is that adolescents' questions can be very direct and probing (Hess, 2008). Congruence and appropriateness, openness and discretion depend upon context and relationship. Being evasive may well impact negatively on alliance, while honest personal sharing can convey respect and value, inspire bond as well as model the way the therapeutic space can be used. The salient question is, is one's response likely to be of benefit? Supervision can give therapists a space to reflect upon complex issues such as this.

Each therapist is unique

Besides ethical and legal concerns, the uniqueness of each particular therapist and the type of supervisor she or he thinks and feels s/he needs has to be taken into account. A therapist new to working with young people, for example, may need a supervisor who is able to draw on significant experience of working with this age group. On the other hand, therapists with sufficient personal experience and understanding of the legal and practical complexities encountered in this field may not prioritise such external knowledge. Instead, he or she might place greater importance upon whether a supervisor will enable him or her to work with more fluidity, facilitate particular areas of self-awareness and help him or her develop certain psychotherapeutic interventions. So, along with issues of a supervisor's theoretical stance, underpinning philosophy, location, availability, hourly rate, as well as felt sense of connectivity, the experience of working therapeutically with young people on the part of the supervisor becomes an important consideration when choosing a supervisor. Just as we consider it vital to tailor therapy to client, likewise the most rewarding supervision fits the needs and style of supervisee.

Functions of supervision

Supervision has been described as having three broad functions: formative, normative and restorative (Inskipp and Proctor, 1993). In brief:

- Formative functions are educational. In the context of working with young people this might include developing youth-friendly techniques, or deepening one's ability to be authentically playful.
- Normative functions involve the maintenance of professional standards: safety and ethical practice, etc.
- Restorative functions include the provision of a safe empathic space in which a therapist can receive support and affirmation, and benefit from expressing his/her experiences and concerns (Pennebaker, 1990).

In many professional organisations, supervision is mandatory. This could lead to practitioners going through the motions (Carroll, 1996), ticking required legal boxes, yet failing to make the most of the creative opportunities inherent in 'good supervision' (Weaks, 2002). Therefore, in the pluralistic counselling spirit that pervades this book, I want to emphasise the collaborative supervisory alliance, at the same time honouring the need to keep well-being of clients centre stage.

The supervisory alliance

[T]here is an intimate connection between how one construes psychotherapy and how one construes supervision (Bordin, 1983, p.35).

From a pluralist point of view there is no one way to do supervision (Cooper and McLeod, 2011). Supervision is understood to be a co-constructed process, emerging from the interaction of supervisor and supervisee, focused upon the supervisee developing her skills, qualities and overall ability to be the best therapist she can be. The underlying purpose of the process is to resource, inspire and support the therapist to be of maximum benefit to the clients s/he works with.

Based upon the wealth of research that demonstrates that the working alliance is a significant indicator of positive therapeutic outcome, it seems feasible to assume alliance between supervisor and supervisee will play a similarly important role (Bordin, 1983). Research into supervision is relatively scant; however, there is evidence that the supervisory relationship is considered the most important factor by supervisees (Weaks, 2002).

Bordin (1979, 1983) proposed three components of a working alliance both in therapy and supervision: an emotional bond, consensus about goals, and agreement upon the means for achieving the goals (this topic is explored in Chapter 8). Goals and tasks of supervision can be agreed upon when forming a supervisory contract and/or evolved as the process of supervision unfolds.

A therapeutic space?

Particular moments in supervision look like and may feel like therapeutic moments; they may even have similar effects and outcomes. What defines them as different is not their nature but . . . their context (Tudor and Worrall, 2004, p.12).

Therapy has been described as the collaboration of two (or more) intelligences (Bohart and Tallman, 1999). Building on the work of Art Bohart (2000, 2006), I propose five ways in which supervisees make supervision work.

1. a safe empathic space in which to develop self-awareness, make discoveries and benefit from self-expression;
2. a meeting of minds with a fellow practitioner, sharing experiences and developing ideas;
3. an interpersonal learning environment that allows for the recognition of patterns of relating and reacting. This then allows for transformation, increased agency and/or transcendence;
4. utilise procedures such as role play, guided imagery or meditation, forms of artistic expression, facilitated by the supervisor. These allow for the discovery of insights or new ways of being that can inspire and inform the therapist's work;
5. receive, reflect upon and learn from a supervisor's more or less formal instruction about skills, metaskills (Mindell, 1995), theory, or other aspects of practice.

Feedback

An ongoing process of feedback seems to be integral to supervision. In an ideal situation, this works reciprocally. Supervisee feedback to supervisor will help shape the process and content of sessions to suit supervisee needs. Supervisor feedback to supervisee enables the latter to tap the intelligence, wisdom and empathically informed perspective of a fellow practitioner. We all have so-called blind spots where we lack awareness. In the context of a trusting, mutually respectful relationship, we can take steps towards greater therapeutic competence and 'presence' (Welwood, 2000; Geller and Greenberg, 2002). The inevitable evaluative component of supervision (Bordin, 1983) can have the tendency to mobilise a supervisee's 'inner critic' (Stone and Stone, 1993), hence the need for a strong alliance and skilfully delivered feedback.

Conclusion

As is evident within this chapter, the infrastructures that need to be in place for counselling psychology services for young people are incredibly complex. The legal issues of working with this group are multifaceted and often interpreted differently. This manifests in services operating with different policies and procedures that place emphasis upon differing priorities (e.g. safeguarding or retaining confidentiality). Within the therapy room this translates into therapeutic contracts (working agreements) that can vary depending upon the practitioner's own belief systems or organisational structures. They do however often have many common elements. For instance, a counselling psychologist is likely to outline at the outset of therapy that if a young person is putting him- or herself or someone else 'at risk' the counselling psychologist is likely to disclose this information to a relevant third party. Such complexities require psychologists to consider the need for supervision that they need, with some needing more guidance and others wanting to reflect more creatively on how to engage this client group.

Here we have just scratched the surface of this issue and the interested reader would be encouraged to look deeper into some of the recommendations of the authors of the chapter (see below).

Summary

- Ethical therapeutic practice with young people can ultimately vary depending on the views of the individual in question. Codes of practice, such as those devised by the Health Professions Council and British Psychological Society, are created to harness features of recommended good practice.
- The law regarding work with young people is constantly evolving as new cases are examined. Different agencies often interpret aspects of the law differently, with complex issues such as the 'competence' of the young client, the confidentiality offered by a service and the amount of information shared with others proving points of contention at times.
- The policies and procedures that services operate often differ depending on the organisational setting. It is notable that services might take differing types of referral and assess individuals differently before offering support. Furthermore, each setting will address the issue of data protection and record keeping in a way that is compliant with national standards and professional bodies.
- The contract that individuals devise when working with this group might vary greatly dependent upon the therapist in question. Common elements to contracts are likely to be administrative content (e.g. the time and place of therapy) and issues to do with the process of therapy itself (e.g. negotiating which goals might be worked upon).
- Fruitful supervision needs to account for both the needs of the therapist and the client group with which that therapist is working. Readers are encouraged to consider what it is that they need when working with young people with a view to creating a successful supervisory alliance.

Further reading

This chapter outlines numerous follow-on texts within the content of the chapter. It is however noteworthy to outline a few pertinent sources that will provide important additions to the youth counsellor's resources. As a resource to extend discussions on the legal and policy aspects of working with children and young people we therefore recommend:

Daniels, D. and Jenkins, P. (2010). *Therapy with Children: Children's rights, confidentiality and the law (2nd edition)*. London: Sage

In relation to the infrastructure more generally, the Welsh Assembly Government has been instrumental in pulling together a freely available resource pack for those working within schools, although much of the documentation is transferable. This provides a great deal of useful information, including recommendations about record keeping and policies regarding sharing information.

Welsh Assembly Government. (2009). *School Based Counselling Operating Kit*. Cardiff: WAG.

References

Alderman, T. (1997). *The Scared Soul: Understanding and ending self inflicted violence*. Oakland, CA: New Harbinger.

Bayne, R., Horton, I., Merry, T. and Noyes, E. (1994). *The Counsellor's Handbook*. London: Chapman and Hall.

Beauchamp, T. and Childress, J. (2008). *Principles of Biomedical Ethics (6th edition)*. Oxford: Oxford University Press.

Bohart, A. C. (2000). The client is the most important common factor: client's self-healing capacities and psychotherapies. *Journal of Psychotherapy Integration*, 2, 17–33.

Bohart, A. (2006). The client as active self-healer. In J. C. Norcross, L. E. Beutler and R. F. Levant (eds) *Evidence-based Practices in Mental Health: Debate and dialogue on the fundamental questions* (pp.218–26). Washington, DC: American Psychological Association.

Bohart, A. C. and Tallman, K. (1999). *How Clients Make Therapy Work: The process of active self-healing*. Washington, DC: American Psychological Association.

Bond, T. (2000). *Standards and Ethics for Counselling in Action* (2nd edition). London: Sage.

Bond, T. and Mitchels, B. (2008). *Confidentiality and Record Keeping In Counselling and Psychotherapy*. London: Sage/BACP.

Bordin, E. S. (1979). The generalizability of the psychoanalytic concept of the working alliance. *Psychotherapy: Theory, Research and Practice*, 16 (3), 252–60.

Bordin, E. S. (1983). A working alliance based model of supervision. *Counseling Psychologist*, 11 (1), 35–42.

British Association for Counselling and Psychotherapy (2010). *Ethical Framework for Good Practice in Counselling and Psychotherapy*. Lutterworth: BACP.

British Psychological Society (2009). *Code of Ethics and Conduct: Guidance published by the Ethics Committee of the British Psychological Society*. Leicester: BPS.

British Psychological Society/Professional Practice Board (BPS/PPC) (2008). *Generic Professional Practice Guidelines*. Leicester: BPS.

Carroll, M. (1996). *Counselling Supervision: Theory, skills and practice*. London: Sage.

Castro-Blanco, D. and Karver, M. S. (2010). *Elusive Alliance: Treatment engagement strategies with high-risk adolescents*. Washington, DC: American Psychological Association.

Children's Legal Centre (2006). *Working With Young People: Legal responsibility and liability*. London: Children's Legal Centre.

Cooper, M. and McLeod, J. (2011). *Pluralistic Counselling and Psychotherapy*. London: Sage.

Daniels, D. and Jenkins, P. (2010). *Therapy with Children: Children's rights, confidentiality and the law* (2nd edition). London: Sage.

Department for Education and Skills (DfES) (2001). *Special Educational Needs Code of Practice*. London: DfES.

Department of Health (DoH) (2008). *Mental Health Act 1983: Code of practice*. London: Stationery Office.

Department of Health/Department for Education and Employment/Home Office DoH/DEE/HO (2000). *Framework for the Assessment of Children in Need and their Families*. London: Stationery Office.

Dishion, T. and Kavanagh, K. (2003). *Intervening in Adolescent Problem Behavior: A family-centered approach*. New York: Guilford Press.

Everall, R. and Paulson, B. (2002). The therapeutic alliance: adolescent perspectives. *Counselling and Psychotherapy Research*, 2 (2), 78–87.

Geldard, K. and Geldard, D. (2010). *Counselling Adolescents: The proactive approach for young people* (3rd edition). London: Sage.

Geller, S. and Greenberg, L. (2002). Therapeutic presence: therapists' experience of presence in the psychotherapy encounter in psychotherapy. *Person Centered and Experiential Psychotherapies*, 1, 71–86.

Hawkins, P. and Shohet, R. (2007). *Supervision in the Helping Professions*. Maidenhead: Open University Press.

Health Professions Council (HPC) (2008). *Standards of Conduct, Performance and Ethics*. London: HPC.

Her Majesty's Government (HMG) (2010). *Working Together to Safeguard Children: A guide to inter-agency working to safeguard and promote the welfare of children*. London: Stationery Office.

Hess, K. D. (2008). Supervising psychotherapy with adolescents. In A. K.Hess, K. D. Hess and T. H. Hess (eds) *Psychotherapy Supervision: Theory, research, and practice*. New Jersey: Wiley.

Horton, I. (2000). Structuring. In C. Felthamand I. Horton (eds) *Handbook of Counselling and Psychotherapy*. London: Sage.

Hughes, D. (2007). *Attachment-Focused Family Therapy*. New York: Norton.

Information Commissioner's Office (2001). *The Data Protection Act 1998: Legal guidance*. ICO: Wilmslow.

Information Commissioner's Office (2009). *The Guide to Data Protection*. Wilmslow: ICO.

Inskipp, F. and Proctor, B. (1993). *The Art, Craft and Tasks of Counselling Supervision, Part 1 – Making the most of supervision*. Twickenham: Cascade Publications.

Jenkins, P. (2003). *Exploring Children's Rights: A participative exercise to introduce the issues around children's rights in England and Wales*. Pavilion: Brighton.

Jenkins, P. (2006). Contracts, ethics and the law. In C. Sills (ed.) *Contracts in Counselling and Psychotherapy* (2nd edition) (pp.109–16). London: Sage.

Jenkins, P. (2007). *Counselling, Psychotherapy and the Law* (2nd edition). London: Sage.

Jenkins, P. and Polat, F. (2006). The Children Act 2004 and implications for counselling in schools in England and Wales. *Pastoral Care in Education*, 24, 7–14.

Miller, A. L., Rathus, J. H. and Linehan, M. M. (2007). *Dialectical Behavior Therapy with Suicidal Adolescents*. New York: Guilford Press.

Mindell, A. (1995). *Sitting in the Fire: Large group transformation using conflict and diversity*. Portland, OR: Lao Tse Press.

Mitchels, B. and Bond, T. (2010). *Essential Law for Counsellors and* Psychotherapists. London: Sage.

Pattison, S., Rowland, N., Cromarty, K., Jenkins, P. and Polat, F. (2009). School counselling in Wales: recommendations for good practice. *Counselling and Psychotherapy Research*, 9 (3), 169–73.

Pennebaker, J. (1990). *Opening Up: The healing power of expressing emotions*. New York: Guilford Press.

Prochaska, J., Norcross, J., and DiClemente, C. (1994). *Changing for Good: The revolutionary program that explains the six stages of change and teaches you how to free yourself from bad habits*. New York: W. Morrow.

Robbins, M. S., Liddle, H. A., Turner, C. W., Dakof, G. A., Alexander, J. F. and Kogan, S. M. (2006). Adolescent and parent therapeutic alliances as predictors of dropout in multidimensional family therapy. *Journal of Family Psychology*, 20, 108–16.

Robbins, M. S., Mayorga, C. C., Mitrani, V. B., Szapocznik, J., Turner, C. W. and Alexander, J. F. (2008). Adolescent and parent alliances with therapists in brief strategic family therapy with drug-using hispanic adolescents. *Journal of Marital and Family Therapy*, 34 (3), 316–28.

Sanders, M.R. (2008). Triple P – positive parenting program as a public health approach to strengthening parenting. *Journal of Family Psychology*, 22 (3), 506–17.

Selekman, M. (2005). *Pathways to Change: Brief therapy with difficult adolescents*. New York: Guilford Press.

Shirk, S., Karver, M. and Brown, R. (2011). The alliance in child and adolescent psychotherapy. *Psychotherapy*, 48 (1), 17–24.

Sills, C. (2006). Introduction: the therapy contract – a mutual commitment. In C. Sills (ed.) *Contracts in Counselling and Psychotherapy* (2nd edition). London: Sage.

Stone, H. and Stone, S. (1993). *Embracing Your Inner Critic: Turning self-criticism into a creative asset*. New York: Harper.

Sutton, J. (2005). *Healing the Hurt Within: Understand self-injury and self-harm and heal the emotional wounds*. Glasgow: Bell and Bain.

Tudor, K. and Worrall, M. (2004). *Freedom to Practise: Person-centred approaches to supervision*. Ross-on-Wye: PCCS Books.

UNICEF. (1989). *The United Nations Convention on the Rights of the Child*. London: Children's Rights Development Unit.

Weaks, D. (2002). Unlocking the secrets of 'good supervision': a phenomenological exploration of experienced counsellors' perceptions of good supervision. *Counselling and Psychotherapy Research*, 2 (1) 33–9.

Welwood, J. (2000). *Towards a Psychology of Awakening*. Boston: Shambhala.

Wibberley, M. (1988). Encounter. In J. Rowan and I. W. Dryden (eds) *Innovative Therapy in Britain*. Milton Keynes: Open University Press.

Worrall, M. (2006). Contracting within the person centred approach. In C.Sills (ed.) *Contracts in Counselling and Psychotherapy* (2nd edition). London: Sage.

Legal references

Axon, R (on the application of) v Secretary of State for Health and Anor [2006] EWHC 37 (Admin).
Bolam v Friern HMC [1957] 2 All ER 118.
Campbell v MGN Ltd [2004] UKHL 22.
Gillick v. *West Norfolk AHA* [1985] 3 All ER 402; [1986] AC 112.
Phelps v *Hillingdon Borough* [1997] 3 FCR 621, [2000] 4 All ER 504.

Chapter 8

Pluralistic counselling psychology for young people

Terry Hanley, Gareth Williams and Aaron Sefi

Overview

As has already been described in Chapter 6, this book takes the stance that there are a multitude of therapeutic responses to the issues that young people bring to therapy. This chapter attempts to take this a step further by providing a glimpse into some of the possibilities that we have encountered within our therapeutic work with this age group. In doing so, we begin by recapping the position of a pluralistic counselling psychology and reflecting upon how this can become even more complex when considering the client group in question. Following this, we provide an overview of the types of goals that young people may have when they enter into therapy, therapeutic tasks undertaken and methods that counsellors often use. Alongside these we also provide reflective activities with a view to getting you, the reader, to enter into a more personal engagement with the topics being discussed. Finally, we present three composite case studies, which aim to clarify what therapeutic work with young people may be like and illustrate the interaction of therapeutic goals, tasks and methods.

Pluralistic counselling psychology for young people

At the heart of pluralist approaches to therapy is the view that there are a variety of potentially helpful ways to approach any significant issue brought to therapy. Such a sentiment reflects the ever-increasing literature noting that therapeutic approaches, when examined thoroughly, display roughly equivalent outcomes (e.g. Wampold, 2001 – although we note that this view has also been challenged by the likes of Beutler, 2002). From this apparent equivalence, a metatheory of therapy has been developed offering a framework embracing all approaches and valuing those components shown to be demonstrably effective (Norcross, 2002, 2011). This framework, described by Cooper and McLeod (2007, 2011; see Chapter 6 for a brief introduction), places emphasis upon the collaborative nature of therapeutic encounters, with a client's needs and preferences being prioritised over and above allegiance to particular therapeutic paradigms. As youth counsellors often utilise a variety of therapeutic approaches, it is felt that a framework such as this can provide a common ground upon which to bring together the diverse work undertaken in this field.

In the sections which follow, we begin to unpack this pluralistic framework with a view to highlighting how it may be utilised with young people. We reflect upon therapeutic goals that young people have when they arrive at therapy, tasks that may be agreed upon by the young person and the therapist, and methods that can be helpful. Prior to this, we will highlight a few principles that inform our understanding and practice of youth-friendly therapy.

Youth-friendly counselling

As has been highlighted within Chapter 3, therapeutic services for young people come in a wide variety of forms, ranging from the very conservative to the more liberal. Furthermore, therapy can be offered in a multitude of settings: some individuals may meet online, some in school, some in a medical clinic, some in a community setting and some at home, to name but a few possible environments. We would remind individuals to consider the environment in which they (plan to) work, as this context is likely to have an impact upon the therapy that follows and therefore should not be taken for granted.

Another area to prefix discussions about therapeutic work with young people is the complex nature of adolescence. Chapter 5 reflects upon the phenomenon of adolescence in more depth; however it is noteworthy here that an individual entering adolescence (at say 11 years of age) will have vastly different life experience and worldview than someone just leaving it (at say 25 years of age).

We do not wish to spend too much time revisiting issues noted elsewhere, so we will move on to reflect upon youth-friendly therapeutic relationships and their constituent goals, tasks and methods. We do however highlight some organisational and developmental issues within the material that follows and hope that the broader contents of this book enable you to see that such issues can impact upon the therapeutic approaches taken and, at times, ethically responsible courses of action.

Youth-friendly therapeutic relationships: the importance of collaboration

Within this section, we outline the importance of collaboration in work with young people. Although many issues overlap with those present in work with adult populations (see Cooper and McLeod, 2011, for a useful summary of this), here we highlight several issues that are pertinent to work with this particular age group. Of particular importance are the likely power imbalance within adult–child professional relationships and the value of taking a creative approach to facilitating a therapeutic alliance.

As discussed in the previous chapter, the therapeutic alliance is viewed as a consistently significant factor in determining the success of therapy. A major part of an alliance is its collaborative nature and this becomes increasingly complex due to the power dynamics between adult counsellor and adolescent client. For instance, for many young people there is a lack of awareness about therapy and a lack of clarity about why they are being asked to attend. It is a common scenario that young people are 'sent' to therapy and the driving force is often a parent, teacher, youth worker or social worker, rather than the young people themselves. Therapists working with this client group are advised to be prepared for this.

Given the potential ambivalence involved in young people's attendance of counselling, we have, at times, found it beneficial to be guided by clients' interests and enthusiasm. 'What are you into lately?' 'Have you got hobbies?' 'What's your favourite music?' Questions such as these can be friendly ways to make and develop psychological contact. Nevertheless, if these inquiries are not expressions of a therapist's authentic interest and simply a technique to try and recruit young people to take part in psychological treatment, they will probably be sensed as such and may prove counterproductive. It may be important to remind readers that for many practitioners and researchers, genuineness on the part of a therapist is considered a key component of psychotherapy (Klein *et al.*, 2002).

For some, music, art and games can be excellent ways to engage with young people. They can be both a bridge between client and therapist – a means of forming and building a relationship – as well as a way to address issues and concerns. Unlike adults, who tend to expect conversation to be the main means of interaction, young people have a range of ways of expressing themselves. For those who are uncomfortable expressing themselves verbally, creative media and games can prove invaluable. We believe that what Ken Robinson (2001) describes in the domain of education is equally relevant in therapy: '[R]ealizing our creative potential is partly a question of finding our medium, of being in our element. Education should help us achieve this, but too often it does not and too many people are instead displaced from their true talents' (p.xvi)

For example, someone with interests in visual arts having problems with getting angry could draw a comic strip of an incident where his or her anger was triggered. The therapist might invite the client to fill in extra boxes that show what went on in between the triggering event and angry response. The therapist might suggest drawing a different response to the angry behaviour or invite the client to draw him- or herself as someone who could handle the situation in a preferable way. This might lead on to a role play, making a badge with a symbol reminding the person of alternatives to aggression or writing a poem. The possibilities are probably endless and depend on the personalities and interests of therapist and client, as well as on the situation they work in together and the materials and resources available.

As noted at the outset of this section, therapy with adolescents might take a relatively traditional/conservative form, similar or identical to work with older populations (particularly when working with older young people). In contrast, creating a non-intimidating youth-friendly intervention may lead to a therapist being more creative or playful in his or her way of working. It is therefore important to remember that therapy can be fun whilst also remaining appropriately focused.

For many young people, it could be argued that the more fun the time with their therapist, the better. A fun experience tends to lead to engagement, both moment to moment and throughout therapy. Castro Blanco and Karver (2010) remind us that 'even the best psychotherapeutic treatments in the world will not matter if no one is there to receive them' (p.x).

Being mindful that replicating adult services in youth settings is not always the most fruitful response proves important when aiming to engage with young people in therapy. In this section we highlight the need for youth-friendly counsellors to be sensitive to what collaboration means with this age group and to consider working in more creative media. Such an ethos runs throughout the following sections in which we discuss the goals, tasks and methods that counselling psychologists might encounter and use in their work with people in adolescence.

Young people's therapeutic goals

Young people arrive at therapy through numerous avenues. Unlike work with adult populations, many individuals are referred for support by someone in a position of authority (e.g. a parent, teacher, educational psychologist, youth worker). Furthermore, services themselves may receive funding for working with particular presenting issues. Factors such as these contribute a peculiar dynamic to a therapeutic relationship; after all, whose goal is it that is being worked towards? Although these external agendas are primarily made with good intent, it is relatively common for referrers' agendas to reflect headlines and to be relatively unsophisticated (e.g. a school-based counselling service may prioritise offering counselling to what they might summarise crudely as 'naughty boys' and 'overemotional girls'). These often have limited value and (1) do not reflect the complexity of an individual's life (i.e. 'What is it that has made John act in the way he did?'), and (2) place the agenda of the referrer at the fore (e.g. 'Is the point of therapy to stop people being so naughty?') Such (implicit or explicit) messages may need exploration with the young person in question and to be considered together with the proposed direction of therapy.

When considering the goals of the young people themselves it is important to distinguish between broader 'life goals' and more 'specific goals' that are potentially attainable within (often relatively brief) therapy. Life goals reflect broad desires within individuals' lives and might be expressed in the following ways: 'I want to feel good about myself', 'I just want to feel better' or 'I want to be more chilled out'.

Goals such as these might prove overly daunting to the young person (and therapist), and potentially be setting unattainable outcomes and unrealistic expectations for the therapeutic work on offer. With this in mind, although it is acknowledged that sometimes such goals have to be a starting point to therapy (and may always remain as hoped-for outcomes), counsellors may work to identify more 'specific goals' that fit within these larger goals. Discussions within an assessment with a young person may therefore look at refining what it is that client and therapist will work on together. For instance, two specific goals for the life goal, 'I want to feel good about myself,' might be: 'I want to understand what it is that will help me feel good about myself' and 'I want to learn what gets in the way of me feeling confident'.

Specific goals are more explicit in focus and provide a tangible starting point to enter into discussions about how they might be achieved. One way of conceptualising specific goals (which we acknowledge might not be appealing to everyone) is to view them as SMART goals (originally devised by Doran, 1981, within the field of management). This acronym stands for:

- specific
- measurable
- achievable
- realistic
- time-limited.

The concepts presented here can be useful to keep in mind when attempting to identify specific therapeutic goals.

When working with young people, identifying therapeutic goals is not always a simple task. For example, it is not uncommon for someone to arrive at therapy without a particular goal in mind other than wanting to feel better. Additionally, specific goals may feel like they vary in intensity. One person may be seeking advice on how to learn to French-kiss ('Do you put your tongue in or not?'), another might not know why she has come to a counselling session, whilst another may be trying to understand why his parents used to burn him with cigarettes when he did something 'wrong'. As a text directed at therapists who are mindful of ethical practice, it does not seem necessary to note the need to respond with respect in all cases and to meet individuals 'where they are at'. It does however feel appropriate to note that this might not be a straightforward matter.

One specific goal that we feel is important to introduce is the goal of 'testing out' therapy. Here we refer to instances where young people work with a counsellor but do not actively bring the material that is predominantly troubling them. They may even behave in such a way that the counsellor feels they are not taking the meetings seriously at all. This phenomenon is commonly talked about within mediated therapy (e.g. online or via telephone) (Hanley, 2004) but is less acknowledged within face-to-face work. Furthermore, such occurrences may be more prevalent within services that are free at the point of delivery, as many youth counselling services are. If a client seems not to be taking the therapeutic process seriously it can be helpful to remember that this may be a process of 'testing out'. Young people may feel the need to challenge their therapist's patience and trustworthiness to ensure that they feel safe enough to continue, or perhaps to return at a later date.

Box 2 provides a list of some of the therapeutic goals that we have come across within our work with this client group. It is in no way a comprehensive list and has been provided to illustrate the wide variety of ways that individuals hope to use therapy.

Box 2 Examples of specific goals that young people have when they approach therapy

A young person may want to:

- Be less anxious during exams
- Get on with family members better
- Cope better with the pain of losing a parent
- Stop angry outbursts that are damaging relationships
- Feel more confident and able to go into town alone and meet new people
- Not worry so much
- Deal with panic attacks
- Stop soiling their pants
- Stop self-harming
- Feel more supported and make better use of different support that is being offered

---

Reflective exercise

Imagine being a teenager again, perhaps aged 14 or 15. Think back to how you used to enjoy spending your time. Perhaps you can remember a piece of music from that time, or a film or television programme. Can you recall some other young person or people from that time? A friend maybe? What about a teacher?

Now, can you imagine deciding to go and book a counselling appointment? How might you or one of the young people you knew back then comfortably meet up for a one-to-one session with a therapist? What would help you to feel ok to go to the meeting? What would support you or that other young person to show up?

Can you imagine what a therapist that you would have liked to have met with would be like? What would be his or her qualities? Would it matter what the room was like? How the therapist spoke with you? Where and when you met?

The counsellor asks: 'What might you hope to get from our meetings?' How might you, or the young person you're thinking of, have responded to this question?

Spend a few moments on this. Perhaps talk it through with a colleague or peer. Or maybe you could record yourself speaking the directions. Take your time. Make some notes or a sketch of any ideas, insights or discoveries.

Therapeutic tasks

Once specific therapeutic goals have been identified and agreed upon, it should hopefully be possible to identify potential therapeutic tasks that would be of benefit to the young person. McLeod (2007) describes such a process as being akin to having a 'counselling menu' whereby the young person and counsellor can work together on discussing and choosing an appropriate strategy to address the presenting issue(s). This process might also be described as a type of collaborative case formulation (Cooper and McLeod, 2011) in which the counsellor aims to utilise everyday language to describe potential ways for therapy to proceed.

Manualised therapies might be seen as one way of responding to particular issues once they have been identified, that is, you have x and so it is recommended that you get y treatment. However, we do not advocate such a one-size-fits-all response. Although such models have been demonstrated to be relatively effective with adult clients with particular diagnoses, the pluralist stance advocated here acknowledges that there may be many plausible therapeutic avenues for any presenting issue and that in some instances adopting a manualised approach could be deleterious (Strupp and Anderson, 1997). We favour responsiveness tailored to each person (Norcross, 2011) and based upon research-informed principles (Duncan *et al.*, 2004), rather than research-directed ones. From this perspective therapeutic menus are potentially vast.

In contemplating how therapists might address and negotiate the therapeutic tasks that are to be engaged in within a session, we return to the menu analogy. We invite therapists to adopt the stance of a waiter or waitress. As such, this involves presenting an overview of various therapeutic means on offer for each goal (the task menu), describing and elaborating upon those that seem unfamiliar to the young person. Discussion might take account of numerous nuances, for instance, one's own skill set, research around the presenting issue, the therapeutic setting and resources to hand, the developmental stage of the young person and one's clinical experience of working with similar issues. Importantly, there is always a need to consider one's competence and confidence in responding in the ways presented.

The developmental stage of the person with whom one is working proves incredibly important when discussing therapeutic tasks. With some young people, such conversations will prove relatively straightforward, but for others it may be very difficult. Issues such as the individual's deference towards adults (or lack of it) may have a huge impact upon the negotiating process (Hanley, 2012) and, as therapists, we are well advised to be mindful of such dynamics.

For many young people, choosing specific tasks can feel overwhelming. Imagine going to a restaurant and being confronted with hundreds of possible meal options that you do not recognise. This unease could be magnified for those with little or no previous experience of working psychologically, not to mention being engaged on such a level by an adult. With this in mind, we acknowledge the sensitivity and flexibility generally needed to navigate such a complex task. It may therefore be appropriate to adopt a 'give it a go' attitude, whilst remaining clear that you are interested to hear if the client is not finding an approach helpful. Keeping such a dialogue open is a skilful endeavour and one we feel is essential for remaining responsive to a client's needs. Within adult therapy, Rennie (1998) describes such a process as metacommunication, and Cooper and McLeod (2011) present a therapy personalisation questionnaire to encourage such discussions to take place (www.pluralistictherapy.com). Adapting the latter form may be helpful in some circumstances. Alternatively, using a simple and brief session-rating scale (such as that developed by Johnson *et al.,* 2000, available at www.talkingcure.com) to monitor how the client perceives the sessions might prove less intrusive. It seems salient to point out that in the adult research literature systematically gathering client feedback has been identified as a significant contribution to positive therapeutic outcome (Lambert, 2010).

Table 3 provides a list of some of the therapeutic tasks that we have negotiated with clients when considering two of the goals presented earlier in this chapter. As with the list of potential goals, it is in no way a comprehensive list of possibilities and has been provided for illustrative purposes only.

Table 3. Examples of negotiated tasks engaged in therapy with young people

Therapeutic goal 1: To be less anxious during exams

Therapeutic tasks
Talking through what it means to be anxious during exams
Practising relaxation activities
Looking at self-talk, and how this can be modified to manage anxiety
Making sense of what it is that is problematic
Supportive work looking at planning systematically for the exam

Therapeutic goal 2: To get on with family members better

Therapeutic tasks
Working through and mapping family dynamics
Co-creating increased awareness of impact of family dynamics on young person
Exploring different ways of managing conversation and interaction
Examining feelings about different members of family
Helping a young person prepare self for open feedback from others

Reflective exercise

Consider the case presentations in the second half of this chapter with a view to creating a counselling menu for each of the individuals. Imagine being in the assessment session with each of the young people introduced. You have just got a good sense of why they have come to the meeting and identified a relatively specific goal: what tasks might you be able to suggest to the young person that might be helpful? Try to come up with at least three options for each of the scenarios.

Therapeutic methods that can be helpful

Finally, once a task has been agreed upon by both the therapist and the young person, the therapist can make use of specific therapeutic methods. These may include very non-directive interventions which aim to facilitate conversation, or they may be more directive in nature, such as cognitive behavioural worksheets or relaxation exercises. This is likely to be the most varied and individual part of the therapeutic process and the one that proves most aligned to the training the therapist has undertaken.

Therapeutic methods can take numerous forms. For some practitioners it may prove useful to delineate categories. Cooper and McLeod (2011, p.95) outline five types of methods. These are outlined in Table 4.

The idiosyncratic nature of the methods we use (and how we use them) means that interventions rely greatly upon us, our personalities and our unique histories. For instance, the training we have completed will mean that we each have very different explicit therapeutic toolkits to offer clients. Ultimately, however, our view of the world, and our experiences within it, will also prove instrumental in what we offer to others. Here we would note that previous work, personal therapy and/or our hobbies might also help to enrich the support and facilitation we offer (e.g. experience with music production has proven helpful within two of the authors' experiences of working with this age group). Additionally, we must not forget that much of what proves helpful in clients' lives is likely to occur outside the therapy room (Asay and Lambert, 2000; Lambert and Barley, 2002). In accounting for this, cultural resources such as music, film, museums and sport might be incredibly significant in an individual's life. Supporting young people to find an appropriate method that fits with their needs and lifestyles is likely to prove fruitful (Hadley and Yancy, 2011).

Table 4. Therapeutic methods and examples of their use

Method	Example(s)
Conversation	Non-directive facilitation; socratic questioning; interpretations; self-disclosure
Structured problem-solving	Keeping a diary of thoughts and emotions; therapeutic homework
Creating new experiences	Gestalt two-chair work; role play; mindfulness and acceptance practices; guided visualisation; graded exposure
Making use of existing strengths	Resource activation; identifying exceptions to an identified problem; affirming previous instances of overcoming adversity
Directly intervening to alter information-processing	Hypnosis; eye movement desensitisation and reprocessing (EMDR)

As with generating a plan of what therapeutic task(s) client and therapist will engage in, deciding upon therapeutic methods should also be a collaborative process. Spending too much time clarifying potential tasks and methods is not going to help create a successful alliance but we do feel that a young person's preferences for certain therapeutic avenues can prove incredibly helpful for guiding the work. For instance, where it becomes apparent that a young person has a leaning towards a particular learning style (e.g. Fleming, 2001, has developed a model around the idea that there are visual learners, auditory learners, reading/writing learners and kinaesthetic learners), tailoring interventions appropriately may be very helpful. A therapist might, for example, discuss the idea of drawing the anger a client feels towards a teacher as a volcano, and the client immediately responds positively saying, 'yeah, let's give that a go!' Such enthusiasm suggests that the therapist has found a medium through which to engage fruitfully. Alternatively, the young person might be much less enthusiastic, or outright dismissive: 'I'm not doing that!' With the latter, one might then explore an alternative medium such as writing a letter to the teacher expressing the emotions, or even banging a drum. Though this description is somewhat simplistic, we hope it helps convey some insight into the potentially rich benefits of a collaborative approach.

In deciding which methods may be useful in therapy, the counsellor should be mindful of the rationale informing his or her decision. This is likely to be informed by training, understanding of psychological theory, skills base and therapeutic supervision, awareness of relevant research and personal experiences. Where possible, therapists are encouraged to describe explicitly to the young person how they would suggest working and why they feel this might be helpful, that is, explaining how a method on offer will help work on particular tasks that can support reaching a therapeutic goal. As far as possible, frame the offer in language that is understandable and relevant to each individual young person. For example, 'I will mainly listen and pick up on some of the things you are saying that seem especially important. Doing this should hopefully help us to gain a better sense of what's going on for you at home.' Or: 'I would like to ask you to do some experiments in between our meetings. These will help us to test whether you are really going to pass out when you feel stressed in class.' Sensitivity around consensus on a way forward seems particularly important within professional–client relationships in which the power of the helper can often be underplayed.

Table 5 provides a list of some of the therapeutic methods that could relate to the two goals mentioned above. As with the previous two tables, this has been provided for illustrative purposes only and we acknowledge the abundance of additional methods that may used.

Table 5. Examples of methods used within therapy with young people

---

Therapeutic goal 1: *To be less anxious during exams*

Therapeutic task 1: Talking through what it means to be anxious during exams

Therapeutic methods
Non-directive empathic reflections
Socratic questioning

Therapeutic task 2: Practising relaxation activities

Therapeutic methods
Breathing exercises
Safe space visualisations

Therapeutic task 3: Exploring self-talk

Therapeutic methods
Identifying and highlighting anxiety-provoking thoughts
Keeping a journal of thoughts and their triggers as they emerge during day

---

Therapeutic goal 2: *To get on with family members better*

Therapeutic task 1: Mapping family dynamics

Therapeutic methods
Creating a genogram
Completing a timeline related to key family events

Therapeutic task 2: Co-creating increased awareness of impact of family dynamics on young person

Therapeutic methods
Two-chair enactments to explore relationships with key family members
Creating a family sculpture using sandtray miniatures

Therapeutic task 3: Exploring different ways of managing conversation and interaction

Therapeutic methods
Problem-solving activity focused on difficult events
Role play

Reflective exercise

Ask yourself what methods you employ within your therapeutic work. Create as comprehensive a list as possible.

Once you have created a list, rate your competence at using each method on a scale of one to ten, with ten being very competent and one being not competent at all. Also consider what it is that has led you to this view (for example, your practice, training or supervision).

Finally, now consider the rationale that might be behind using such a method and how you might introduce this to a young person (potentially aged 11, aged 15 and aged 20).

Examples of how the pluralistic framework may look in practice

So far we have discussed the pluralistic framework in a predominantly theoretical way. Although we have introduced small examples from clinical practice, we have not described how this may look within live therapeutic work. Within this section we present work with three very different young people to illustrate how this framework may be applied in practice. Each case is presented in an abridged version of the systematic case study format recommended by Fishman (1999). Within each case example, the different goals, tasks and methods used within the work are outlined. Furthermore a psychological rationale for the approach adopted is also briefly stated. In acknowledging that such work is usually not straight-forward (e.g. clients do not often have just one neat and tidy goal that they work on throughout therapy), the examples also reflect some of the complexities inherent in such work. So that we are not using client material without appropriate consent, each of these cases is a composite of our work with clients. These have been carefully constructed so that they do not reflect work that we have undertaken with any one person.

Case example 1: Terry and Jade

Context

This example reflects therapeutic work taking place within a secondary school in a UK inner city. I visit the school one morning a week and commonly meet with pupils for sessions of 50 minutes (a time that matches the length of time of the timetabled classes); however sometimes this is shortened depending upon the needs of the client. Many of the young people I meet have been referred to the service by a teacher who has noticed they may be in need of additional support. The room in which we meet is a private room which is also used by other support services that visit the school.

Jade's referral

Jade is a 13-year-old girl who has been asked to meet with me following a period of difficulty at home. Her head of year at school had noted within a brief referral letter that Jade had been having difficulties keeping concentration within class due to problems at home. This had led to her having to leave class on occasions and sit quietly in the learning support facility while she composed herself to return to class. Jade had consented to meet with me and had agreed with the teacher that it might be helpful to talk about what was going on for her. Jade's parents were not informed about the referral to me. No more information was given at this stage.

The counsellor

As a counselling psychologist I am heavily influenced by humanistic psychologists such as Carl Rogers and my approach places a great deal of emphasis upon the quality of the relationship (Gillon, 2007; Roth *et al.*, 2009). However, as I do not adhere to one particular psychological model, I would describe my practice as pluralist, combining approaches depending on the client I am meeting.

Assessment and formulation

Jade and I met during the first session of the school day to say hello and discuss the potential of meeting for counselling. This began with me briefly describing how I work and how our meetings might proceed, outlining the parameters that I saw to this initial meeting and potential future ones (e.g. time boundaries, limits to confidentiality) and very explicitly noting that she didn't have to attend sessions with me and that she could choose to go if she wished. Once this information had been given I asked: 'Would you mind telling me a bit about yourself and what you feel you might gain from meeting with me?'

This question facilitated Jade to begin talking about herself and why she thought her head of year had asked her to attend counselling. In doing so, Jade mentioned that she was having a tough time at home due to consistent arguments between her mum and dad. She was not involved in the arguments but was getting increasingly worried about what may happen as her parents had split up briefly about two years ago and she was worried that this might happen again.

As Jade discussed her situation she become increasingly sad, contemplating what might happen at home. After about 30 minutes of listening to Jade introduce her difficulties, I tentatively asked her how she was finding talking about everything that was going on. At this point I was mindful of not asking, 'How could things change to make you happier?' as I would have anticipated her stating that she did not want her parents to split up – a potential event that was likely to be out of the influence of our meetings. With this in mind, the question that I asked therefore aimed to gain insight into whether she was finding having the space to talk useful. This question received a resounding yes.

Following this question, I reflected that counselling can sometimes be about having a space to get things off your chest and talking through difficult things. Additionally, as she was finding the process of talking useful it seemed appropriate to acknowledge that I had observed this and this might be a major component of what I could offer. However, in mentioning this, it was also important to clarify whether she had any differing hopes or expectations from me. Jade didn't know what to expect, but was happy that I had not asked lots of questions and agreed that she would like meet again.

As a way forward, I made the suggestion that we meet for six sessions in which she could have a space to talk about the difficulties she was facing (the task). I would predominantly be there to listen and engage in conversation within the sessions (the method) and be a companion in her trying to make sense of the complexities at home (goal 1). Additionally, this may support her in reducing the amount of times that she has to leave class due to feeling tearful in school (goal 2). When presented with this idea Jade agreed that she would be willing to give the plan a go.

Course of therapy

We met for the six sessions that we had arranged. As the sessions progressed Jade engaged in the meetings very actively by primarily talking through and processing the week's events. Although nothing had changed at home, she noticed that she didn't have to leave class so often during the week, a factor that she attributed to our meetings and having somewhere to get things off her chest.

During the fourth meeting Jade presented very differently. During this session Jade was preoccupied by an upcoming exam. We had a very brief update on what Jade described as a relatively good week and then she left after a few minutes to attend a revision class.

Within the final two sessions, Jade's intrusive thoughts about her parents appeared to have subsided greatly. Things at home had calmed down and, although not perfect, felt manageable to Jade. Our focus therefore went towards discussing: (1) what happens if things worsen again; (2) celebrating success in the exam; and (3) reviewing our meetings.

Therapy monitoring and use of feedback

At the onset of counselling, Jade had completed a well-being measure which was indicative that she was in a lot of distress. This was completed at the beginning of every session and fluctuated greatly throughout the meetings: scores varied depending on what had happened in the week. These measures were incorporated into the work and discussed when they had been completed. Jade mentioned finding them useful in deciding what to talk about. Interestingly, although Jade's level of distress had reduced greatly, it had not moved below a clinical cut-off when we agreed that it would be appropriate to end therapy.

Concluding evaluation

The meetings with Jade were reviewed on the final session and in supervision. Although Jade indicated, both in the questionnaire completed and in the final review session, that things could still improve, the work was viewed positively. The two goals that had been discussed during the assessment were felt to have been achieved, with Jade feeling that she had more of a sense of what was going on at home and that she was no longer being tearful in class. Importantly Jade had expressed finding the meetings very helpful and had recommended a friend to approach a counsellor as a consequence too.

Case example 2: Gareth and Ged

Context

I have been working in community-based young people's counselling/support agencies for about ten years. My roles have included providing face-to-face and online counselling, group work and supervising volunteers.

I have long believed that being creative can be inherently therapeutic and that the expressive arts offer a non-stigmatised way of facilitating recovery and healing (Richards, 2007; Williams, 2010). This has led me to organise and facilitate a variety of arts-based projects.

Referral

Ged was a young man when I met him – 17 years old. His mother brought him to meet me, having heard from a friend of her family that I was a musician as well as a therapist. The referral form told me he was suffering from depression, had a history of being bullied at school and hardly ever went out of the house. It also said he had an interest in rock music and playing the guitar. Ged had refused to engage with other services but Mum was hopeful that his interest in music might overcome his reluctance to accept help.

For some (young) people the notion of counselling is tainted by an idea that it is for those who are ill or weak. I do not believe in this notion; in my mind we all face difficult times and can benefit from an empathic creative space. It is too large an issue to address here; suffice it to say that how we promote our services can go some way to addressing the prejudices surrounding mental health.

The counsellor

My background is in person-centred (Rogers, 1961; Mearns and Thorne, 2007) and process-oriented (Mindell, 1989, 1992) approaches to therapy. I aspire to remain open-minded rather than governed by theory and have a strong affinity with the active client model (Bohart and Tallman, 1999). Recognising many different ways people can benefit from therapy, this humanistic-integrative approach considers each person as the central agent of change in his/her therapeutic process.

Taking an improvisational, collaborative approach to therapy, I try to draw upon research lightly so that it informs, but does not dictate, how and what I practise. I view the therapeutic alliance as the heart of therapy and have a commitment to ongoing processes of feedback. Feedback strikes me as a crucial component of therapy (and any improvised activity), sourced both from one's own felt sense of a therapeutic process, from client (verbal, non-verbal and written) communication, as well as from supervision.

Assessment and formulation

When he first came into the room, it was clear that Ged was unhappy. Stooped over, it looked as though he was burdened by a heavy load. No smiles, no laughter, lots of self put-downs. This first meeting demonstrated how self-critical he was and how aversive he considered counselling to be.

Gareth: Hi, man. Good to meet you.

Ged looks down, doesn't reply.

Gareth: You are welcome here. As you are. 'Come as you are,' as Nirvana [Nineties rock band] put it.

Ged: Yeah. I bet!

Gareth: You're not sure you're really welcome. Perhaps you think I'm just saying that.

Ged: Probably. It's your job, isn't it.

Gareth: (Slightly flustered) It's my job to be here, that's true. And I genuinely have a feeling of welcoming you as you are. I like meeting people. And from what I hear, you are a musician. Me too. Perhaps we'll have a jam!

Ged: I'm rubbish.

Gareth: How long you been playing guitar?

Ged: Too long for how rubbish I am. I'm not interested in counselling. I tried that at school and it was crap.

[In this context, words like assessment and formulation are unhelpful to the client. Though assessments can be carried out in a collaborative and informal manner, they tend to convey a clinical tone and carry a sense of power imbalance. For many young people such an approach is off-putting.]

Ged: If someone really wants to help me then they would help me do my music or something.

Gareth: Really?! That sounds like fun. Maybe we could work together and produce a few tracks.

Here I find myself challenged to take a leap of faith (Spinelli, 2001), abandon the traditional role of counsellor/therapist and draw on my (congruent) passion for music production. Not all agencies would support such an unconventional step but at this time I was involved in a lot of outreach and could frame it as such. Outreach can be geographical, reaching out into the community; it can also be a reaching out beyond the conventions of the counselling room. In this instance the idea was to reach out into music and audio technology. Here we are on the borderline of therapy and youth work, where music, arts, games and activities can function first, as a bridge facilitating psychological contact, and second, as a means for personal development. One way of describing this type of working is as a radical form of therapeutic alliance, with worker and young person collaboratively negotiating a therapeutic pathway, using client-directed (Duncan *et al.*, 2004) methods and goals.

Course of therapy

Over the months of working together on Ged's music project, a relational bond developed. As we spent time recording and editing, we would drink tea and talk, not just about music but about philosophy, the meaning of life, even painful personal history. Often the lyrics of Ged's songs would be a starting point for conversation. It seems likely that a willingness to be open about personal life experiences on my part facilitated Ged to open up. The therapeutic benefits of self-disclosure have been well documented (Pennebaker, 1990; Farber, 2006).

I suspect that 'going the extra mile' played an important role in the successful progression of this therapeutic process (Cooper, 2008). For example, when Ged failed to arrive for his third appointment I decided to phone him:

Gareth: Where are you, man? The studio is ready, the microphone is plugged in.
Ged: I've overslept. I couldn't get to sleep last night. Shite! I've been thinking about this all week. That just shows how crap I am, doesn't it! Can't even get there on time. Just wasting your time.
Gareth: It can happen to anyone. I've missed appointments myself. It's easy to get sucked into inner criticism and putting yourself down. Personally I would wish for you not to do that. Look, I've actually had a cancellation at noon, so if you can get here in 30 minutes we can start the session then.
Ged: Yeah. Ok. I'll be there. I'll go and get ready now.
Gareth: I can't always be so flexible.
Ged: Thanks. That's great.

I also obtained some free software that enabled Ged to use his personal computer for audio production. This meant he could develop his compositions at home.

For many people, being recorded, especially one's voice and especially in front of another person, can constellate self-criticism. In the context of this project I was able to support Ged in overcoming his embarrassment and developing his self-confidence.

When the tracks were completed my manager offered to host Ged's work on the organisation's website. I considered this doubly positive in that it affirmed and appreciated Ged's work and helped promote the organisation as non-pathologising, creative and youth-friendly.

Therapy monitoring and use of feedback

Gareth: So how d'you think it's gone so far?

Ged: It's gone really well. I wish I was better on the guitar but I really like how it's come together. It means a lot to me coming here.

Gareth: That's good to hear. Do you think it's helped in any other ways?

Ged: What do you mean?

Gareth: Well. I dunno. Like confidence or happiness. Anything like that . . . [no response]. Have I gotten too therapisty?

Ged: I still think I'm a $#*! if that's what you mean. [Laughs.]

Gareth: I don't know whether to laugh or not.

Ged: Only joking. Sorry. I shouldn't say that. It's definitely helped me. Shall we just get on with burning that CD now?

Ged and I arranged a follow-up meeting six months after ending. With a smile he told me he was now playing in a band and doing some part-time work in a local studio. Clinical Outcome Measures in Routine Evaluation measures demonstrated a ten-point decrease in reported distress. Ged's mum made a point of letting me know how much she appreciated the organisation's help.

Concluding evaluation

My challenge was to trust and respect Ged's ability to know what would help him develop. From a cognitive-behavioural perspective, one might frame what happened as behavioural activation (Martell *et al.*, 2010) and support to move in a valued direction (Hayes *et al.*, 1999). In this case, these therapeutic processes emerged organically, in a nondirective context.

Person-centred approaches rest upon the facilitator congruently embodying unconditional positive regard and empathy, and this being received by the client. Would this hold in contexts other than traditional counselling? Why not? In his integrative statement, Rogers (1957) described how the core conditions could be communicated in a wide variety of ways. One can support and challenge as a fellow human being and, in this case, as a collaborative producer whose aim is to get the best out of the artist. Creative collaborative approaches to supporting people involve tailoring therapy to the unique characteristics and context of each client (Norcross, 2011).

Case example 3: Aaron and FreedomFighter

Context

This example reflects therapeutic work taking place online as part of the service Kooth (www.kooth.com). The service caters for 11–25-year-olds, offering a blend of synchronous chat, asynchronous messaging and moderated forums for support. Users can choose a made-up name and avatar, and remain anonymous. They can be offered booked chats (sessions) or 'drop in' during opening times, which extend to late evening and weekends.

FreedomFighter's referral

FreedomFighter logged his details as a 16-year-old boy from an inner-city area. It emerged during our first session that he had been recommended Kooth by the head of year at his school. He was falling behind with class work, and had self-described 'issues' with authority and self-control. His carers remained unaware of his use of the service.

The counsellor

Trained in gestalt psychotherapy (Perls, 1969), I (AS) have a tendency towards humanistic models of practice, with a readiness to employ techniques and strategies in a pragmatic 'what works' approach. The overriding value of meeting a young person 'where he is at' and feeling most comfortable drew me towards online work and continues to inform my practice. With a strong draw towards research-informed practice, I have embraced a pluralistic framework as a means of eliciting goals as a valid form of self-reporting (Cooper and McLeod, 2011).

Assessment and formulation

Initial contact with FreedomFighter was through a message he sent to me with the subject line of: 'anger issues' and stating that he gets really angry sometimes and doesn't know why. In my reply, as well as offering validation for the fact he had made contact, and explaining how the service ran, I asked him to describe a bit more about what happened when he got angry. In the course of numerous messages, I began to get a picture of a young person who was at odds with every aspect of his life – he was angry with his foster carers for being too nice, with his teachers for being too strict and his friends for being too unreliable.

We agreed to a time to have a booked session, in which we contracted for an initial six booked sessions with instant messaging in between. At the outset of the work, FreedomFighter identified that he wanted to be able to communicate better with his foster parents (goal 1), get into less trouble at school (goal 2) and find a new friendship group (goal 3). When we looked a bit more at this last goal, and how our work could facilitate change, he agreed to modify that goal to focusing his attention on friendships that supported the aims of goals 1 and 2. It is note-worthy that these goals were identified in a spirit of collaboration, which, in itself, helped form the basis of, and underlying dynamic for, an alliance.

The tasks that filtered down from goals 1 and 2 were to work on ways of managing and releasing anger in a safe manner through letting him talk through his feelings (task 1) and by exploring his negative automatic thoughts about friends and family members (task 2). Task 1 would therefore be worked upon by facili-tating a conversation in which I utilised rogerian core conditions (Rogers, 1980) to promote respect and self-autonomy (a method). As I had identified through assessment that he might benefit from more directed work, it was also agreed that he would complete a mood diary on the site to explore potential faulty thinking about situations (another method).

Course of therapy

FreedomFighter attended the first two booked sessions, cancelling the next, then choosing to 'drop in' as and when our free time coincided. Whilst the majority of these sessions lasted 50 minutes, some were as short as 20-minute 'catch-up' sessions, where we would check in with the life events of FreedomFighter as well as evaluate how the achievement of set goals was going.

During the course of the work, there were significant crises in FreedomFighter's life that took the conscious focus away from the goals he had set. He had been involved in a street fight and was awaiting court proceedings. Whilst the temptation was to focus exclusively on finding new friends (goal 3), it had been determined that the achievement of goals 1 and 2 would be causal, and go to the heart of the issue for FreedomFighter. After this fight, FreedomFighter became angry with me, and a challenging rupture formed in the alliance: 'You are just like everyone else, trying to fix me when I ain't broke'. In this instance, setting aside goals was important for a moment to re-establish the pillars of trust, respect and self-autonomy. This was facilitated by another method – that of role play, which helped him focus and redirect his anger.

By our seventh and final session (to date), FreedomFighter reported that he had enjoyed using a 'mood diary' to identify triggers for his anger and had felt that we had developed a good bond: 'I feel like I can talk to you, and you won't tell me what to do'. He continues to message me occasionally to let me know about significant life events.

Therapy monitoring and use of feedback

At the onset of counselling, FreedomFighter had completed a well-being measure which suggested he was experiencing a moderate to severe level of distress. This level fluctuated throughout the course of our work, and ended marginally lower.

The service also utilises a goal-based outcome measure, which allows for measuring the statistical improvement of personalised identified goals. FreedomFighter achieved his goal of communicating with foster parents (goal 1). He was significantly on the way to achieving goal 2 – getting in less trouble at school – but had made little progress in finding a new friendship group (goal 3). As research in this area is in its infancy, there are no benchmarks against which to compare this attainment.

Concluding evaluation

Ongoing reviewing was indicating that FreedomFighter was developing a good bond with me and with the work itself, and was steadily working towards his goals. He was appreciating the tasks, and took well to the mood diary. He said he would continue to fill this in even if he did not drop in to talk to me.

It is notable from this study that working towards explicitly set goals within a pluralistic framework can at times be conducive towards forming a bond, and at times set a challenge. There is a need on occasions to step back from the trajectory, and 'free-float' within the relationship. This requires a willingness to switch between tasks that have differing outcomes, and work towards the integration of these within the process as a whole.

Conclusion

This chapter presents an overview of what the pluralistic framework devised by Cooper and McLeod (2011) might look like when working with young people. In doing so, the way in which therapeutic alliances manifest in such work is considered, utilising this pantheoretical framework. Initially caution is needed not to assume that therapeutic work with this age group will echo that undertaken in adult services. In particular, therapists will need to be mindful of environmental and developmental issues before considering the interpersonal therapeutic relationship. Following on from this, the wide range of goals that young people present with are discussed, the way that these can be broken down into achievable therapeutic tasks introduced and the types of methods used contemplated. Each of these requires skill to work collaboratively with young clients in a way that navigates sensitively adult–young person relationships.

In the second half of this chapter we have presented three composite case studies of work with this client group. These are fictional relationships but present an accurate overview of what it can be like working with this age group. In pulling these together we hope that the reader is provided with a helpful view of how the pluralistic framework might work in practice.

Summary

- Given the wide array of therapeutic approaches used with young people, a pluralistic perspective (Cooper and McLeod, 2011) offers a unifying framework, without compromising diversity. Acknowledging a multiplicity of bona fide therapeutic avenues, this pluralistic approach draws upon concepts that are demonstrably effective within the research literature.
- As with all (therapeutic) relationships, youth-friendly counselling is complex in nature. However, in addition, therapists working with young people need to be mindful of the context and developmental level of each individual client. Putting a collaborative approach centre stage often calls for more creativity to help overcome some of the potential barriers between adult therapist and young person.
- Where possible, it is generally useful to identify young people's therapeutic goals. This is likely to involve breaking down broader life goals into more tangible specific goals.
- Therapeutic tasks outline the ways in which identified goals can be worked on. This can be considered as a kind of therapeutic menu in which counsellors aim to describe what they feel they can offer to support clients with their goals. The keywords here are 'offer' and 'menu'. The process of formulation and choice of therapeutic tasks proceeds collaboratively.
- Therapeutic methods are the ways in which counsellors attempt to support the client in working towards completion of the therapeutic tasks. This can be viewed as the 'toolkit' that therapists draw upon within their work. It is likely to be heavily influenced by core therapeutic training.
- Within this chapter, three vignettes have been presented. These represent the type of therapeutic work that individuals enter into within schools, community settings and online. They are far from comprehensive accounts but hope to give the reader a sense of the type of work engaged in, and the way in which the alliance might begin to form.

Further reading

For a more detailed overview of the theoretical positioning of pluralistic therapy we recommend the following text:

Cooper, M. and McLeod, J. (2011). *Pluralistic Counselling and Psychotherapy*. London: Sage.

When considering the reasons why young people access counselling and what they want from it, the British Association for Counselling and Psychotherapy has an interesting short video on its website: www.bacp.co.uk/information/school Toolkit.php.

For ideas relating to the use of creative media in therapy, the reader is pointed to the following book by Carl Rogers' daughter, Natalie:

Rogers, N. (2000). *The Creative Connection: Expressive Arts as Healing*. Ross-on-Wye: PCCS Books.

References

Asay, T. and Lambert, M. (2000). The empirical case for the common factors in therapy: quantitative findings. In M. Hubble, B. Duncan and S. Miller (eds) *The Heart and Soul of Change: What works in therapy* (pp.33–56). Washington, DC: American Psychological Association.

Beutler, L. E. (2002). The dodo bird is extinct. *Clinical Psychology: Science and Practice*, 9, 30–4.

Bohart, A. C. and Tallman, K. (1999). *How Clients make Therapy Work: The process of active self-healing*. Washington, DC: American Psychological Association.

Castro Blanco, D. and Karver, M. S. (2010). *Elusive Alliance: Treatment Engagement Strategies with High-Risk Adolescents*. Washington, DC: American Psychological Association.

Cooper, M. (2008). *Essential Research Findings in Counselling and Psychotherapy: The facts are friendly*. London: Sage.

Cooper, M. and McLeod, J. (2007). A pluralistic framework for counselling and psychotherapy: implications for research. *Counselling and Psychotherapy Research*, 7 (3), 135–43.

Cooper, M. and McLeod, J. (2011). *Pluralistic Counselling and Psychotherapy*. Sage: London.

Doran, G. (1981). There's a S.M.A.R.T. way to write management's goals and objectives. *Management Review*, November, 35–6.

Duncan, B. L., Miller, S. D. and Sparks, J. A. (2004). *The Heroic Client: A revolutionary way to improve effectiveness through client-directed, outcome-informed therapy*. San Francisco: John Wiley.

Farber, B. A. (2006). *Self-disclosure in Psychotherapy*. New York: Guilford Press.

Fishman, D. (1999). *The Case for Pragmatic Psychology*. London: New York University Press.

Fleming, N. D. (2001). *Teaching and Learning Styles: VARK strategies*. Christchurch, New Zealand: N. D. Fleming.

Gillon, E. (2007). *Person-centred Counselling Psychology: An introduction*. London: Sage.

Hadley, S. and Yancy, G. (2011). *Therapeutic Uses of Rap and Hip-Hop*. New York: Routledge.

Hanley, T. (2004). E-motion online. *Counselling and Psychotherapy Journal*, 15 (1), 48–9.

Hanley, T. (2012). Understanding the online therapeutic alliance through the eyes of adolescent service users. *Counselling and Psychotherapy Research,* 12 (1), 35–43.

Hayes, S. C., Strosahl, K. D. and Wilson, K. G. (1999). *Acceptance and Commitment Therapy: An experiential approach to behavior change*. New York: Guilford Press.

Johnson, L. D., Miler, S. D. and Duncan, B. L. (2000). *The Session Rating Scale 3.0*. Chicago: Authors.

Klein, M. H., Kolden, G. G., Michels, J. L. and Chisholm-Stockard, S. (2002). Congruence. In J. C. Norcross (ed.) *Psychotherapy Relationships that Work: Therapist contributions and responsiveness to patients* (pp.195–216). New York: Oxford University Press.

Lambert, M. J. (2010). Yes, it is time for clinicians to routinely monitor treatment outcome. In B. L. Duncan, S. D. Miller, B. E. Wampold and M. A. Hubble (eds) *The Heart and Soul of Change: Delivering what works*. Washington, DC: American Psychological Association.

Lambert, M. and Barley, D. (2002). Research summary on the therapeutic relationship and psychotherapy outcome. In J. Norcross (ed.) *Psychotherapy Relationships that Work. Therapist contributions and responsiveness to patients.* Oxford: Oxford University Press.

McLeod, J. (2007). *Counselling Skill.* Maidenhead: OU Press.

Martell, C.R., Dimidjian, S. and Herman-Dunn, R. (2010) *Behavioral Activation for Depression: A clinician's guide.* New York: Guilford Press.

Mearns, D. and Thorne, B. (2007). *Person-Centred Counselling in Action* (3rd edition). London: Sage.

Mindell, A. (1989). *Working with the Dreaming Body.* London: Penguin-Arkana.

Mindell, A. (1992). *Riding the Horse Backwards.* London: Penguin-Arkana.

Norcross, J. (ed.) (2002). *Psychotherapy Relationships that Work. Therapist contributions and responsiveness to patients.* New York: Oxford University Press.

Norcross, J. (ed.) (2011). *Psychotherapy Relationships That Work: Evidence-based responsiveness.* New York: Oxford University Press.

Pennebaker, J. W. (1990). *Opening Up: The healing power of expressing emotions.* New York: Guilford Press.

Perls, F. S. (1969) *Gestalt Therapy Verbatim.* Lafayette, California: Real People Press.

Rennie, D. L. (1998). *Person-centred Counselling: An experiential approach.* London: Sage.

Richards, R. (ed.) (2007) *Everyday Creativity and New Views of Human Nature.* Washington, DC: American Psychological Association.

Robinson, K. (2001). *Out of our Minds.* West Sussex: Capstone.

Rogers, C. R. (1957) The necessary and sufficient conditions of therapeutic personality change. *Journal of Consulting Psychology*, 21, 95–103.

Rogers, C. R. (1961). *On Becoming a Person.* Boston: Houghton-Mifflin.

Rogers, C. R. (1980). *A Way of Being.* Boston: Houghton Mifflin.

Roth, A., Hill, A. and Pilling, S. (2009). *The Competences Required to Deliver Effective Humanistic Psychological Therapies.* Retrieved 19/09/11 from www.ucl.ac.uk/clinical-psychology/CORE/humanistic_framework.htm.

Spinelli, E. (2001). *The Mirror and the Hammer: Challenging orthodoxies in psychotherapeutic thought.* London: Continuum.

Strupp, H. and Anderson, T. (1997). On the limitations of manuals. *Clinical Psychology: Science and Practice*, 4 (1), 76–82.

Wampold, B. (2001). *The Great Psychotherapy Debate: Models, methods, and findings.* New Jersey: Lawrence Erlbaum.

Williams, G. (2010). *The Role of Creativity in Transformation and Healing: An inquiry.* Unpublished Masters dissertation. University of Manchester.

Chapter 9

Assessing therapeutic outcomes

Neil Humphrey, Terry Hanley, Clare Lennie, Ann Lendrum and Michael Wigelsworth

Overview

This chapter focuses upon assessing the outcomes of therapeutic interventions. We begin by discussing the importance of research and routine outcome measurement, before introducing a number of commonly applied research designs and measurement tools, including their inherent strengths and weaknesses. The emphasis here is on the application of these designs and tools in professional practice, and the opportunities and challenges this presents. The chapter continues by exploring issues in interpreting and analysing outcome data. We then shift to consideration of methods that more actively and explicitly incorporate the views and perspectives of user groups and allow for the concurrent assessment of process, such as interviews and focus groups, before we conclude with a suggested model for assessing therapeutic outcomes in adolescent counselling psychology.

Research with children and young people

Each of the authors of this chapter has been involved in conducting research with children and young people over a number of years, and can testify that it is at once challenging, enlightening, frustrating, enjoyable and, above all, extremely valuable in terms of the insights it can yield. We can each also attest to the fact that the idealised world of research presented in methodological textbooks is often very different from the reality of research conducted in complex real-world settings such as schools and counselling services. Indeed, in terms of general research issues there is way more to discuss than can be attempted in this brief chapter. In this vein, our first recommendations by way of further reading are:

- Lewis' (2004) book on the realities of research involving children and young people
- McLeod's (1999) text on practitioner research in counselling
- Barkham *et al.*'s (2010) overview of issues involved in developing and delivering practice-based evidence.

The model we present for research with children and young people in this chapter emphasises the combination of assessment of outcomes (often, but not always, using quantitative data) and assessment of process (often, but not always, using qualitative data). This 'mixed' model is advantageous for a number of reasons. First, it reflects the diversity of real-world research on counselling with young people (Cooper, 2009). Second, it ensures that the voice and perspectives of young people are directly sought in a number of ways. Third, it balances the strengths and weaknesses of diverse approaches to research, ultimately yielding greater insights than any single approach used in isolation.

The importance of research and outcome measurement

Research and outcome measurement is an essential component of children's mental health services, and recent years have seen a substantial rise in the importance attributed to empirical evidence in counselling and psychotherapy (Cooper, 2010). The reasons for this are manifold, and include the increasing need for conformity to the 'evidence-based practice' model, justification of ongoing public funding, feedback to clients on treatments and outcomes and clinical management/ monitoring functions (Johnston and Gowers, 2005). However, there is also a more fundamental reason for gathering sound data to monitor and evaluate the effectiveness of therapeutic interventions. As Wolpert (2010) points out, 'natural biases in reasoning mean that people make decisions and draw conclusions based on prior assumptions, traditions, or influenced by charismatic leaders, and will do things that "feel" right, rather than introduce things that have been shown to be effective' (p.7).

However, making decisions about practice based upon evidence produced in the research literature is not as straightforward as one might hope. Cooper (2010) raises a number of issues and tensions in this regard. He questions whether an increased reliance on research evidence will lead to a greater dehumanisation of clients, and also asks what use it is to know that clients, on average, respond well to a particular type of intervention, when what counsellors or therapists are naturally concerned with is the individual with whom they are working. Hoagwood (2001) highlights other problems, including the discord between the conditions under which particular interventions have been 'proven' to be efficacious and those of routine practice. Indeed, there is an ironic truism that as the internal validity (e.g. the experimental rigour and control imposed in order to allow causal inferences to be made) of a piece of research increases, its external and ecological validity (e.g. the generalisability of the study findings to real-life settings) often decreases. The implications of this issue are neatly summarised by Shucksmith (2007), whose review of research on school-based mental health interventions concluded:

> their applicability to real life classroom settings is . . . suspect on several levels
> . . . studies have seen the investment of massive sums of money . . . the results
> that emerge are very useful in showing the way towards the design of more

effective interventions, yet there must be serious doubts as to the availability of such resources within normal education budgets (pp.4–5).

Commonly applied research designs

Despite the issues and tensions inherent in the increasing push for evidence-based practice, research and outcome measurement does have a useful role to play in helping us to make decisions about practice, and as such it is worth briefly considering some commonly applied research designs.

Evaluation methods in health and related fields are often presented as a 'hierarchy' in terms of the quality of evidence they produce (remembering, as noted above, that 'quality' here favours internal validity). Such hierarchies typically focus on basic questions of efficacy, and as such those methodologies from which one can most rigorously determine that an intervention has produced a given effect on an outcome are given precedence. The most commonly utilised hierarchy, reported by Harbour and Miller (2001), is outlined below:

1. systematic reviews and meta-analyses of randomised controlled trials
2. randomised controlled trials
3. non-randomised controlled trials
4. observational studies
5. non-experimental studies
6. expert opinion.

Given the emphasis on practical application, and the fact that the reader is unlikely to have the resources or inclination to implement designs leading to any of the first three types of evidence highlighted above, our focus will primarily be observational studies (a full and detailed discussion of the hierarchy can be found in Rawlins (2008); his analysis of the limitations of the 'gold standard' randomised controlled trial in particular is worth reading). Observational studies are a family of research designs that involve some form of comparison in order to examine treatment effects, including:

- historical controlled trials – where the effects of an intervention are compared with retrospective treatment-as-usual data
- non-randomised contemporaneously controlled trials – where the effects of an intervention on client outcomes are compared to those for a group of clients who are either left untreated or treated with an alternative intervention during the same time period
- before-and-after designs – also known as 'phase change' or 'pre-to-post' designs, where measures are taken among a group of clients before, during and after the intervention has taken place
- case series – where the outcomes of a group/series of clients who have taken part in an intervention are studied; although there is no formal comparison

group, internal comparisons may be made, e.g. between individual clients (Rawlins, 2008).

How might such designs be applied in practice? Beginning with before-and-after designs, there are two useful examples in the recent literature. Humphrey and Brooks (2006) utilised this approach in an evaluation of a short, four-week cognitive-behavioural anger management intervention for 12 pupils at risk of exclusion from secondary school. They took outcome measures relating to the pupils' social, emotional and behavioural difficulties four weeks before, at the onset of the intervention, at the end of the intervention and at four-week follow-up. Similarly, Hanley *et al.* (2011) used a before-and-after design to evaluate the impact of school-based counselling on nine adolescents. They took measures at the point of referral, the onset of counselling, the completion of counselling and at two-month follow-up. In both studies, the before-and-after design was advantageous in that it allowed the researchers to establish a baseline period (from the first measure to the second) against which to compare change in the intervention period (from the second measure to the third), the durability of which could then be explored in the follow-up period (from the third measure to the fourth). Furthermore, as participants effectively act as their own comparison group in this design, there are no ethical quandaries regarding withholding of treatment. However, to implement such a design appropriately does require careful planning so that measures can be taken at each of the four key points in time.

Another common application of observational study designs is the non-randomised, contemporaneously controlled trial. In particular, waitlist and/or alternative/usual treatment control groups are commonly used in this approach (Eyberg *et al.*, 2008). For example, Wiggins and Wiggins (1992) compared the effectiveness of classroom guidance to individual counselling in improving outcomes such as self-esteem and behaviour in 48 pupils. The advantage of research that incorporates some kind of control group – as in the aforementioned study – is the increased rigour associated with being able to compare change in young people who have undergone the intervention of interest with a similar group who have been left untreated (or have received an alternative intervention) (Cooper, 2009). However, unless allocation to one group or another is random (as in a randomised controlled trial), there can be ethical and design issues associated with decisions about which clients join each group. For example, creating a control group from clients who are on a waitlist for treatment might seem advantageous, but one would need to consider their comparability with an intervention group. It may be that clients are allocated to a waitlist because initial assessment suggests they are experiencing less severe distress or fewer problems than those referred immediately for treatment.

Therapeutic outcome measures

How might we assess the outcomes of a given therapeutic intervention using one of the designs outlined above? The number of measures available for assessing therapeutic outcomes among adolescents is staggering. For example, in a systematic review, Johnston and Gowers (2005) identified 113 measures of mental health outcomes for children and young people. Similarly, a survey of UK Child and Adolescent Mental Health Services (CAMHS) by Wolpert *et al.* (2008) found over 100 different measures routinely used by clinicians. Providing coverage of each of these is, of course, way beyond the remit of this chapter. In the case of the review by Wolpert and colleagues, a very useful guide to the measures, including brief descriptions and information on different versions, length, scales and subscales, response format, example items, cost and references/contacts, can be downloaded from www.ucl.ac.uk/clinical-psychology/EBPU/publications/pub-files/. Here, we provide a brief overview of a small number of commonly used measures that are available free of charge.

The decision as to which measure(s) to use in outcome evaluation should rest on key issues such as:

- availability
- cost
- ease of use/interpretation
- appropriateness for the client group, e.g. age
- psychometric properties
- sensitivity to change
- different versions available, e.g. self-report, parent and/or teacher report
- brevity
- theoretical grounding.

However, ultimately one needs to select a measure or measures that can accurately measure the specific outcomes that the intervention is designed to affect. A useful starting point in this regard is to think about why clients have been referred in the first place. In adolescent counselling psychology, the difficulties experienced by clients can be manifold and complex. Cooper's (2009) review of school-based counselling in the UK revealed a large number of presenting issues among young people who had been referred for treatment, such as family problems, anger, relationship difficulties, behavioural issues, depression and anxiety. Many of the measures that have been developed in the field attempt to incorporate this diversity by either providing a generic measure of distress or well-being (as with the Young Person's Clinical Outcomes in Routine Evaluation (YP-CORE), below) or providing a multidimensional instrument through which subscale scores can be calculated covering different presenting issues (as with the Strengths and Difficulties Questionnaire (SDQ) and Health of the Nation Outcome Scales for Children and Adolescents (HoNOSCA), below).

Young Person's Clinical Outcomes in Routine Evaluation

The YP-CORE was developed by Twigg *et al.* (2009) and consists of ten items. Each provides a statement, to which respondents indicate how frequently it has applied to them over the last week on a five-point scale from nought ('not at all') to four ('most or all of the time'). A sample statement is 'I've thought of hurting myself'. Item responses are summed to give a total score of 0–40, with higher scores being indicative of greater difficulties. Two risk/clinical cut-off scores are provided to aid interpretation.

Initial analyses by Twigg *et al.* (2009) indicated that the YP-CORE had acceptable psychometric properties. It is also very quick and easy to administer and score, and therefore is ideal for use to investigate change in brief interventions. However, it provides only a single, generic index of emotional well-being, and as such is not as comprehensive as other measures.

More information about the YP-CORE can be found at www.coreims.co.uk.

Strengths and Difficulties Questionnaire

The SDQ was developed by Goodman (1997) and consists of 25 items, covering emotional symptoms, conduct problems, hyperactivity/inattention, peer relationship problems, and prosocial behaviour. The first four of these domains can be added together to generate a 'total difficulties' score. Each item provides a statement, to which respondents indicate the extent to which it has applied to them over the last six months, on a three-point scale from nought ('not true') to two ('certainly true'). A sample statement is 'I get very angry and often lose my temper'. Item responses are summed to give a score of 0–10 (0–40 for total difficulties), with higher scores being indicative of greater difficulties (except in the case of prosocial behaviour). Two risk/clinical cut-off scores are provided to aid interpretation. There are three versions available for use with adolescents: self-report, teacher report and parent report.

Goodman (1997) reports that the SDQ has good psychometric properties. It is quick to administer and score, and benefits from being both multidimensional and multi-informant, enabling a more comprehensive picture of a young person's emotional well-being to be developed.

More information about the SDQ can be found at www.sdqinfo.org.

Health of the Nation Outcome Scales for Children and Adolescents

The HoNOSCA was developed by Gowers *et al.* (1999) and consists of 13 items, covering behaviour, impairments, symptoms and social functioning. Each provides a statement, to which respondents indicate how much it has applied to them in the last two weeks, on a five-point scale from nought ('not at all') to four ('severely'). A sample statement is 'Have you been feeling in a low or anxious mood, or troubled by fears, obsessions or rituals?'. Item responses are summed to give separate scores for each of the four domains, but a total score can also be calculated. There are three versions available for use with adolescents: self-report, clinician report and parent report.

Gowers *et al.* (1999) report that the HoNOSCA has good psychometric properties. It is quick to administer and score, and benefits from being both multidimensional and multi-informant, enabling a more comprehensive picture of a young person's emotional well-being to be developed. However, there are no risk/clinical cut-off scores to aid interpretation.

More information about the HoNOSCA can be found at www.liv.ac.uk/honosca.

CAMHS Outcome Research Consortium (CORC)

For further recommendations related to the assessment of therapeutic work with young people, see the CORC website: www.corc.uk.net/.

Issues in interpreting and analysing outcome data

Interpreting and analysing outcome data comes with its own set of issues. These include, but are not limited to, statistical significance, effect size, reliable and clinically significant change and differential results.

Statistical significance

When analysing outcome data it is important for us to know whether any change we have observed in a client group (whether in a before-and-after or control group design) is genuinely the result of a given intervention. Part of this comes through selecting methodologically rigorous designs in the first place, but data analysis also plays a vital role. Inferential statistical techniques rely on the concept of statistical significance, which refers to the probability (expressed as P) that a given result/effect/difference observed is due to random variation or chance. A threshold of probability that is considered acceptable is less than five times in 100 (five per cent), expressed as '$P < 0.05$' (see Joseph *et al.*, 2005, for a more detailed explanation). Although this an extremely widely used approach (indeed, it is the standard consideration in the analysis of quantitative data in the social sciences), it is also flawed in a number of ways (Cohen, 1993), including the fact that the threshold of $P < 0.05$ is completely arbitrary, and also that statistical significance is inherently tied to sample size (larger samples lead to more sensitive tests, meaning that small differences that are of little practical utility can be flagged as significant; conversely, with small samples tests are much less sensitive, meaning that potentially important differences can be missed).

Effect size

A complementary/alternative approach to the concept of statistical significance is that of effect size. Effect size analysis considers the magnitude of the effect/ difference/pattern observed. Effect sizes are calculated in standardised units, which help us to compare the outcomes of different interventions across numerous studies that have used different outcome measures. There are a number of different indices of effect size associated with different designs – see Cohen (1992) for a review – but the most common (and simplest to understand) is Cohen's *d*. This is a simple measure of effect size that is most often associated with a control group design, and is calculated by subtracting the average (mean) score of one group (e.g. the control group) from the average score of the other group (e.g. the intervention group), before dividing the resulting value by the standard deviation of scores for the sample as a whole. The value this produces can be thought of as a measure of the number of standard deviations' change in the outcome measure that can be attributed to the intervention in question. Cohen's *d* values of 0.2, 0.5 and 0.8 are traditionally thought of as small, medium and large effects respectively. A handy effect size calculator for Cohen's *d* can be found online at www.uccs.edu/~faculty/ lbecker/.

Cohen's *d* values can also be converted to U^3 index scores, which represent the percentile point improvement in a given outcome measure associated with being part of the intervention group as compared to the control group (assuming that the average member of a control group is, by definition, at the 50th percentile). For example, a Cohen's *d* value of 0.25 corresponds to a U^3 index score of 0.60 (or 60%); in this example, being part of the intervention group led to a ten per cent improvement in the outcome measure (60 – 50 = 10). A handy tool for converting Cohen's *d* to U^3 index scores can be found at www.wilderdom.com/research/ ZCalc.xls.

Reliable and clinically significant change

Although effect size analysis can provide us with an index of the amount of change in an outcome measure that has occurred as a result of a given intervention, it arguably tells us relatively little about the reliability of that change or its importance in clinical terms (Jacobson and Truax, 1991). Thus, we might ask two questions: (1) does the amount of change observed exceed that which could be attributed to measurement error? (reliable change), and (2) is the amount of change observed socially and/or clinically meaningful? (clinically significant change) (Evans *et al.*, 1998). In relation to the former, there are formulae that can be applied that take into account the fact of the inherent consistency/reliability of the instrument to produce a threshold above which change can be considered reliable (Evans *et al.*, 1998). In relation to the latter, there are several approaches, but it has been suggested that the fundamental principle is the extent to which individuals have moved from the 'dysfunctional population' range to the 'functional population' range on a given measure (Jacobson and Follette, 1984). So, for example, we might examine the relative probability of the SDQ scores of adolescents undergoing counselling moving from the 'abnormal' to the 'normal' range when compared to an equivalent group of young people in a comparison group.

Differential results

One of the inherent advantages of using outcome measures that allow for multiple informants (for example, self-report, parent and/or teacher informant report) is that findings can be triangulated, increasing the validity of the study in question and potentially giving us more confidence in the effectiveness of a particular intervention. For example, we might be more confident that an intervention is effective if we see change across measures completed by young people, their parents and their teachers. However, research findings are rarely this straightforward in this field! More often than not, studies using multi-informant outcome measures often produce differential findings. For example, Humphrey *et al.* (2010) evaluated the impact of a short, social-emotional intervention on children at risk of developing mental health difficulties in primary schools using child self-report, and parent and teacher informant report measures. They reported significant changes on the child measure, but null results (that is, no change) for the teacher and parent measures. In such situations, consideration needs to be given as to whose perspective is prioritised when deciding whether the intervention can be deemed 'effective', alongside the inherent advantages and disadvantages of that particular perspective. For example, self-report is advantageous in that it allows for introspection of feelings and thoughts that are not directly accessible by other means, but its reliability may be questionable in some cases (Cooper, 2009).

Assessment of process (and perspectives)

It is a great truism, attributed to Albert Einstein, that 'not everything that counts can be counted, and not everything that can be counted counts'. Thus, we now turn to consider approaches that more actively and explicitly incorporate the views and perspectives of user groups and allow for the concurrent assessment of process. Exploring therapeutic process through the perspectives of clients and other stakeholders is an essential component in evaluation research in this field. Approaches such as interviews and focus groups can aid our understanding of how an intervention has (or hasn't!) worked, as well as raising important issues such as helpful and unhelpful factors (Cooper, 2009). They may also allow additional insights into areas of perceived impact that cannot be adequately captured in a quantitative outcome measure.

Interviews

Interviews can offer a systematic, comprehensive way of obtaining views from a range of perspectives to develop a more holistic understanding of therapeutic process in a particular context. Interviews are time-consuming, however, for both the researcher and the interviewee. In addition, Fontana and Frey (2005) warn that researchers often overprivilege interview data, believing that they are trustworthy and accurate, when in fact they are as subject to bias as any other method. Interviewees, as individuals, have their own concerns and beliefs and will present themselves in a particular way, perhaps to provide socially desirable or 'appropriate' answers or to further their own agendas. However, such issues of bias are unavoidable and as long as all data are analysed with due consideration of their origins and intent, the interview can be a very useful method. An example of its utility can be seen in the aforementioned evaluation of a short cognitive-behavioural anger management intervention for adolescents at risk of exclusion from secondary school by Humphrey and Brooks (2006). The second author conducted interviews with each participating adolescent, and the resultant data provided a wealth of useful information pertaining to both the process of the intervention and its outcomes. For example, in relation to the intervention, the interviews highlighted issues in relation to trust and sharing of information in group contexts (the intervention was group-based). In relation to the outcomes, the generalisation of skills to contexts beyond the intervention setting emerged as a critical factor.

Focus groups

A focus group is a group interview that makes use of interaction and communication between participants in order to generate data. Rather than the researcher asking a series of questions in turn, the emphasis is on the focus group members asking questions, sharing anecdotes and reflecting on each other's experiences and views (Kitzinger, 1995). The process is not entirely unstructured though, and the researcher may use prompts in order to keep the discussion 'on track'. This is a particular consideration when the focus group members are children and young people, who may prefer to talk about what they did at the weekend rather than discuss their experiences of the therapeutic process! When implemented properly, focus groups can generate data through discussion among participants that would/could not have emerged in a standard one-to-one interview. However, it is not an appropriate technique to use in every evaluation, and consideration needs to be given as to whether the topics to be discussed are likely to cause issues in relation to confidentiality and emotional distress among participants. An example of the use of focus groups with adolescents is seen in Humphrey and Ainscow's (2006) exploration of vulnerable pupils' experiences of an innovative intervention (Transition Club) to facilitate successful adjustment to secondary school. Through the discussions between pupils that took place in their focus group interview, the authors were able to identify the ways in which the intervention has impacted upon their early experiences of secondary school, including promoting a sense of belonging, helping them become familiar with the school environment and making learning fun.

Conclusion – a suggested model for assessing therapeutic outcomes in practice

Throughout the course of this chapter, we have examined the importance of research and routine outcome measurement, explored different research designs and their applications, presented exemplar measures for assessing therapeutic outcomes with adolescents, discussed key issues in interpreting and analysing outcome data and finally highlighted a couple of methods through which one might generate qualitative data that could yield insights into the therapeutic process that underpins any measured change. In concluding, we offer a tentative model for assessing therapeutic outcomes in practice, defined through the following fundamental principles:

1. The combination of qualitative data to highlight the therapeutic process with quantitative data to assess therapeutic outcomes is essential. Either alone will not yield sufficient information to allow for a clear picture of the success of an intervention to emerge.
2. The research design chosen obviously needs to fit the particular context of the therapeutic intervention; however, some form of comparison is essential, whether this be through historical records or comparison within or between participants. Whatever the design chosen, measures also need to be repeated over time so that analysis of change can occur (e.g. from beginning of therapy to end of therapy).
3. Given the variety of therapeutic outcome measures available, the decision as to which to use needs to be made carefully, and should incorporate key issues such as cost, ease of use/interpretation, appropriateness for the client group and psychometric properties.
4. Wherever possible, the views and/or ratings of a range of informants should be incorporated into the evaluation design.
5. Consideration needs to be given to how the outcome data that will be collected are analysed and interpreted. Issues such as statistical significance, effect size, reliable and clinically significant change and differential results need to be taken into account.
6. Methods like interviews and focus groups that more actively and explicitly take into account the views of user groups – such as clients themselves – should be incorporated into the evaluation design alongside outcome measurement.
7. Fundamental ethical considerations (e.g. consent, anonymity, right to withdraw) must always be taken into account, particularly given the dual role of the practitioner-researcher.

8. Above all else, high-quality evaluation is always underpinned by good planning and preparation.

Summary

*   Conducting research and measuring outcomes have become essential components of young people's mental health services. This trend goes hand in hand with a general move within the therapeutic world towards an increased importance in empirical evidence and raises numerous new challenges.
*   Research is often judged using a hierarchical system. At the top of this hierarchy, systematic reviews and randomised controlled trials are often viewed as the gold standard. Such methods are often out of the range of attainable designs for individual practitioners.
*   Practice-based research designs are beginning to develop in the field of youth counselling. A design that has become commonplace is the before-and-after (or pre-to-post) research design. This collects data at the outset of therapy and compares this score to that at end, thus indicating potential change due to therapy. A number of more complex designs are also introduced in this chapter.
*   There are numerous outcome measures available for work with this client group. Presently there is not a tool that stands out from all the others. The choice of questionnaire should therefore be carefully considered in relation to the information that is hoped to be captured. Three measures that are often used with this client group are the YP-CORE, the SDQ and the HoNOSCA.
*   When you have collected quantitative research data it is likely that the data will be reported in terms of a statistical significance, effect size or clinical/ reliable change. It is important that consumers of research understand what these figures mean and are aware of some of their limitations.
*   Qualitative research approaches can be used to add depth to a quantitative investigation. Such investigations might utilise one-to-one interviews or focus groups to explain quantitative research findings from the perspectives of the various stakeholders (e.g. the young clients, parents and teachers).

Further reading

At the outset of this chapter we identified several texts that would provide readers with resources to continue their explorations into the worlds of practitioner research and research with young people. This brief section therefore aims to complement these generic recommendations by outlining a few extra complexities that we decided would have complicated issues within the main body of the chapter. These are: (1) the complexity of mixed methods research; and (2) the integration of research techniques into the therapeutic process. These are noted in turn below.

Within our conclusion we make the recommendation that numbers should be accompanied by a rich explanatory narrative. Such designs are often under-considered and readers are urged to familiarise themselves with mixed methods designs before embarking upon them (Creswell and Plano Clark, 2010). Another area in which mixed methods have evolved in a systematic way is case study design. Within the world of therapy, John McLeod's text in this area would be heartily recommended (McLeod, 2010).

In relation to the second point noted above, it is increasingly recognised that the integration of monitoring therapeutic progress (and the associated process) as a therapeutic activity can actually improve outcomes. Such an approach can often be described as client-directed and outcome-informed. As a starting point we refer you back to Chapter 6 for an overview of such a way of working and related references. This is also exemplified to varying degrees within Chapter 8.

Finally, and in keeping with the approach discussed in the text, we do not refer to goal-based outcome measures. These are very simple tools, of which one can be found on the CORC website, noted earlier in this chapter. Presently these have potential and are developing; however little has been written about them with this client group.

References

Barkham, M., Hardy, G. and Mellor-Clark, J. (2010). *Developing and Delivering Practice-based Evidence: A guide for the psychological therapies*. Chichester: Wiley-Blackwell.

Cohen, J. (1992). A power primer. *Psychological Bulletin*, 112, 155–9.

Cohen, J. (1993). The earth is round (p < .05). *American Psychologist*, 49, 997–1003.

Cooper, M. (2009). Counselling in UK secondary schools: a comprehensive review of audit and evaluation data. *Counselling and Psychotherapy Research*, 9, 137–50.

Cooper, M. (2010). The challenge of counselling and psychotherapy research. *Counselling and Psychotherapy Research*, 10, 183–91.

Creswell, J. and Plano Clark, V. (2010). *Designing and Conducing Mixed Methods Research* (2nd edition). Thousand Oaks: Sage.

Evans, C., Margison, F. and Barkham, M. (1998). The contribution of reliable and clinically significant change methods to evidence-based mental health. *Evidence-Based Mental Health*, 1, 70–3.

Eyberg, S. M., Nelson, M. M. and Boggs, S. R. (2008). Evidence-based psychosocial treatments for children and adolescents with disruptive behavior. *Journal of Clinical Child and Adolescent Psychology*, 37, 215–37.

Fontana, A. and Frey, J. (2005). The interview: from neutral stance to political involvement. In N. Denzin and Y. Lincoln (eds) *The Sage Handbook of Qualitative Research*. Thousand Oaks: Sage Publications.

Goodman, R. (1997). The Strengths and Difficulties questionnaire: a research note. *Journal of Child Psychology and Psychiatry*, 38, 581–6.

Gowers, S. G., Harrington, R. C., Whitton, A., Lelliott, P., Beevor, A., Wing, J. and Jezzard, R. (1999). Brief scale for measuring the outcomes of emotional and behavioural disorders in children. Health of the Nation Outcome Scales for children and Adolescents (HoNOSCA). *British Journal of Psychiatry*, 174, 413–16.

Hanley, T., Sefi, A. and Lennie, C. (2011). Practice-based evidence in school-based counselling. *Counselling and Psychotherapy Research*, 11(3), 300–9

Harbour, R. and Miller, J. (2001). A new system for grading recommendations in evidence based guidelines. *British Medical Journal*, 323, 334–6.

Hoagwood, K. (2001). Evidence-based practice in Child and Adolescent Mental Health Services. *Psychiatric Services*, 52, 1179–89.

Humphrey, N. and Ainscow, M. (2006). Transition club: facilitating learning, participation and psychological adjustment during the transition to secondary school. *European Journal of Psychology of Education*, 21, 319–31.

Humphrey, N. and Brooks, A. G. (2006). An evaluation of a short cognitive-behavioural anger management intervention for pupils at risk of exclusion. *Emotional and Behavioural Difficulties*, 11, 5–23.

Humphrey, N., Kalambouka, A., Wigelsworth, M., Lendrum, A., Lennie, C. and Farrell, P. (2010). New beginnings: evaluation of a short social-emotional intervention for primary-aged children. *Educational Psychology*, 30, 513–32.

Jacobson, N. S. and Follette, W. C. (1984). Psychotherapy outcome research: methods for reporting variability and evaluating clinical significance. *Psychotherapy Research*, 352, 336–52.

Jacobson, N. S. and Truax, P. (1991). Clinical significance: a statistical approach to defining meaningful change in psychotherapy research. *Journal of Consulting and Clinical Psychology*, 59, 12–19.

Johnston, C. and Gowers, S. (2005). Routine outcome measurement: a survey of UK Child and Adolescent Mental Health Services. *Child and Adolescent Mental Health*, 10, 133–9.

Joseph, S., Dyer, C. and Coolican, H. (2005). What does p<0.05 mean? *Counselling and Psychotherapy Research*, 5, 105–6.

Kitzinger, J. (1995). Introducing focus groups. *British Medical Journal*, 311, 299–302.

Lewis, V. (2004). *The Reality of Research with Children and Young People*. London: Sage Publications.

McLeod, J. (1999). *Practitioner Research in Counselling*. London: Sage Publications.

McLeod, J. (2010). *Case Study Research in Counselling and Psychotherapy*. London: Sage

Rawlins, M. (2008). De testimonio: on the evidence for decisions about the use of therapeutic interventions. *Lancet*, 372, 2152–61.

Shucksmith, J. (2007). Mental wellbeing of children in primary education (targeted/indicated activities). Teeside: University of Teeside.

Twigg, E., Barkham, M., Bewick, B. M., Mulhern, B., Connell, J. and Cooper, M. (2009). The young person's CORE: development of a brief outcome measure for young people. *Counselling and Psychotherapy Research*, 9, 160–8.

Wiggins, J. D. and Wiggins, M. M. (1992). Elementary students' self-esteem and behavioral ratings related to counselor time-task emphases. *School Counsellor*, 39, 377–81.

Wolpert, M. (2010). What does it mean to be a scientific practitioner? Developing evidence-based and outcomes-informed CAMHS. Retrieved from www.ucl.ac.uk/clinical-psychology/EBPU/presentations/presentation-files/BPS talk.pdf.

Wolpert, M., Aitken, J., Syrad, H., Munroe, M., Saddington, C., Trustam, E., Bradley, J., Nolas, S. M., Lavis, P., Jones, A., Day, C., Fonagy, P., Frederickson, N., Humphrey, N., Meadows, P., Rutter, M., Tymms, P. Vostanis, P. and Croudace, T.*et al.* (2008). *Review and Recommendations for National Policy for England for the Use of Mental Health Outcome Measures with Children and Young People*. Nottingham: DCSF Publications.

Chapter 10

Summary

Terry Hanley, Neil Humphrey and Clare Lennie

Throughout this text we have covered a great deal of territory. Unfortunately, as is the nature of a textbook such as this, its content is primarily didactic in its nature and there is no opportunity for dialogue around each of the topics presented. In considering this, we would like to remind the reader that, in presenting this text, we are by no means attempting to claim this to be a definitive text on the subject of adolescent counselling psychology. The subject is expansive, as partially indicated in the further reading sections throughout, and ever-growing. However, as noted at the end of the introduction, we do hope that you found it useful and enjoyable. Below we attempt to pick out several of the major elements that we feel are the headlines within this text.

Youth-friendly counselling psychology

Counselling psychology is well situated to find a niche within the field of therapeutic work with young people. Its ethos (as outlined in Chapter 2) is founded upon the principles of humanistic psychology and is openly challenging of the medical model. Such an ethos does not aim to dismiss the medical model view of the world, but acknowledges that the reductionist way in which it can often manifest is not always the most helpful to clients. Often such assumptions are made without full regard to the complex nature of the lives of young clients and this is something that this text considers throughout. In particular we could highlight the variety of settings in which therapeutic services are offered. These can include medical, community, school or technologically mediated settings (see Chapter 4) and are often delivered in ways that help to break down the professional–adolescent power dynamic that can often play such a large inhibiting part in work with this client group. Importantly, this dynamic is often greatly influenced by the developmental stage that the individual is in whilst in therapy (see Chapter 5), with adolescence being an incredibly varied life stage in which great changes occur.

Therapeutic work with young people can be potentially challenging due to the complexities specific to the age group. This may include liaising with other professionals who work with young people (see Chapter 4 for introductions to some of these individuals) or manifest in the infrastructure of the counselling services.

Within Chapter 6 some of the key elements related to the service delivery are discussed. Specifically, these outline how legal nuances can be interpreted into good policy and safe working contracts. Additionally, consideration of appropriate supervisory support for therapeutic work with this age group is considered. Although we do not in any way attempt to outline a comprehensive overview of the types of issues young people bring to therapy, Part 3 of the text (particularly Chapter 7) does attempt to provide bring much of the thinking together related to the practice of youth-friendly counselling psychology.

Research-informed practice

One of the major messages within this text is that research can be used to inform therapeutic practice helpfully. This is encapsulated in the description of research-informed practice outlined in Chapter 6 and contrasts with the more prescriptive notion of evidence-based practice. It is argued that such a model is more commensurate to counselling psychologists and more in tune with an audience that can be sceptical about the part research plays in their work. For instance, research is sometimes looked at by therapeutic practitioners as first, something that they do not do, or even worse, second, something that intrudes upon the therapeutic encounter. Within this text we challenge both of these assertions.

In relation to the first assertion, noted above, we would argue that counselling psychologists are in a great position to adopt a research-informed position (as are many applied psychologists who utilise research in such a way within their everyday work). Research is therefore weighed up in a mature manner alongside other influencing factors. For instance, your personal background, skill set, supervision, training and therapeutic practice will all influence the decisions that you make. For one person, one therapeutic method will be the most beneficial to a client, whilst a completely different method might be best coming from someone else. Within the text the multiplicity of responses could be reflected in Gareth's therapeutic work with Ged (see Chapter 8). In particular, how many of us could truly utilise a portable music studio to support the creation of a therapeutic alliance? This may not be something many of us could offer; however, we will all have individual strengths that can play an important part in developing strong relationships with a young person.

In contesting the second statement, made above, we would argue that research need not intrude upon the therapeutic relationship. In fact, there is compelling evidence to suggest that such techniques are a means of improving the outcome of therapeutic practice (see Chapter 6). In such an approach, research techniques become part of the therapy, rather than intruding upon it, and support the dialogue between counsellor and client. Such a technique has a research base itself and acknowledges that clients are not always forthcoming in how they are finding or using therapy (to the therapist, anyhow). It also acknowledges that those in therapeutic disciplines are not always very accurate at judging their own work. These important discoveries (or at least discussions, if that proves too grand a term) heighten the need for therapeutic work to be scrutinised in depth. The field of applied psychology is an emerging science and there is much we still do not understand, and there is much we can improve in the work that we do. In our minds, it would therefore not be appropriate to remain stationary and treat the works of eminent individuals such as Freud, Rogers or Beck as gospel which remains unchallenged or undeveloped. Let's not forget that research methods (such as those discussed in Chapter 9) often proved the staple diet of the key proponents whose theories often guide us.

Pluralistic counselling psychology

As a means of bridging the gap between research and practice we have utilised the pluralistic framework originally put forward by Professors Mick Cooper and John McLeod to harness our discussion. As pluralism is a philosophical position that values the multitude of possible avenues, it will be an area of potential dispute within this text. This particularly becomes the case when it is laid out as a potential framework, as we have done (see Chapters 6 and 8). However, we do so as it provides a means of articulating an approach that can provide a framework for all models of therapy (e.g. pure model, integrative, eclectic). Importantly, it also provides a framework that creatively engages with research findings and focuses our dialogues about therapy towards the factors that have shown themselves to be demonstrably effective. Such discussions are in their relative infancy, particularly in relation to working with young people, and hopefully they will provide a starting point rather than an end to your thinking.

A final thought

Now, before closing the text and filing it nicely on your shelf, e-books collection or returning it to the library, we invite you to consider the content one last time.

Reflective exercise

During Chapter 9 the authors discuss numerous ways of evaluating therapeutic work with young people. One of the ways discussed is the notion of goal-based outcome measures. Here we invite you to consider this book in a similar way.

Instruction I

At the outset of the book, what were your goals? What did you hope to get from reading it? Now, if we invite you to rate on a scale of one to five (one being it didn't address your goals at all and five being it did exactly what you hoped), how much did the book meet these goals?

Instruction 2

Now, if you take each goal separately:

- In the instance that you rated it highly, which bits proved fruitful? Why was this the case?
- In the instance that you rated it moderately, or lowly, how do we think you could have improved the contents of the book to fit with your goals?
- In your reflections you might identify elements that met your needs and other bits that did not. Furthermore, you might identify an additional need in yourself that might be met by one of the recommended texts noted throughout. In the spirit of the pluralistic framework discussed in this text, all of this feedback is likely to provide useful for the authors/ publishers. Do feel free to contact us with your comments.

Index

For Product Safety Concerns and Information please contact our EU
representative GPSR@taylorandfrancis.com
Taylor & Francis Verlag GmbH, Kaufingerstraße 24, 80331 München, Germany

www.ingramcontent.com/pod-product-compliance
Lightning Source LLC
Chambersburg PA
CBHW070333270326
41926CB00017B/3861